# *Solutions for a*
# *Small Planet*

## Volume Two

# *Gaia Speaks*
## THROUGH PEPPER LEWIS

# Solutions *for a* Small Planet

### Volume Two

## *Gaia Speaks*

### THROUGH PEPPER LEWIS

 Light Technology Publishing

Some of the material in this book includes articles previously printed
in the *Sedona Journal of Emergence!*, a monthly magazine
published by Light Technology Publishing.

ISBN: 1-891824-84-8
ISBN-13: 978-1-891824-84-5

Published & Printed by

800-450-0985
www.lighttechnology.com
PO Box 3540
Flagstaff, AZ 86003
publishing@lighttechnology.net

# *Acknowledgments*

*I* am still amazed by how we help each other accomplish great things. For some reason, we often do for others those things that we would not do for ourselves—perhaps so we can see our own true reflections, as Gaia would say. We are selfless more often than we are selfish, and we say yes more often than we say no, even if we think differently about it later on.

My life has been fortunate in unique and unexpected ways, and I have been loved and supported even when it did not look like that was what was happening. Simply put, I am grateful for all of the simple and profound moments I have experienced, for family and friends, and for all those who have become part of my extended family as I have traveled around the world sharing Gaia's messages.

— Pepper

# About Pepper Lewis

*P*epper Lewis is a world-renowned author, teacher and channel. She has been the primary voice for Mother Earth (Gaia) for over fifteen years and has carried Gaia's unique wisdom and guidance to many corners of the globe. Her channeling is rich, clear and profound. Pepper is the author of dozens of audio programs and several books, including *Gaia Speaks: Sacred Earth Wisdom,* *Gaia Speaks: Wisdom for an Awakening Humanity* and *Transition Now, Redefining Duality, 2012 and Beyond.*

Pepper is passionate about passing her art on to others and has developed an exceptional program for teaching channeling to every skill level, from beginner to professional. Her unique methods are a blend of time-honored traditions with a few new twists on an ancient art. Pepper explains her passion as follows: "Channeling continues to be a mutually enriching synthesis of prayer and meditation. In prayer, you offer gratitude and ask, and in meditation you receive answers. In channeling you can do both at the same time. It is the most fulfilling practice I know."

Pepper lives with her husband Glenn in the hills above Ashland, Oregon. She enjoys time spent in nature, gardening, reading and needlecraft, and an occasional motorcycle ride on a country road. For more information about seminars, How to Channel workshops, and audio programs, including Gaia's Voice, a new downloadable subscription (also found at www.DailyOm.com), please visit www.pepperlewis.com.

# *About Mother Earth (Gaia)*

*G*aia (the sentience/soul that animates the Earth) is humanity's partner, caregiver and creative resource. Gaia animates the planet, gives it purpose and makes life on Earth possible. Her words are soothing and uplifting, sometimes gently stern, endlessly compassionate, a little humorous and somehow strangely familiar.

We receive Gaia's guidance through the gift of channeling, a form of communication that allows the qualities of higher frequencies and dimensions to be heard and felt in our own language. Channeling is unique in that the messages are designed to touch each of us in an individual and purposeful way. It is likely that you will feel Gaia's energy profoundly and be able to recognize its "compassionate corrections" in several areas of your life.

Gaia is truly the sentience of Earth. She is to the planet what our souls are to us: a nonphysical pure awareness that is alive, awake and in service 100 percent of the time. Gaia guides and enlivens all that is upon and within the planet. She animates the air we breathe and the water we drink yet is so much more than that. Gaia's words are warm and endearing, they are the words of a mother who loves unconditionally and does not judge, not even those who harm her out of ignorance or arrogance. Her words are practical and precise; they are meant for this time and for everyone within earshot.

You may want to keep this book nearby, as you will find yourself referring to it frequently. It will carry you through good times and bad. As Gaia says, "Humanity is not in a freefall or a tailspin and Earth is not inside-out or upside-down, yet there is not a moment to lose, for life is long, but time is short."

# Table of Contents

Preface . . . . . . . . . . . . . . . . . . . . . . . . . . . . . . . . . . . . . . . . . . . . xv
Introduction . . . . . . . . . . . . . . . . . . . . . . . . . . . . . . . . . . . . . . . . xvii

### Resources and Responsibility

1. Healing the World One Meditation at a Time . . . . . . . . . . . . . . . . 1

    Blessings in Disguise . . . . . . . . . . . . . . . . . . . . . . . . . . . . . . . . . . . . 2
    Difficult Questions, Experiential Answers . . . . . . . . . . . . . . . . . . . . . . . . . . 3
    Do Not Succumb to Overly Dramatic Urgency . . . . . . . . . . . . . . . . . . . . 4

2. The Conscious Development of Land . . . . . . . . . . . . . . . . . . . . . . 7

    Ownership versus Custodianship of Land. . . . . . . . . . . . . . . . . . . . . . . . . 7
    Tuning into Sound Resonance . . . . . . . . . . . . . . . . . . . . . . . . . . . . . . . . . 8
    Visualizing Image Resonance . . . . . . . . . . . . . . . . . . . . . . . . . . . . . . . . . 9

3. Lack of Resources in a World of Plenty . . . . . . . . . . . . . . . . . . . . 11

    The Ebb and Flow of the Economy. . . . . . . . . . . . . . . . . . . . . . . . . . . . . 11
    Reshuffling the House of Cards . . . . . . . . . . . . . . . . . . . . . . . . . . . . . . 13
    Tapping Undiscovered Resources . . . . . . . . . . . . . . . . . . . . . . . . . . . . . 14
    The Coming Changes. . . . . . . . . . . . . . . . . . . . . . . . . . . . . . . . . . . . . . 15
    Antidotes for the Poisons . . . . . . . . . . . . . . . . . . . . . . . . . . . . . . . . . . 16

4. Hope for a Spiritual Economy. . . . . . . . . . . . . . . . . . . . . . . . . . . 19

    Principles in Today's World and Workplace . . . . . . . . . . . . . . . . . . . . . . . 19
    Why Do People Struggle Financially?. . . . . . . . . . . . . . . . . . . . . . . . . . . 20
    The Beggar and the Preacher . . . . . . . . . . . . . . . . . . . . . . . . . . . . . . . 21
    The Value of Wealth. . . . . . . . . . . . . . . . . . . . . . . . . . . . . . . . . . . . . . 24
    The Balance of Spirit and Matter. . . . . . . . . . . . . . . . . . . . . . . . . . . . . . 25

5. Solutions for a Small Planet . . . . . . . . . . . . . . . . . . . . . . . . . . . 27

    The Advent of the Pod Car . . . . . . . . . . . . . . . . . . . . . . . . . . . . . . . . . 27
    New Transportation Technologies on the Horizon. . . . . . . . . . . . . . . . . . . 29
    Five-Dimensional Minds in Our Future . . . . . . . . . . . . . . . . . . . . . . . . . 30
    The Law of Attraction and Our Changing World . . . . . . . . . . . . . . . . . . . 31

6. Developing a Personal Philosophy for Life. . . . . . . . . . . . . . . . . . 33

    Nature's Message . . . . . . . . . . . . . . . . . . . . . . . . . . . . . . . . . . . . . . . 33
    It Is Not Too Late . . . . . . . . . . . . . . . . . . . . . . . . . . . . . . . . . . . . . . . 34
    Developing Personal Morality. . . . . . . . . . . . . . . . . . . . . . . . . . . . . . . . 35
    The History of Studying Philosophy. . . . . . . . . . . . . . . . . . . . . . . . . . . . 37
    Avoiding Troubled Philosophies . . . . . . . . . . . . . . . . . . . . . . . . . . . . . . 38
    You Are Part of a Changing World. . . . . . . . . . . . . . . . . . . . . . . . . . . . . 39

7. Making the Most of Your Spiritual Toolbox . . . . . . . . . . . . . . . . . 41

    Live a Fulfilling Life . . . . . . . . . . . . . . . . . . . . . . . . . . . . . . . . . . . . . . 42

Rise Above and Think New Thoughts . . . . . . . . . . . . . . . . . . . . . . . . . . . . . . . . . 42
Redefine Your Outlook on Economics . . . . . . . . . . . . . . . . . . . . . . . . . . . . . . 43
Moving Transportation into a New Direction . . . . . . . . . . . . . . . . . . . . . . . 45
Trust the Voice of Spirit . . . . . . . . . . . . . . . . . . . . . . . . . . . . . . . . . . . . . . . . . . 46
Look for the Good News Within Yourself . . . . . . . . . . . . . . . . . . . . . . . . . . 47

**8. Righting the Wrongs: 2006 and Beyond . . . . . . . . . . . . . . . . . . . . 51**

There Are Beings Already among You . . . . . . . . . . . . . . . . . . . . . . . . . . . . . . 52
Contact with the Travelers . . . . . . . . . . . . . . . . . . . . . . . . . . . . . . . . . . . . . . . 53
Meeting a Traveler . . . . . . . . . . . . . . . . . . . . . . . . . . . . . . . . . . . . . . . . . . . . . . 55
The New Children Are Highly Disease Resistant . . . . . . . . . . . . . . . . . . . 56
They Are Your Future . . . . . . . . . . . . . . . . . . . . . . . . . . . . . . . . . . . . . . . . . . . 57
The Great Separation Is Over . . . . . . . . . . . . . . . . . . . . . . . . . . . . . . . . . . . . 58
You Are the Key to Your Wellness . . . . . . . . . . . . . . . . . . . . . . . . . . . . . . . . 59
Natural versus Artificial Medicine and the Avian Flu . . . . . . . . . . . . . . . . 60
Strengthening the Immune System . . . . . . . . . . . . . . . . . . . . . . . . . . . . . . . 61
Beware the Medicine Makers! . . . . . . . . . . . . . . . . . . . . . . . . . . . . . . . . . . . . 62
War Does Not Just Happen; War Is Chosen . . . . . . . . . . . . . . . . . . . . . . . . 64
It Is One War . . . . . . . . . . . . . . . . . . . . . . . . . . . . . . . . . . . . . . . . . . . . . . . . . . 65
A Turning Point . . . . . . . . . . . . . . . . . . . . . . . . . . . . . . . . . . . . . . . . . . . . . . . . 65
Many Fronts, Many Places, Many New Weapons . . . . . . . . . . . . . . . . . . . 66
No Life Is Better or Worse than Any Other . . . . . . . . . . . . . . . . . . . . . . . . 68
Humanity Created Currency and Accepts Its Debt . . . . . . . . . . . . . . . . . . 68
Loosen the Binds of Your Identity and Loosen the Burdens of Debt . . . . . . . . 69
New Financial Systems Based On Bargaining . . . . . . . . . . . . . . . . . . . . . . 70
Take Care of Your True Self . . . . . . . . . . . . . . . . . . . . . . . . . . . . . . . . . . . . . 71
Anticipate Change . . . . . . . . . . . . . . . . . . . . . . . . . . . . . . . . . . . . . . . . . . . . . 72
Revive Your Awareness of Being at Cause . . . . . . . . . . . . . . . . . . . . . . . . . 74
Melting Ice and Changing Coastlines . . . . . . . . . . . . . . . . . . . . . . . . . . . . . 75
You Are a Community-Based Species . . . . . . . . . . . . . . . . . . . . . . . . . . . . . 76
The Life of a Secret . . . . . . . . . . . . . . . . . . . . . . . . . . . . . . . . . . . . . . . . . . . . . 77
New Autonomical Technology Is Designed to Watch People . . . . . . . . . . . 78
You Are a Collection of the Best of All Things . . . . . . . . . . . . . . . . . . . . . . 80
A New Language . . . . . . . . . . . . . . . . . . . . . . . . . . . . . . . . . . . . . . . . . . . . . . . 81
Questions and Answers . . . . . . . . . . . . . . . . . . . . . . . . . . . . . . . . . . . . . . . . . 82
World Leaders, the Divine Feminine and the Space Brotherhood . . . . . . . . . . 84
True Solutions Exist in Your Ability to Remember . . . . . . . . . . . . . . . . . . 85

## Where the Past Meets the Future

**9. The Lemurian Changelings . . . . . . . . . . . . . . . . . . . . . . . . . . . . . . . 87**

The Sky Is Falling . . . . . . . . . . . . . . . . . . . . . . . . . . . . . . . . . . . . . . . . . . . . . . 88
A Time of Individual Choice . . . . . . . . . . . . . . . . . . . . . . . . . . . . . . . . . . . . . 89
They Live among You . . . . . . . . . . . . . . . . . . . . . . . . . . . . . . . . . . . . . . . . . . . 89

**10. The Long and Short of It . . . . . . . . . . . . . . . . . . . . . . . . . . . . . . . . 91**

The Beginning of the New Age . . . . . . . . . . . . . . . . . . . . . . . . . . . . . . . . . . . 91
The Third Dimension Will Be Thought of as a Relic . . . . . . . . . . . . . . . . 92
Drawing a Distinction between Joy and Happiness . . . . . . . . . . . . . . . . . . 93

Bliss, Misery, Ecstasy and Agony . . . . . . . . . . . . . . . . . . . . . . . . . . . . . . . . . . . 94
The Memory of Our Births and Deaths . . . . . . . . . . . . . . . . . . . . . . . . . . . . . 95

## 11. Rounding the Corner to the Fifth Dimension . . . . . . . . . . . . . 97

The Distillation of Thought . . . . . . . . . . . . . . . . . . . . . . . . . . . . . . . . . . . . . . . 97
Move from the Third Dimension to the Fifth . . . . . . . . . . . . . . . . . . . . . . . 98
A Leap Forward. . . . . . . . . . . . . . . . . . . . . . . . . . . . . . . . . . . . . . . . . . . . . . . . . . 100

## 12. Understanding Your Cosmic Lineage . . . . . . . . . . . . . . . . . . . . 103

Your Cosmic Lineage Is One with Source . . . . . . . . . . . . . . . . . . . . . . . . . . 103
Understanding Your Energetic Waveband . . . . . . . . . . . . . . . . . . . . . . . . . . 105
Your Purpose Is to Grasp Your Totality . . . . . . . . . . . . . . . . . . . . . . . . . . . . 106
The Red Race: What Was . . . . . . . . . . . . . . . . . . . . . . . . . . . . . . . . . . . . . . . . 107
The Indigo Race: What Will Be. . . . . . . . . . . . . . . . . . . . . . . . . . . . . . . . . . . 108
The Indigos Carry Great Power and Great Burden . . . . . . . . . . . . . . . . . . . 110
Do Not Make the Indigos' Burdens Your Own. . . . . . . . . . . . . . . . . . . . . . . 111
You Can Link with Your Own Cosmic Lineage . . . . . . . . . . . . . . . . . . . . . . 112
You Must Claim Your Life. . . . . . . . . . . . . . . . . . . . . . . . . . . . . . . . . . . . . . . . 114
The Crystal Kin Will Hold a Light. . . . . . . . . . . . . . . . . . . . . . . . . . . . . . . . . 116
Coming from Another World . . . . . . . . . . . . . . . . . . . . . . . . . . . . . . . . . . . . . 118
Those Who Go Beyond Will Have Opportunities to Choose From . . . . . . . . 119
Message from a Crystalline Child. . . . . . . . . . . . . . . . . . . . . . . . . . . . . . . . . . 120
Baby Boomers and the Invasion of New Light . . . . . . . . . . . . . . . . . . . . . . . 121
Your Evolution of Consciousness. . . . . . . . . . . . . . . . . . . . . . . . . . . . . . . . . . 121
Your Children Are Your Parents. . . . . . . . . . . . . . . . . . . . . . . . . . . . . . . . . . . 123
The Crystalline Children Will Change the World. . . . . . . . . . . . . . . . . . . . . 123
You Are an Art Form . . . . . . . . . . . . . . . . . . . . . . . . . . . . . . . . . . . . . . . . . . . . 125

## 13. The Wars of Humankind in Heaven . . . . . . . . . . . . . . . . . . . . . 127

The Star Gate in Orion's Belt. . . . . . . . . . . . . . . . . . . . . . . . . . . . . . . . . . . . . 128
Discord Began to Alter the Web of Harmony . . . . . . . . . . . . . . . . . . . . . . . 129
A New Virus Arrived . . . . . . . . . . . . . . . . . . . . . . . . . . . . . . . . . . . . . . . . . . . . 131
No World Was Safe from the Darkness . . . . . . . . . . . . . . . . . . . . . . . . . . . . . 132
Light Arrived to Balance the Darkness . . . . . . . . . . . . . . . . . . . . . . . . . . . . . 133
The Star Gate Was Reopened. . . . . . . . . . . . . . . . . . . . . . . . . . . . . . . . . . . . . 134
The Star Gate Continued to Heal and the Earth Continued to Evolve . . . . . 135
The Earth Was a Planetary Hospital . . . . . . . . . . . . . . . . . . . . . . . . . . . . . . . 136
The Star Gate Collapses and the Story Begins . . . . . . . . . . . . . . . . . . . . . . . 136
Souls Healed and Gaia's Role as the Sentience of Earth Started. . . . . . . . . . 137
The Collective Soul of Humanity Began to Awaken. . . . . . . . . . . . . . . . . . . 138
Kingdoms and Evolution on Pangaea, the Supercontinent . . . . . . . . . . . . . 140
Physicality . . . . . . . . . . . . . . . . . . . . . . . . . . . . . . . . . . . . . . . . . . . . . . . . . . . . . 140
The Original Form of Duality. . . . . . . . . . . . . . . . . . . . . . . . . . . . . . . . . . . . . 142
Adaptation, Mutation, Extinction. . . . . . . . . . . . . . . . . . . . . . . . . . . . . . . . . 143
History Is Not Linear . . . . . . . . . . . . . . . . . . . . . . . . . . . . . . . . . . . . . . . . . . . . 144

## 14. The Walk-In Experience . . . . . . . . . . . . . . . . . . . . . . . . . . . . . . . 145

The Soul Is in Control . . . . . . . . . . . . . . . . . . . . . . . . . . . . . . . . . . . . . . . . . . . 146

Reasons for Walk-Ins. . . . . . . . . . . . . . . . . . . . . . . . . . . . . . . . . . . . . . 147
The Process of the Walk-In. . . . . . . . . . . . . . . . . . . . . . . . . . . . . . . . . . 148
The Period of Unity . . . . . . . . . . . . . . . . . . . . . . . . . . . . . . . . . . . . . . . . 149
The Experience of the Outgoing Personality . . . . . . . . . . . . . . . . . . . . . . . 150
The Path of the New Walk-In. . . . . . . . . . . . . . . . . . . . . . . . . . . . . . . . . . 151
Final Notes on a Vast Subject. . . . . . . . . . . . . . . . . . . . . . . . . . . . . . . . . 152

## Accelerating Evolution

**15. Keeping Time** . . . . . . . . . . . . . . . . . . . . . . . . . . . . . . . . . . . . . . **155**
Pushing Our Clocks Forward . . . . . . . . . . . . . . . . . . . . . . . . . . . . . . . . . 156
A Few Notes from Gaia. . . . . . . . . . . . . . . . . . . . . . . . . . . . . . . . . . . . . . 158

**16. Evolution versus Creation Revisited Again and Again** . . . . . . **159**
Choice Is the Meaning of Life . . . . . . . . . . . . . . . . . . . . . . . . . . . . . . . . . 159
The Truth Lies in the Original Thought of Divinity. . . . . . . . . . . . . . . . . . 161

**17. The Acceleration of Evolution** . . . . . . . . . . . . . . . . . . . . . . . . **163**
The Age of Humanity. . . . . . . . . . . . . . . . . . . . . . . . . . . . . . . . . . . . . . . 163
Light Will Define Language . . . . . . . . . . . . . . . . . . . . . . . . . . . . . . . . . . 165
Assisting the Collective Mind of Humanity. . . . . . . . . . . . . . . . . . . . . . . . 165
Know How to Send Light . . . . . . . . . . . . . . . . . . . . . . . . . . . . . . . . . . . . 166
Life in the Shifting Paradigms . . . . . . . . . . . . . . . . . . . . . . . . . . . . . . . . 167

**18. Predictions Packaged "To Go"** . . . . . . . . . . . . . . . . . . . . . . . . **169**
How the Black Box Was Created . . . . . . . . . . . . . . . . . . . . . . . . . . . . . . . 169
Fact and Fantasy Make Interesting Bedmates. . . . . . . . . . . . . . . . . . . . . . 170
Did the Black Boxes Predict the Attacks on September 11, 2001?. . . . . . . . 171
An Unprecedented Shift. . . . . . . . . . . . . . . . . . . . . . . . . . . . . . . . . . . . . 173
The Battle against Separation. . . . . . . . . . . . . . . . . . . . . . . . . . . . . . . . . 173
Some of You Walk a Precarious Path . . . . . . . . . . . . . . . . . . . . . . . . . . . . 175

**19. Living on Prana.** . . . . . . . . . . . . . . . . . . . . . . . . . . . . . . . . . . . **177**
Human Behavior and Food. . . . . . . . . . . . . . . . . . . . . . . . . . . . . . . . . . . 177
The Ability to Live Without Food . . . . . . . . . . . . . . . . . . . . . . . . . . . . . . 179
To Live on the Wholeness of Light. . . . . . . . . . . . . . . . . . . . . . . . . . . . . . 181
Prana Advantages and Disadvantages . . . . . . . . . . . . . . . . . . . . . . . . . . . 182
Physical Transitions. . . . . . . . . . . . . . . . . . . . . . . . . . . . . . . . . . . . . . . . 183
The Future of Textiles. . . . . . . . . . . . . . . . . . . . . . . . . . . . . . . . . . . . . . . 183

**20. Compassion Knows No "Other"** . . . . . . . . . . . . . . . . . . . . . . . **185**
Assembling Your Year with Creativity . . . . . . . . . . . . . . . . . . . . . . . . . . . 185
History, Free Will and the Path of Evolution . . . . . . . . . . . . . . . . . . . . . . 186
Dissolving Old Thoughts and Patterns. . . . . . . . . . . . . . . . . . . . . . . . . . . 187
Cautionary Influences and (R)evolutionary Developments . . . . . . . . . . . . . 188
Healing Division and Duality. . . . . . . . . . . . . . . . . . . . . . . . . . . . . . . . . . 188
Exposing Injuries and Injustices . . . . . . . . . . . . . . . . . . . . . . . . . . . . . . . 190
Cautionary Notes: Reducing Risk and Vulnerability . . . . . . . . . . . . . . . . . 191
You're Moving into a Tertiary System. . . . . . . . . . . . . . . . . . . . . . . . . . . . 192

Do Not Hold Back Compassion . . . . . . . . . . . . . . . . . . . . . . . . . . . . . . . . . . . 193
The Purpose of Life Is Life Itself . . . . . . . . . . . . . . . . . . . . . . . . . . . . . . . . . . 193

## Earth Body, Gaia Spirit

### 21. Does Gaia Believe in God? . . . . . . . . . . . . . . . . . . . . . . . . . . . . . 195

Forms of Belief. . . . . . . . . . . . . . . . . . . . . . . . . . . . . . . . . . . . . . . . . . . . . . . 195
Knowledge and Faith. . . . . . . . . . . . . . . . . . . . . . . . . . . . . . . . . . . . . . . . . . 196
The Many Versions of God. . . . . . . . . . . . . . . . . . . . . . . . . . . . . . . . . . . . . . 197
The Living Mind. . . . . . . . . . . . . . . . . . . . . . . . . . . . . . . . . . . . . . . . . . . . . . 198

### 22. The Once and Future Pope . . . . . . . . . . . . . . . . . . . . . . . . . . . . . 201

Prophecy and Prediction . . . . . . . . . . . . . . . . . . . . . . . . . . . . . . . . . . . . . . . 201
The Most Recent Pope Hoped to Live through the End Times. . . . . . . . . . . 202
The New Pope Faces Challenges from the Powerful . . . . . . . . . . . . . . . . . . . 203
An Interpretation of the Bible and Organized Religion. . . . . . . . . . . . . . . . . 204
The Authority of Spirit. . . . . . . . . . . . . . . . . . . . . . . . . . . . . . . . . . . . . . . . . 205

### 23. The Gift of Life Continues to Give . . . . . . . . . . . . . . . . . . . . . . 207

It Is Not Possible to Impair the
Progress of Those Who Have Passed On . . . . . . . . . . . . . . . . . . . . . . . . . . . . 208
Following the Trail Left by a Loved One . . . . . . . . . . . . . . . . . . . . . . . . . . . . 209
On Organ Transplants . . . . . . . . . . . . . . . . . . . . . . . . . . . . . . . . . . . . . . . . . 210
Body Regeneration Is a Gift from Humanity's Ancient Ancestors . . . . . . . . . 210
Organ Transplants Are Proof That You Are All One . . . . . . . . . . . . . . . . . . . 211
Advice for Hopeful Recipients, Kind Donors and Brokers of Organs . . . . . . . 212

### 24. Earth Changes Update. . . . . . . . . . . . . . . . . . . . . . . . . . . . . . . . . . 215

Acclimatizing to Change . . . . . . . . . . . . . . . . . . . . . . . . . . . . . . . . . . . . . . . 215
Earthquakes and Human Practices. . . . . . . . . . . . . . . . . . . . . . . . . . . . . . . . 217
Listening to the Earth's Messages . . . . . . . . . . . . . . . . . . . . . . . . . . . . . . . . . 219
Understanding Natural Changes . . . . . . . . . . . . . . . . . . . . . . . . . . . . . . . . . . 221
Healing in the Aftermath. . . . . . . . . . . . . . . . . . . . . . . . . . . . . . . . . . . . . . . 223
Preparing for Upcoming Changes. . . . . . . . . . . . . . . . . . . . . . . . . . . . . . . . . 224

# Preface (Pepper)

## DEAR FRIENDS AND FAMILY OF GAIA,

*B*ehind these polite and cultured words the Gulf of Mexico is in the midst of one of the largest oil spills in modern human history, and every environment and being—plant, animal, mineral and human—seems to be under assault. I have always introduced Gaia's words to you as uncompromisingly compassionate and nonjudgmental, yet when I sat down to do the same this time, a part of me wondered whether it would still hold true. "Even now?" I asked aloud with the television on in the background displaying images of wildlife mired helplessly in the oil slicks. And yet without even waiting for an answer, I already knew that, yes, even now.

Still, some part of me feels that we have crossed an invisible barrier that will have long-lasting effects on our present and future Earth experiences and that of future generations. About fifteen years ago, when I began to channel Gaia's words and energy, she showed me mental pictures of Earth in its various stages of evolution. I understood that some of these were possibilities, others were probabilities and a few were already certainties. Large environmental catastrophes seemed very probable, but I felt confident back then that we would avert most of them, even if it was just in the nick of time. Gaia says we have averted some, but we cannot avert them all because there is simply not enough consciousness on the planet yet to do so. In the meantime, there are some "compassionate corrections" in store for us. The good news is that if we learn to clean up some of our messes, we can clean up others too—perhaps all of them.

Earth can resource itself and has done so many times. We, collective humanity, are one of Earth's resources. We cycle and recycle ourselves through lifetimes upon Earth, learning, sharing and contributing to Earth in a variety of ways. Gaia truly benefits from our company, and her sentience enjoys the varied history we have shared with the planet. That being said, this is a time of great change for humanity and for Earth. We are on the cusp of a New Age, and time is running out on our present—soon to be recent past—age. Some of the problems that have persisted in this age will follow us into the next. We cannot simply dismiss them because the calendar indicates it is time to flip the page onto the next bright image. Fortunately, some of the solutions and changes that we have resisted will also follow, allowing us the dignity of knowing that we have truly evolved instead of wondering if we imagined it.

Gaia's love and compassion will follow us wherever we go, whether it is here or somewhere else. Her empathy for humanity sounds a universal note; the kind that strikes a balance between friends and foes, garish nightmares and golden days, the third dimension and the next. She will continue to assist us in discovering the kind of solutions that we need most given our present-day circumstances. And we must do our part as well. Although we have been supportive of and supported by the systems we all know, we must admit that at times they have been unsatisfactory and inadequate.

The material in this volume does not point fingers at our less than honorable moments. Instead, it makes suggestions, offers course corrections, gently describes the errors and omissions of previous civilizations, and sheds light on corridors of thought that are still new to us. Gaia cannot offer us complete solutions to our difficulties and dilemmas, but she can instill within us the knowingness to see through our predicaments to solve the puzzles of our time.

— Pepper Lewis

# Introduction (Gaia)

*I* present this book to you as a laboratory, a think tank and a supply store where you can acquire the tools and ideas you need most. The planet is my body, but your world is simply something that has been constructed atop it. It is a temporary structure and was never meant to be permanent. One of the best things that can be said about it is that it serves a variety of different purposes. Many different worlds call Earth home, each one is unique and separate from the rest for the most part. Each is refreshingly different and no two are alike, yet some share common interests and resources. Some of the worlds are aware of each other, but most are not. Mostly they imagine other worlds in the way that you do: far away and distant, in galaxies that you will never know unless foreign-looking visitors were to come calling.

The evolution of a planet also means evolution is in store for those things that are associated with or attached to the planet. This nonexclusive arrangement applies to all worlds and all realities, including thought processes, ideas, feelings, truths, and those physical things that the foregoing have constructed. In other words, change for one means change for all. Is Earth being forced to change because humanity has erred in its assumptions about the role of Earth as consummate mother and resource, or is humanity changing because the elemental environment it calls home is remaking and repositioning itself in response to an inner directive? Is one or the other at fault in a process that is older than time?

This is a burdensome time for humanity, mostly because it has forgotten that worlds, like days, overlap. This time of overlap is like an intersection that has one too many directions to choose from. This intersection is the meeting place of bridges and tunnels, carports and skyports, choices and ideas. My suggestion to you is that you observe your response to each of the ideas that visit you, making sure that a visit does not turn into an extended stay. Cherish these moments, because they are the last before the first. Come together in community whenever possible so that your souls will recognize the light within each other.

One candle can light ten or more others without stress or strain, but the same candle cannot illumine the way for even one other, thus the two will not see beyond the shortest distance. Continuing on, they would extinguish each other, both blinded by too little light.

This book will help you to overcome real and imagined burdens. It will teach you how to think and dream a new world and then to create it. You do not need to wait until this one, like a candle, no longer illumines your path. There are still joys to be had on your journey, and many successes and solutions to savor. Earth is a very resourceful planet, perhaps even more than others that follow a similar path around their own suns. Humanity is made of that same material, one part earth and one part sky, with two poles to tether and temper new ideas—always leaning in, as if to hear the secrets that are whispered in the wind.

— Gaia

# Healing the World
# One Meditation at a Time

*Several weeks ago I participated in a global meditation event based upon an inspirational and widely circulated email. Are you able to say the event was a success? If so, can you describe how? Was the specified date and time as relevant as was publicized? Also, and I mean no disrespect, it seems that every time I turn around there is yet another call to action and another date that is supposed to be even more vitally significant than the last. Is our world really that fragile? Would everything we believe in unravel if we did not respond to these urgent requests? Lastly, are these events more noteworthy than our individual moments of prayer or contemplation with Spirit?*

Your questions, though well thought out and expressed, are reminiscent of something that has been swallowed but cannot be entirely digested. Your generous deeds and desires for humanity and for the Earth juxtapose the obvious contradictions that you feel. Know that you are not alone in your concerns, as countless other well-intentioned members of a growing community of consciousness think and feel as you do.

Your participation in the global mediation, and that of others, was perceived at a deep vibratory level throughout the globe. This means that for the duration of the cycle of intention, the Earth was in direct resonance with a shared concentrated vibration that transcended the common and the known. The known has many relative boundaries, and most of these are based on agreed beliefs. Certainly there are many beliefs regarding the limitations of the third dimension, but there are even more beliefs entirely dedicated to the limits of the human mind. These belief systems are as dense and outmoded as the concrete and glass buildings that imprison your creativity far too much of the time.

The limiting belief systems that humans hold about themselves are the very reason they now consign themselves to address the challenging and potentially life-threatening situations that have the power to free them forever. In order to do so, humans must break through the old, ironclad half-truths that have long stood as substitutes for original and creative thought. With many present-day systems bound for collapse and failure, humans must rise above the problems they have created with solutions that benefit their tomorrows rather than those that expired yesterday.

## BLESSINGS IN DISGUISE

The event you participated in was the brainchild of a moment in which inspiration and desperation became one. Odd as it may appear, these two seeming opposites are more complimentary than not. Opposites both attract and repel one another—the further the stretch, the quicker the rebound effect. Thus dramatic moments, however unfair or inconvenient they may seem at the time, can be thought of as blessings in disguise. Moments of divine inspiration are ones in which an isolated or limited thought becomes quickened by the intensity of limitlessness. This creates a combustible catalyst—a fire that must consume itself—and because the law governing the infinite surpasses the more temporary law of the finite, a potential solution emerges in place of a persistent dilemma. The solution is born as pure potential; it is an immaculate conception. It is a potential solution, in that it can all too easily be dissolved in a moment of ignorance, doubt or fear. Very few original thoughts become actions, at least not in the third dimension.

This original thought became a prime directive for the individual who conceived it. Divine will, when coupled with human will, is a match made in heaven and made creative on Earth. It is both creative principle and that which the principle created. Please follow along carefully. Do not allow yourself the luxury of becoming sluggish or glossing over these words! You will find the virtues of this law useful in almost every aspect of life should you apply it carefully and measure it equally in all directions. Natural law, like universal law, is diverse and specific, always supporting that which is greater than itself and never undermining it as human law often does.

An original thought is almost always a success, if for no other reason than it puts true creativity first. But true creativity, like an infant child, must be protected and nurtured until it can sustain itself. Ignorance, more than anything else, will subdue and even smother it before it has even known the breath of life. Such is the case with many grand and creative ideas that seemingly fall over the mirage called the horizon as if the Earth were truly flat. The individual whose efforts sustained the idea of a global meditation until it became a force of its own reckoning held its vision beyond the point of no return. That this is the principle behind all creation is more important than the event itself, those who participated in it and its overall effect.

The event can be deemed a success, but it is one of many in a succession of events. When hearts and minds come together, there is no limit to what can be achieved. The benefit of this event is that it became a living mediation—one whose directed energy was empowered by those who, themselves, felt powerful in their participation. The Earth as a whole was able to draw upon that power and use it purposefully for the well-being of the all and the All. Do not assume, however, that a global meditation with awareness on peace means that the Earth must use the energies gathered for that purpose alone. Energy flows, based upon both necessity and creativity, via the path of least resistance. Your bank account, for instance, does the same. Why does it seem to flow to your debts more quickly than to your creative notions? Because those to whom you owe have no resistance in allowing the repayment of that debt. The act of receiving is both creative and natural, do you see? As your creative instincts become first nature to you instead of second instinct, you will have more funds in your bank account with which to accomplish your creative means.

## DIFFICULT QUESTIONS, EXPERIENTIAL ANSWERS

You wish to know about the specific success of this event, which is difficult to format into words. Can you specifically describe what makes you awaken to a more profound sense of purpose one day and not another? Or what makes you feel that you are part of a galactic race of beings whose evolution is linked to an indivisible net of consciousness? Can you explain what makes this unique awareness available to you in one moment and absent in the next? It is not that these questions cannot be answered so much as that the answers are found at the experiential level. These experiences are at the root of why, as individual souls, you risk everything again and again as units of human potential. There simply is nothing else like them in the universe. To be in service to the wholeness is to be whole. To be whole is to be everything and All. Moments such as these approximate the experience of being All rather than one with the All.

The specific date and time, in this case, was of less relevance to the global interests that can be considered Gaian or human. It was a catalyst, an agreement that touched hearts and minds alike. The depths of sorrows and the heights of amazement to which the human spirit can soar are unequalled in the galaxy as far as the third dimension is concerned. The prime directive of the third dimension is experiential growth—not escape—through and beyond the veils of perceived suffering. Your participation in events such as those reflected in your questions indicate a desire to be a part of something greater than your individual thoughts. By the way, it does not matter if your motives are selfless or selfish; the effect is the same because your point of origin is the same. Energy is energy; the electrical outlet does not care if you are plugging in a refrigerator or a television. Do not confuse intent and motive, as one applies to focused thought and the other to reason and motion.

## DO NOT SUCCUMB TO OVERLY DRAMATIC URGENCY

The date became something like the "shot heard 'round the world," but that is the nature of this period in time. Humanity is looking for signs and symbols in every crevice and under every rock. It is in consummate fear that it may miss the one and only link between its past and its future. May I promise you that this will not be the case? May I plead my case with you in this regard? You are made of the breath and substance of the One and the All. There is no error in your thinking and no temporary forgetting that would make it possible for you to get lost or left behind. Even the dust beneath your feet knows this. Please do not succumb to the urgency that you see in the hungry eyes of those who continue to dine at the table whose host is but the maker of the latest doomsday device.

Are all global meditation dates insignificant? No, but for the most part, they are coordinates, indicators of humanity's ability to come together as a community for a common cause. The inner knowing that guides you to join in thought to effect change will one day guide you to join in thought to cause change. Events such as these promote the growth of certain cells within the brain that recognize the family of humanity. In other words, they recognize the signature call of divine human will. Does this mean that those who choose not to participate in these events will not develop this cell structure? No, this is one of many triggers that will guide you beyond doubt and into true instinctual knowing.

The world you live in is not fragile or brittle. Life upon Earth is not tenuous. It is sound, secure and stable. It is currently in a state of adaptation; it is in the process of changing to fit new circumstances and conditions. All of life upon the Earth is being modified to suit a greater purpose, and there are no exceptions in this. All of life is undergoing the development of physical and behavioral characteristics that will allow it to thrive under new and different circumstances. These conditions will continue to prevail, and some will increase in intensity. That being said, some of your more difficult reactions will diminish as your sensory responses become more able to sustain new vibrations and other stimuli.

Please do not respond to the pleas of those who insist that your participation in these events is necessary to save the world or save yourself. There is a tendency within those who advertise and broadcast these messages to unreasonably magnify their importance, making them into a mockery of the unjust and the unconscious. Let each invitation stand on its own merit. Whether you accept or decline an invitation is up to you. Both heaven and Earth will look favorably upon you either way. Refrain from believing in lack, and instead celebrate the abundance of resources at your disposal.

Your individual moments of contemplation are intimacies whose secrets rest within the divine. There is no comparison between these and the global moments of which you write. One does not stand in place of another. Each is a sacred act unto itself. Many believe that the inability to meditate prevents them from communicating with Earth and heaven. It is not so; a simple desire to share and expand your beingness, placed in or near your heart, is strong enough to melt the lead of resistance and gain a foothold with Spirit! There is no substitute for this, and your silence is not necessary. Sing your thoughts and your prayers if you like; do not underestimate Spirit's ability to understand all languages. Do not measure yourself by the rewards or lessons of others. Be one as a conscious community and unique as a creative individual.

Do allow yourself to celebrate the solstices and the equinoxes. Soon enough these dates will change. Do not chastise the melting of the poles! Good things will yet follow the thawing of that which has been long frozen. Your beliefs have also been frozen in time and have prevented you from seeing beneath and beyond the limitations of this life. Whenever possible, acknowledge the new moon and the full. Give thanks that the Sun returns each day and the Moon at night. What you struggle with today, you will look back on in sweet nostalgia.

# The Conscious Development of Land

*I own a few parcels of land that are unique and special to me. Over the time that I have owned this land, I have experienced encounters with a variety of animals, both common and uncommon, as well as elementals and other energies. I am sure that all of these beings enjoy and appreciate this land, which pleases me very much. Strangely, I also feel that the time may be right to either sell these parcels or to develop them, and I am currently exploring these possibilities. Any decision I make would have to acknowledge and include a sense of good will for and from the land itself. How can I be confident that I am acting correctly?*

*I*t is best to begin by reintroducing yourself, even if you and the land have been intimately acquainted with one another before. It is likely that either you or the land have changed in some significant way, so becoming reacquainted will benefit you both. A parcel of land can be identified by certain characteristics. Like a personality, its terrain might be rough around the edges but soft on the interior, or gnarly and thorny, or even overly soft—like quicksand. Interestingly, land can also be influenced by several other criteria, including whether its owners are local or live elsewhere, as well as how and by whom the title for the land is held. Land that is owned by an individual has different characteristics than federal land or land that is corporately owned.

## OWNERSHIP VERSUS CUSTODIANSHIP OF LAND

Some would be quick to correct these words—almost before they have been spoken—by reminding me (as if I didn't know) that the Earth cannot be truly owned, and rightly so! And now that we have gotten that out of the way, we can proceed with an answer that is of use to you. For if we were to negate your ownership, we would also do away with the question itself, and it is one that is far too valuable to you and to others. Truth be told, you cannot own anything. You do not even own your body—at best, it is

7

leased for the duration of your life, after which it is returned to the Earth, as its elements belong to the clay from which it was formed. The only things that can be owned are your experiences, which are maintained infinitely and lovingly by the compassionate observer of miracles called your "soul."

The Earth cannot be owned, though attempts to do so have marred its surface, your history and the availability of certain resources. Over time, the Earth will be rearranged many times over, and its uses will be many. Imagine, just for a moment, the variety of resources your land currently offers—not simply those on the researched and recorded deeds that your current protocol requires, but those that may extend beyond that. How many times might have the boundaries around this land been drawn and redrawn? This land is much older than your memories, but you are much older than the land—a paradox best left for another day, yes?

As the land's current owner, you can do much, and as its custodian, you can do even more. A custodian is someone who is sworn to protect and uphold something that is considered both valuable and precious. A custodian is linked in some inexplicable way to that which they have sworn to protect. Those who recognize this relationship as sacred also know that it entails a moral concordat, one that exists beyond the social or legal entitlements of a deed. If you are not certain that you are your land's custodian, ask it. Yes, it is that simple! Place yourself comfortably upon it and ask the land to speak to you in one voice—rather than through its elemental makeup—so there will be less confusion.

If you discover that you are not the most appropriate custodian, then you can evaluate the choices that present themselves, including selling or turning over the land to a more appropriate owner. If you discover that you are its custodian, you will enter a new wisdom within yourself that binds you to the land's well-being. This does not mean that you cannot develop or sell the land; it simply assures that your decisions will be made in the highest good.

## TUNING INTO SOUND RESONANCE

Because there seems to be a shortage of land, it also seems that what remains must be stayed from development, but that is not necessarily so. All that is life is designed to be useful and purposeful. In your time, this has come to mean that something of use to humanity's commerce must be erected atop it, and this has led to certain imbalances, as you already know. So it is for the nature outside of you that is yours, and the nature within that is you, to co-create a conscious response to the questions that arise.

A response is not the same as an answer. An answer is the result of your reasoning and logical thinking; it is based upon the vibrations of linear time. A response is the natural knowing that emerges from the resonant harmonic of life itself. Do you remember hearing or reading about how the great stones of the pyramids were lifted into place by the science of sound? A resonant harmonic response is based upon the same science, and it is available to all who acknowledge and attune themselves to the kingdoms of nature. It requires a bit of practice, so do not abandon the idea if nature does not immediately make itself known to you.

You and the land are both part of Earth's resources, and you are not as different from it as you may imagine, at least not while your essence is merged with your journey here. Your body is made of a mix of the same minerals the Earth requires. When these are included in your diet, you are more apt to respond from a naturally resonant place, but if your body is devoid of these important elements, it will be more difficult for you to be in your natural knowing. Therefore it is important to be a careful caretaker of your own well-being as you evaluate the future of this parcel of land.

## VISUALIZING IMAGE RESONANCE

As you continue the practice of sound resonance, begin to include image resonance, or the process of actively envisioning the future you would like to share with others. If you envision the best of all worlds, you will live in the best of all worlds. Image resonance is an activity that is enhanced and protected by the third eye center. This center regulates your well-being and connectivity to all of your environments, including all that you participate in on the Earth plane; it is not limited by your personality, though it can be influenced by it. The third eye center is always present in the Now, which is one of the reasons why so many of you have difficulty connecting with it. Most of you are still anywhere but here!

Image the present moment as you envision the highest potential it (and you) can attain. You may begin to feel a distortion in your electro-magnetic field similar to the sensation associated with crossed eyes. This sensation is due to the merging of two semi-realities (soft potentials) into one. Stay in the moment until the distortion passes. Other side effects of this exercise may include dizziness and a slight headache, though these are not mandatory. Resist the temptation to manifest these symptoms in order to ensure or confirm that you have done the exercise correctly.

Last, be honest with yourself, for any attempt to do otherwise will result in a condition that is less than desirable. If you wish to become a developer of land and to profit by it, then say so and do so. Let your thoughts match your words and your words match your deeds. If you wish to be a protector of wildlife, then be an inspiration to including other lands in the scope of your imagineering. And if you wish to sit upon your good fortune for a bit longer before deciding what to do, then pull up a rock or two and invite a tree, a squirrel and a bear to share a meal as kin. The canopy of stars by moonlight will set the mood, and the god within all will be language enough.

# Lack of Resources in a World of Plenty

*T*he surface of the Earth bears certain scars, witness to events of major historic perspective. Beautiful canyons, rivers and lakes erase, or least hide, evidence of massive and unexpected devastation. Likewise, deserts lie naked and exposed, unclothed and unable to mask the corruption that changed verdant green resources into dry sand. History has also left scars behind where wars have changed the course of events, and monuments now stand in place of men. Catastrophic events are a natural part of the evolution of the planet, and they have helped to shape the course of history. Many unnatural events have also had a catastrophic effect upon events on Earth and have altered the course of history significantly. Events associated with the condition of the world economy can be attributed to both natural and unnatural causes, and history will more than likely record them as extremes of the same polarity.

The solar system of which the Earth is a part is pulsing its way toward a light of a different order, changing everything and inspiring an evolutional leap that is natural within the great scheme of time in which universes are measured. This soon-to-be-experienced light is of a cosmic order, and though you cannot see it from your current perspective, it has temporarily cast the Earth in shadow. The Earth will emerge from this pale cast as it always has, and the light that has temporarily eclipsed a clearer vision of a bright future will return, opening the eyes of all—even those of the blind who would not see.

## THE EBB AND FLOW OF THE ECONOMY

The Earth is part of a solar system that is vast, powerful and sometimes difficult to fathom. World economic markets and the currencies that represent them are also part of a much larger system, one that is vast in its holdings, unimaginable in its power and equally difficult to fathom. Inevitably, the ocean tides rise and fall, oblivious to the rise and fall of world leaders, currencies or the markets they have invested in. Their rhythm is perfect and timed by a relationship with something greater than the moment or the day. Currencies and markets on the other hand, are artificial instruments and can be controlled—or left uncontrolled— quite easily. These too follow a rhythm that is perfectly timed and guided by a relationship to something unseen.

Please understand that forces, even those that are natural, can be influenced or controlled to a certain degree. Like a serpent, they can be tamed and hypnotized to act in a certain way even while everyone is watching. Such is the case with world markets at this time; they have been coaxed into behaving in a manner that has dissolved many assets into thin air. But not all assets have fallen, nor have the fortunes of those who understand the system and how it works. Modern people believe that like their destiny, they are in charge of their own money, but that is only partially true. There are systems, of which humans are a part, that exert a great deal of influence upon the world, and because they are a part of this same world, they are, both by participation and agreement, a part of this same system.

The banking systems and the currencies they trade in are experiencing an orchestrated crisis, a well-organized and carefully crafted freefall that will remake the face of the world and those who govern it. Modern people own a part of their world, but a part of their world also owns them. Modern people do not own the currency they trade in—it is leant to them. They do not own their homes or that of their ancestors, as that too is given to them on conditions that are governed by sovereignties greater than their own. That people are not sovereign in their world or in their homes may be an outrage, but it is not a new outrage. Modern people live within the same system as ancient humans, and that system lives within them. Is there a plan for this to change? Yes, but humanity must first emerge from its own shadow. It cannot follow a lighter path without until it discovers its own light within.

The causes for the downturn in the economy are both natural and unnatural. The universal laws that govern the rhythmic rise and fall of the tides are the same ones that ensure the pendulum of fortune will swing through large and small fortunes alike. This is nature at work; one season infallibly yielding to the next, resting and preparing for the dawn of its return. The ocean has a floor, and although its depth is sometimes difficult to measure, it is always there as a foundation of support to all that depends upon it. The economy was not so fortunate. Without a firm foundation, it has been tossed to the waves to do with as they please.

At least for a time the economy will continue to drift, and as long as it does, it will be difficult to build a boat that is strong enough or swift enough to outmaneuver the currents. The tides take with them many things, and this economic movement will mirror the tides in many ways. The tides also return lost items and forgotten relics from times long past. Therefore, carefully hidden truths can be expected to emerge in moments and places where they are least expected. This will expose some of the minor players [pawns] in the system, but the lords and masters of this game can afford to sacrifice many pawns and still protect their well-built fortresses. Modern people must take their finances and obligations seriously, yet in doing so, they may overlook the point of the game in which they are both participant and observer. It is better to ride the pendulum across the sky of illusion than have it slice through one's reality on Earth.

## RESHUFFLING THE HOUSE OF CARDS

As it has been said, global economies will continue to be buffeted by winds of change amid uncertainty. Elected officials will continue to seek counsel among their own experts as well as participate in global showings of support and strength with other world leaders. Even a house of cards looks better built while it is being propped up by more than one hand. But like a deck of cards that must be reshuffled from time to time, there will be a great shift in the distribution of wealth that will raise capital for some countries and threaten to pull down others. Those who emerge seemingly unscathed may have sold their souls in the process—or those of their citizens, more likely.

None of the world currencies have any long-lasting value, so most will see their value sink. They do not have value because they are not aligned with anything of value. The wealth that is attributed to most nations is no longer owned by them and is, in some cases, owned by another country altogether or by the corporations that represent them. Some of the corporations that have been branded as nasty culprits in certain world markets may yet emerge as heroes when it is discovered that they are able to rescue some governments from their own volatility. There is a certain stench associated with greed, but the stench of fear is even worse.

Corporations will be seen as stabilizing forces in some markets and will enjoy a sovereignty of sorts they did not have previously. Even corporations with large business complexes in other countries will be protected by international law in much the same way that embassies and their grantors are protected today. Some countries will default on their most basic obligations, and they will watch on the sidelines as their sovereignty is purchased or annexed by another country whose resources are more "in play" than their own. Trading partnerships between countries will extend into other areas as resources are pooled together in hopes of strengthening global positions.

## TAPPING UNDISCOVERED RESOURCES

Long ago, countries vied for trading routes and for the discovery of new lands to claim in the name of the crowns they represented. Today crowns are out of fashion and most lands–though not all—have been claimed. Their resources have been converted to cash or refinanced into further debt. An economy cannot grow unless there is room for it to grow, and that is virtually impossible given today's schema, making new and vital resources a necessity.

The Earth does have new and undiscovered resources. Some of these have been, until recently, buried underneath the ice, at and near both poles. As the ice thaws, plans on how and when to access these regional resources are already being put in place. Several countries have already led exploratory missions in this regard and have even begun the process of claiming them in the name of those they represent. Already there are a variety of flags posted on the ocean floor, awaiting acknowledgment. But there is no precedent for claiming the ice or what is potentially beneath it, and political minds are already preparing for competition and more. Some of these regional resources include natural gas and oil, but there are a few surprises in the area as well.

Not all countries or economies will have access to these new resources, yet they know that in order to thrive in a new world, they must find ways to expand or face other imaginable perils. Those who cannot find treasure in the depths of the oceans will look to space instead. Many countries, even those you might not consider players in the space race, are already there and beyond. Set aside what you imagine to be exploratory missions to space and nearby planets and consider instead that mining new and profitable resources upon both the Moon and Mars is already possible. In fact, contracts are already in place with government and private sector contractors for transporting resources, housing projects for potential workers and much more.

Those who have recently lost confidence and interest in currency and commodity trading upon the Earth may be coaxed into investing in the new satellite markets. Understand that while some people are doing their best to protect their real estate holdings upon the Earth, others have already projected their fortunes elsewhere and are even now preparing to stake claims elsewhere. "The sky is the limit" is no longer just a saying. Certainly this topic could be developed further, but it is not the intended subject now.

## THE COMING CHANGES

Markets and currencies on Earth will continue to be volatile, and it will be difficult for even the best economic minds to predict what will happen. It is not a level playing field, and those who know how to play the game know this. Those who do not know how to play the financial games of the day will continue to be hurt by the process. As alliances between countries continue to evolve, there will be less need for as many different currencies. Paper money will become less necessary and therefore less available. New ways to manage credits and debits will soon emerge. As with all things of a nature that seem to be a threat, there will be resistance at first. But deepening volatility of other choices combined with several consumer incentives and an unprecedented campaign for public confidence will make this choice an eventual success.

The world's stock markets will be completely revamped and overhauled. They will be renamed and managed in different ways than they are today. Not all companies will be allowed to issue stock. Private investment houses will be able to represent those who cannot participate in the larger scheme of trading. Higher risks will, as always, reap higher rewards. An under-the-counter market will parallel the over-the-counter one, in legal but casino-style investments that resemble the online gaming of today.

Commodity trading will continue to entice investors. However, the future of many commodities, including those in the farming and ranching fields, will continue to be uncertain. They will be worthwhile investments for those with a stomach for it. New food sources of both natural and unnatural origin will also spur interest. The declining health of the average citizen will make the food supplement market among the most lucrative, particularly as the medical community finds that it is less able to diagnose or cure.

As the relationship between biotic and abiotic systems is better understood, it will reveal new insights to the maintenance and rebuilding of ecosystems that are near the brink of death. Those who profit from the demise of these systems will continue to do so. The evolution of consciousness where many are concerned comes slowly, and their new dawn is further away than that of others. Some hunger for food and others for profit. Either way the cost to life is great. Hunger and thirst will continue to worsen, especially in third world countries, though certainly not limited to these alone. Even the world's richest countries, cannot or will not provide for all. Those who live beneath the misery indexes will more than likely remain in misery unless they rise above it by demanding it of the God within. They will find less-than-adequate support without.

## ANTIDOTES FOR THE POISONS

Local and community economies will thrive if they are able to find common ground. The needs of the entire community must be taken into account so there will not be too many pockets or holes that are left ignored or to chance. Open community systems will fare better than closed communities in the long run, but this will not be the first choice for many. Hoarding food and other resources will protect the moment but not the heart. Most hearts dwell in the land of plenty unless they have been driven through deserts of fear into the land of lack. Even the desert feeds its hungry with courage and stamina.

Lack of creativity and vision is the first poison. Fear is the second and greed is the third. Certainly the times ahead will offer other poisons as well. To every poison and every ill there is an antidote, but it must first be discovered and then administered in good time. Like it or not the Earth is changing, and more quickly than most would think. Humanity must rethink and then remake itself creatively now or the future will belong to the next human race. The evolution of the All and the all is capable of setting the scene for that to happen. The old rules by which humanity lives still apply, but not for long. It is time to dream a new dream, because the old one belongs to a timeline that is eroding beneath the feet of those who still cling to it.

The economies that value life will return to balance more quickly than those that do not. There is no inherent value in money. That is why its value rises and falls and why its purchasing power brings temporary happiness at best. The value of a nation is in its natural resources of which humanity is a part. Unless and until the value of human life and life in general is appreciated more generously, the world will seem out of balance and artificial. Before the skies fell and the heavens touched the Earth, there was a sound that resembled silence. Those who entered the silence found themselves in a dream of their own spinning. The pale cast of the dream wanes now, signaling that it is time to dream a new dream. This world is but a dream spell. That is how it came to be heaven on Earth.

# Hope for a Spiritual Economy

*Is there hope for a world economy based upon spiritual principles? I would like to change how I earn a living to something that feels more fulfilling and supportive of a world I would like to live in. I have watched others become healers, practitioners and channelers, but most are barely surviving financially, and the stress of not making ends meet seems to be the same regardless of one's work. I know that many make a practice of exchanging or bartering services, but that doesn't pay the rent. Topping this off, the spiritual community I am familiar with seems competitive and petty at times. I have seen compromises in principles that rival any in the hardcore business world! Is there a solution for this? Can we make a difference in the world and still earn a respectable income? Can we be spiritual and wealthy?*

*S*piritual principles are no different than other principles when they are supported, upheld and considered vital. A principle is an essential and underlying standard that assumes moral and ethical thinking and action. A principle is a primary thought—one that comes before all others. Principles, or right-thinking, are under the direction of first cause, or that which came before itself: the first before there was a first, and the zero before there was one. This principle, an absolute cause, assumes that right thinking will lead to right action, the most natural and obvious effect.

## PRINCIPLES IN TODAY'S WORLD AND WORKPLACE

This may surprise you, but the world is based upon spiritual principles, and for the most part they are upheld. Why doesn't it look that way? Because principles and higher laws are transparent and invisible. You cannot see cause, but you can see effect. Cause, being subtler than effect, is also more refined. Divine law is the foundation upon which human law rests, but human law does not rest lightly just now; in fact, it barely rests at all!

The difficulty with today's workplace is that very few feel that they are making a difference in their environment or the world they share with countless others. There is a nagging and persistent emptiness that remains largely unfulfilled. Starved for the kind of affection that only Spirit can bring, humanity goes in search of a more fulfilling job instead of a more fulfilling path. With so many hours spent at work per day, per week and per year, it is not difficult to imagine why humanity would want to change to a more satisfying endeavor.

Why is the spiritual community brimming over with healers, channelers, teachers, facilitators and practitioners of every kind? Because those who have invited, welcomed or stumbled upon the warmth of Spirit into their lives cannot help but want to share it with others. There is a throne-like place within every being, a seat for the soul. Once Spirit enters this place and warms it with agni, or soul-fire, a change unlike any other takes place, one that transforms lives and sets purpose on course.

As if intoxicated by a love potion, matter and Spirit—now joined—set a course that will take them beyond the Sun and back again. While on this journey, the being is able to revisit many of its previous expressions, and at each of these crossroads, another memory and another gift is added or recalled. Eventually the raging fire becomes a controlled furnace, and the inflamed being settles into a new pattern where matter is sustained by Spirit. Patterns are natural emulations of perfection, which is why they are so attractive and inviting. Inspired by perfection, or cause, one cannot help but want to share in the expansion of perfection. Those who offer themselves in this way describe a nearness to Source that they feel is less available to them elsewhere.

## WHY DO PEOPLE STRUGGLE FINANCIALLY?

Why are so many of these well-meaning, well-intentioned and deserving individuals barely surviving financially? In some cases, the individual and his endeavor are not well suited for one another. The same fire that can never be extinguished can and does burn. When matter and Spirit are not kept in balance, perfect law cannot be upheld. As perfect law is the foundation beneath human law, a less than perfect foundation will lead to a less than perfect pattern. Perfect patterns expand perfectly, but less than perfect patterns expand in less than perfect ways, often creating challenges in their attempts to rejoin perfection. Even those who are guided by Spirit must use that guidance to create or manifest in and with matter. Nowhere is this law more in evidence than upon third-dimensional Earth where suffering and ignorance of natural law reflect one another irrevocably.

Conditions where lack persists are reflections of a skewed polarity. Using the above premise, we must conclude that Spirit or matter—or both—are out of balance where the individual or his work are concerned. Perhaps the desire to heal must be expressed in another way. Often, those who have a strong desire to heal others must first heal themselves. Higher law requires this and demands it when necessary. The world will be healed one heart at a time regardless of whether currencies or favors are exchanged in the process. Oysters are irritated into making pearls by persistent grains of sand. Humans are not unlike oysters.

Modalities and techniques belong to the moment and to the day. Certificates of completion, like diplomas, are remembrances of energy already spent. Empowerment to heal or to teach emerges from the inner spark that alone re-creates itself because it is a reflection of light. Those who approach their practice as students of life will find that they prosper more than those who profess knowledge from the divine. Divinity is wholeness undivided. Modalities and teachers who divide and decry the works of others obscure their own light, slowing its progress and miring it in shadow.

## THE BEGGAR AND THE PREACHER

Long ago a preacher who believed in a blissful heaven and fiery hell began circulating an unhealthy rumor about who might be worthy enough to guide his chariot to the kingdom above. He told his parishioners that heaven and hell were in competition to see who could attract more candidates. To prove his point, he set two of the town's shoemakers against each other by whispering to each that the other would secretly like to see them out of business. For a time, the two shoemakers eyed one another suspiciously, counting their coins in secret and wondering how many coins the other was counting. When their workload became less, they imagined a conspiracy was at work, and they began to plot in counter-measure. They dreamed of the heaven they deserved and of the hell that awaited the other. Bitterness filled their hearts, and vengeful thoughts filled their minds. Each became ill and was certain the other had cast a spell of ill-will upon them. Good fortune eluded them both. Bias overtook the town, and many fell ill under a consequential moon that seemed in shadow for a quarter too long. One day a hungry beggar entered the town barefoot and with a rag for a cloak. He offered the first shoemaker a week's work in exchange for a few warm meals and a used pair of shoes, but he was turned away gruffly. He approached the second shoemaker and offered him two weeks of work in exchange for a soft cot, a few warm meals and a used pair of sandals. He was turned away, albeit more gently. As day turned to night, the beggar sought refuge in the town's parish, hoping for a bench to lie upon.

Staggering and leering as the delirium of hunger and exhaustion threatened to claim him, he startled the preacher who promptly had a heart attack and died. The beggar feared for his life and thought it most likely forfeit, especially given current circumstances. Thinking that it was never too late to make a better first impression, he decided that he would prefer to meet his maker on a full belly and wearing some better clothes. He supped well on the pantry stores and later dressed himself in some of the deceased preacher's clothes. Try as he might, he could not fit the preacher's shoes and sadly, remained barefoot.

The beggar set off in search of the town jailor, but on the way encountered the first shoemaker who did not recognize him dressed and pressed as he was in the deceased preacher's garb. The shoemaker welcomed him to the town and promptly offered him a custom made pair of shoes, which the impostor could not help but accept. He weighed the harm in accepting the gift and found that it was little, comparatively speaking. Continuing on his way, he all but collided with the second shoemaker who apologized profusely and insisted that he repay the unfortunate injustice with a new pair of sandals. Afraid of being recognized before he could confess his crime, the impostor accepted the gift and made his escape.

By offering gentle greetings and making polite inquiries, the beggar discovered that the jailor, a resourceful and kind man, had received some training in the medicinal arts and was even now away gathering yet another round of herbs to add to the latest balm and salve in an attempt to heal the different symptoms that were beginning to afflict the entire town. The beggar returned to the parish promising himself that he would return on the morrow to be judged and most likely sentenced.

In the meantime, he allowed himself the pleasure of another bath and yet another meal. He could not imagine what hell would be like, but he thought this current moment as close to heaven as he had known thus far. He lifted his head as if to heaven, and gave his thanks. Then he dropped his head and whispered to hell that he would come calling soon enough. Silently, and from opposite sides of the room, the two shoemakers entered the parish, bowing low as to not disturb a prayer in progress lest it not be answered because of their intrusion. As the moment became more appropriate, they greeted the imposter, who was already looking and sounding somewhat like a real preacher.

Noting that he was no longer alone, but somehow comfortable in his new environment, the beggar accepted and fawned over the gifted new shoes and sandals as they were presented to him by each of the shoemakers. Convinced that they could no longer identify him as a beggar, and as an extension of his gratitude, he invited his new shoemaker friends to share a cordial with him and to sit by the fire, which they gladly accepted. A sweet melancholy permeated the three as each in turn told of goodness bestowed upon them in moments least expected. Unbeknownst to the beggar/preacher, the two shoemakers looked upon each other with sorrowful sidelong glances. Interestingly, no one asked what had happened to the original preacher or where he had gone.

Sunday morning came, and the jailor had not returned. The beggar was beside himself with angst. He emerged from the small room he had allowed himself to live in to find a room full of parishioners. In a frightful moment he asked hell to claim him now, but nothing happened. Too embarrassed to ask heaven for any favors, he took his place at the pulpit and bowed his head in shame. As he did, so did all of the parishioners. Moved to tears, he began to speak of unenviable hardships that sometimes befall the good until they begin to look bad. His simple words tumbled out of a soft heart that had survived in a harsh world and was now telling its tale. Without knowing it, he had performed his first oratorical.

A grateful and gladdened parish responded to him and stood in respect as he walked past them. They shook his hand and thanked him as they shuffled past him and said their fare-thee-wells. A few could not help but bait his soft eyes with promises of dinners, cakes, firewood and more. All offers were joyfully accepted. Strangely, no one asked what had happened to the original preacher or where he had gone.

Legend has it that heaven and hell meet once a year to exchange residents and to claim new ones. Legend also has it that a barefoot reformed preacher greets each new arrival and mediates on his or her behalf. Before doing so, he is known for saying, "Lest ye not judge, and be neither beggar, lender, borrower or thief."

✻    ✻    ✻

*The above is a true story—I was there. It is a parable, a simple truth that is meant to illustrate and to inspire. There is no grand lesson here, and certainly none that is new. Competition, whether between shoemakers or teachers, tethers one to one's own fear, whatever it may be. Fear tends to consume passion, extinguishing it before it has even warmed the soul. In a competition against oneself, who can be the winner? Pettiness comes from small thoughts, and generally those that are based upon the perception of unfair yesterdays. It is best to speak less and to contemplate more, particularly before casting a vote of no confidence. Even silent words, like a magical salve, will make all that is invisible appear in plain sight. Less than honorable words will also be seen in the garish light of day. Surround yourself with those whom you admire and welcome, and allow others to do the same.*

## THE VALUE OF WEALTH

Compromises in principles are based upon lack of self-respect as well as a diminished trust in the field of plenty. Higher law will not bow down to lower law, thus human law must raise itself or suffer its faults. A compromise is a settlement in which two or more sides agree to accept less than they originally hoped for or thought possible. Most often the dispute is between the higher and the lower self, which is where principles are studied and tried. The hardcore business world is constructed of the same energy platform as that of the New Age or the Stone Age. Many of today's healers and teachers have only recently escaped the business environments that threatened to consume them. The new language they are learning to speak has not erased the platitudes of their pasts. Patience must prevail as they settle into the task at hand.

The bartering of goods and services is an old and established tradition. It upholds the exchange of useful commodities without engaging coin or currency. Long ago those of a lesser class were forbidden from owning property. As they were also unable to sign or fulfill the obligations of a promissory note, they created a system of their own, one that established and maintained a value based upon a word and a handshake. It was an excellent system and still is, except for the fact that those who abide by it most are still under the illusion that they somehow belong to or are related to a lesser standard of living. Uncertain as to their worthiness, or that of their unique talents, they offer them to friends, family and even strangers at reduced, minimal or non-existent rates. They barter and trade for skills, products and services without establishing a true value or upholding their banner of life.

It is good to be well-schooled in many different systems of thought, both social and economic. It is also important to know one's worth and to be as honorable with oneself as one is with others. In all things, there is a point of balance, and in each exchange, its equivalent must be achieved so that the results will be optimal. The unfolding of value is the expansion of wealth. Wealth is not the accumulation of money. It is the gathering of resources, as well as the knowledge, that accompanies all things to their rightful places. This includes the swift repayment of debt when owed and the delightful blend of Spirit and matter as it enters every place in and throughout one's life.

Spirit and matter are parts of every system of measuring abundance. Wealth of Spirit knows that matter is its companion, and Spirit dwells even in the densest matter. Those who bank and trade and confer value upon the current monetary system enjoy their task. One is not less than spiritual because he or she has found a chord of balance in this system where others have not. When the current system yields to the next, perhaps others will become more prosperous. Accumulate as much as you care to or discard that which no longer serves; it matters not, other than you will be best served when the decision is your own and not that of another. Where Spirit and matter are well in balance, there is no difference between spiritual wealth and monetary wealth.

## THE BALANCE OF SPIRIT AND MATTER

Matter wants to do, and Spirit wants to be. God is a divine being not a divine doing because God is the Spirit that animates matter. Humanity is both matter and Spirit; it is both a who and a what, and one cannot live long without the other. Humanity is at its best when both are in balance. One's job, or doing, does not secure a spiritual foundation anymore than being a spiritual visionary feeds a hungry family. On the other hand, finding one's own chord of life, that unique frequency that speaks from a deep and profound place, stimulates and fulfills an essence of perfection that eases and brings peace to even the most ancient stirrings and yearnings.

Does the world have a solution for the casually employed or those who are dismally unhappy in their current positions? Yes, but it involves stepping outside and beyond the belief systems that bind the ankles and trip the first step as easily as the last breath. The third dimension is heavily steeped in density. It is one of the heaviest dimensions as evidenced by its gravitational pull. You cannot escape the pull of gravity any more than you can ignore the many expressions of suffering that manifest daily. The third dimension is as the third dimension does. In other words, being comes before doing. Spirit comes into being before matter. Again, Spirit enters matter and then creates through it. That is why questions that begin with "what can I/should I do?" are so difficult to answer— Spirit has not entered them yet, so there is no matter yet. "Nothing is the matter" means that Spirit has not yet been detected in matter.

In order to create a new reality, a change must be detected in the current one. That change is called beingness; it is also called divinity, creativity and activity. Activity is an aspect of being, not doing. An active being, like an active principle, is a dynamic expression of possibility. A dynamic is a full range of energy, not unlike full spectrum light; it is will (pure desire) expressed as a force (energy), and it is characterized by the production (and secretion) of an activity (being and doing) that produces change, development and motion. Do you see? This is the formula for how to be the change you will also see!

This is how to change your world, one thought at a time, one job at a time, one currency or system at a time—or all at once! You do not have to destroy your world or your beliefs; you can replace them with a higher truth and a higher law. It is a science; it cannot deceive or mislead. It cannot be manipulated or controlled. The understanding of this law will free you to escape the sentence that your belief systems have imposed upon you. The law is the key, and as you may remember, there is no jailor, only a gentle metaphysician gathering of all that might yet heal the ills of the world. Will you be my companion in this?

# Solutions for a Small Planet

*A few months ago, sandwiched in between all of the questions posed to Gaia, she put forth a question of her own. Her question, posed in the form of a problem currently facing humanity was: What is the most probable future of the automobile given that there is an overabundance of cars in almost every corner of the world and taking into account a gradual movement away from fossil fuels? Here is Gaia's answer in its entirety.*

The most pleasant time to consider a problem is before it becomes a problem, or better yet, when it is not your problem. Another good time is when a variety of solutions are present, and such is the case with the automobile. It is a good idea at the outset of any exploration to acknowledge that the subject of inquiry, or problem, is also part of the solution. As another example of this concept, we might note that although diseased cells might pose a serious problem, the intelligence inherent in healthy cells might provide a solution. Therefore, as we begin our exploration, please take a moment to acknowledge just how important an invention the automobile has been, particularly during the last fifty years. The automobile has facilitated individual mobility, increased humankind's ability to make job-related tasks easier, furthered the exploration of remote places and much more. It will continue to be humanity's favored tool of transportation for a few more years, but not too many.

## THE ADVENT OF THE POD CAR

The automobile is already beginning to yield its noble position as a primary stakeholder in the global economy. This trend will continue and will further deteriorate interest in next year's model and the one after that. Even hybridized vehicles will lessen in popularity, at least until a vehicle that is powered by a unique and different fuel emerges on the common market. The true successor of the automobile will be a smaller, podlike vehicle that can be piloted by one or more individuals traveling in the same pod, in other words, the driver need not be the one seated in the driver's seat given today's configuration. A passenger could become the pilot [driver] at any time, even once the vehicle has been engaged and without the need to change seats. All seats will be driver-enabled and a simple computer will transfer command from one to another. Our pod-vehicle will be able to "daisy chain" onto other pods to create a small-scale version of a mass transit system. Pods will have built-in navigation systems so that as each pod nears its destination, it will separate from the others, semi-automatically at first and automatically as advances in the vehicle industry continue to unfold. Although these vehicles will still require a pilot, driving as it is understood today will be virtually obsolete. But we are getting a little ahead of ourselves as we have not yet dismantled the old in favor of the new.

Already there is a small decrease in the number of individual vehicles on the road, and fewer vehicles are being purchased and/or repaired. The worldwide popularity of the automobile will make it the most likely target of increased fees and taxations on both local and national levels. The financing of newer and more efficient toll roads that can accommodate present and future vehicles will be funded at least in part by these additional or increased fees. The cost of fuel will rise and fall many times, leaving the average consumer dazed as to what to expect next. The more creative minds have already turned their attention elsewhere; therefore, newer models will offer less features and incentives than those of previous years. In order to reduce the cost of living, an average family may downsize to one vehicle and an average student might forego a vehicle altogether in favor of their tuition. Automobile sharing arrangements will gain in popularity such that insurance companies will advertise their willingness to discount premiums when drivers choose this feature. Steel from obsolete and totaled vehicles will continue to be compressed and condensed, most of it being shipped to countries whose cost of labor allows for profitable reworking of these metals. And then, suddenly and at long last, just as the Iron Age and other ages before it succumbed, the Age of Steel will yield to the next and number its days as short.

## NEW TRANSPORTATION TECHNOLOGIES ON THE HORIZON

Not every theory or solution is spiritual, but everything that is spiritual is solution oriented. Bear this in mind as we consider the age-old alchemical theory of converting lead into gold. While the initiatic journey has been known to reveal many mysteries, the process by which lead can become gold is a creative one that involves transmutation under the more expansive laws of physics. In other words, when higher laws act upon lower laws, the lower laws become attracted, or attached, to the higher laws. This use of the law of attraction will bind an obsolete thing or thought with one of a higher order for the purpose of advancing a more creative need or desire.

As the desire to emerge from under the weight of the automobile—financially and otherwise—becomes paramount, creativity will surge within minds that lend themselves to such a task. The result will be a series of successful experiments, particularly if minds that have already been working on space-age projects lend their support. Currently this is not the case and competition between scientific frontiers threatens the future of both. To simplify the subject, the emergence of new alloys that are environmentally sustainable and economically feasible will make the automobile worth more in its recycled state than in its previous new or used condition. While this development is not near enough timewise to mark on your calendar, it is worth mentioning and is indeed just rounding the corner of the next obsolete thought

These new alloys will be excellent conductors of electrical and magnetic properties. They will also adhere well to some non-metallic [not plastic] substances. While most current alloys are carbon based these are not, making them the first in a new family of alloys that feature crystalline intermetallic compounds—a solution whose constituent elements has not been previously combined and does not follow the ordinary rules of valency. Where previous alloys have required strength, such as that found in steel, current needs will favor eutectic alloys, or those with a lower melting and freezing point. Such alloys will also have better physical characteristics than their predecessors, such as a much higher resistance to corrosion. While it would be unfair to remove the mystery from the human discovery process, it is fair to say that once a set of desired characteristics is entered or programmed into the equation, the result will be the same as that which allows lead to become gold. It goes without saying that these alloys must be light in weight, quite strong and able to sustain high temperatures. A second look at beryllium and niobium would be an excellent place to begin. At this point it may become necessary to study and then reveal the findings of the few who have been included in the knowledge associated with prior spacecraft interventions, otherwise known as ET technology, for that which will take you into space came from there first.

Quite obviously, the solar system contains the same material as is found on Earth, but in different quantities and in unique combinations. Some of these combinations have landed on Earth, and by one means or another new material has become available. Technology regarding some of these materials has eluded those who have studied it, but that is directly attributable to the secrecy that has surrounded and protected certain events and processes. Matters have changed substantially in this regard, particularly given the economics of the day. Currently, there is a branch of the military that is at least partially dedicated to civilian pursuits and crossover projects. These programs and those who manage their resources have a greater range of freedom with which to explore new ideas, particularly those that are born in the genius of the young mind, which dwells in this moment and the next more often than other minds do. Those whose minds wander the corridors of the gaming technology, particularly within 3D and holographic environments, are prime targets and highly recruitable.

## FIVE-DIMENSIONAL MINDS IN OUR FUTURE

Younger minds, particularly those that carry more ET genetic material have a tendency to bend dimensionally, rather than to the left or the right where the brain is concerned. While the left and the right brain have been known to argue and resist one another in a results-oriented environment, a dimensional mind will yield a more natural, economic and expansive result. Why? Dimensional minds are more harmonic and expositive than linear minds; they see not only the current horizon but the next one as well. These 5D minds are your future as well, as your current minds would defeat you otherwise and humanity would become obsolete within a few more generations. Another way to put this is that humanity's genetic future requires an influx of something else from somewhere else.

The pathways taken by younger minds will be different than those that have already been explored, therefore the same question will be posed in a variety of different ways, each one leading down, or through, a different path and yielding a new and different result. Some of these results combined with our earlier discussion on practical alchemy and given the additional ET perspective will birth at least four new sciences within the next two generations. Two of these will be "edge sciences" and at the forefront of productive and economic revitalization. Two others will become viable explorative sciences that are more adaptable to environments, such as those found on the Moon and on other celestial bodies.

## THE LAW OF ATTRACTION AND OUR CHANGING WORLD

We will still be left with excess material in the form of too many vehicles, and what shall we do with them? As time hastens forward, you will take the problem to task in ways that will be practical at first, then useful and finally exemplary. Like other problems, you cannot wish it away nor point fingers away from you. Desire is the cause, intention the effect and creativity the fuel that will accelerate the resulting ideas and actions. As you might already imagine, steel from some of the surplus automobiles will be reforged and shaped in order to reinforce the needs of an aging infrastructure, including bridges, commuter trains, airplanes and even additional compartment for the original space station and the one that will follow. While wind technology will not be long lasting, it will be the bridge to other explorations and will require its share of steel.

Eventually, new forms of technologies called aspect, or aspected, technologies will arise and quickly gain in popularity. Based upon this particular aspect technology, which will be derived from the alchemy of metallurgy, most of the components, metal and otherwise, associated with automobiles will be reduced to a reusable material that resembles metallurgic compost. This newly composted material will aid in the construction of new housing models, reducing consumption of other more costly and less resourceful material. It will become quite fashionable to live in these futuristic model homes and for a time—while it lasts—it will be a wise commodity investment as well.

Although we have not made the subject of carbon credits or green engineering a part of this work, it is worth mentioning that, at least for a time, some of the world's economies will be tied to a tiered and structured currency based upon the sale and trade of carbon credits and other biologically exchangeable material. Sustainable engineering in reciprocal environments will be another emerging bioscience and an important one at that. This science will find that even where artificial material is concerned, some is more environmentally adaptable than others. These newer human-made materials will offer themselves in ways and uses that are impossible today.

All things and all people respond to both higher and lower laws, regardless of their orientation in heaven or earth. Higher laws are made of a lighter substance and therefore are more evolution oriented. Lower laws, or human-made laws, are enacted to serve a present purpose but rarely a future one. The law of attraction, all too often reduced in scope, is a great binder of obsolete thoughts and things. It, along with other laws of higher order, is capable of advancing and directing the purposeful needs and desires of present and future humankind. Through creative progression, humankind's ability to transport themselves from here to there—regardless of where that is—will be represented by the ingenuity they brought from the stars and will now take them beyond them.

# Developing a Personal Philosophy for Life

*You'd have to be completely aloof these days to miss the messages that nature is sending us. My question is, given that everything is in such turmoil, what can we really do about it? Everything I think about doing seems like "too little, too late," and doing nothing seems equally disagreeable. I want to be socially and morally responsible, but I feel somewhat helpless. Can you please point me in the right direction?*

*P*lease begin by becoming aware that the world is not in as much turmoil as is being painted for you "in living color," as a previous generation once pointed out. Also notice, that in every landscape painting, one color seems to stand out more than the rest. In your current landscape/timescape, green is the most outstanding color—green as in the color of your currency and green as in the color of your environment. Sometimes even a trained eye can be fooled into believing that it is seeing the outstanding color when it is absent altogether! How? Because the absence of something is felt more strongly by the emotional body than that same item's presence. That is why a loved one is missed more dearly once they have departed than while they were present. It is also why hindsight seems clearer than the light of the present moment. With this primer—that things are not always what, why or how they appear—we will explore your question more deeply.

## NATURE'S MESSAGE

To be specific, nature is not sending you messages that the world is in turmoil Those messages are being broadcast by those who do not see nature as natural, as well as by those who would further their interests in commanding nature as they see fit. It might seem that their interests and yours are similar, but that is not true. Nature is sending a message, but the message is not a new one—it is still the same. Basically the message is this: "We are what you are, without exception. Why be without, when you can be within? Why stand outside the circle of life as if you were apart from it when you have always been a part of it without exception?"

Nature's message has never wavered and it has never been louder or softer. Humanity's perception of the message, on the other hand, has wavered. The volume at which nature speaks, as well as the language (gentle or harsh) that nature employs has varied over time, depending for the most part on how humanity perceives itself in relationship to everything else, including nature. Then, as now, humanity has not looked favorably upon itself, judging all too quickly that which it has barely begun to understand. What is the hurry? Why castigate and condemn? In attempting to cut away a cancer, another grows before the first has healed. Since nature is incapable of judging [itself or you], it is also incapable of thinking thoughts of scarcity. The "too little, too late" schema does not apply to nature. It is too busy being what it is and doing what it does within the greater context of things. And here, as we arrive at the main difference between humanity and nature, it becomes more obvious. Humanity does not regard itself as creators of its world or its experience. At best, it believes it has inherited its world. At worst, it believes it has been marooned upon this world by another race, by a less than compassionate God or a variation of both.

## IT IS NOT TOO LATE

Humanity is a species, a kaleidoscopic vehicle of light, a spiritual organism and much more. Humanity as a whole can best be described as a "conservatorship." A conservatorship is an entity that is responsible for the preservation and protection of something of great value and consequence to many—a guardianship and trust to ensure a future for the competent and the less than competent alike. While being fascinated by its individual nature, humanity has forgotten the cardinal laws that providence has imbued it with. Cardinal laws, or those rules that lesser things hinge upon, are pivotal, and to overlook them is folly. In ignorance, humanity—as less than whole or a fractionalized version of itself—has set itself apart from its true constitution of being part of nature. The answer, then, or its beginning, is the restoration of that which is natural as and within nature, beginning with humanity itself and extending to all that is native to humanity as a whole.

Is it possible to restore the Earth and its relationship with humanity or is it too late? Let's explore the "too late" schema first: Using this mental pattern, humanity would judge itself destined to endure misfortune, disaster and finally failure. But what then? What happens after that? Imagine the worst-case scenario—as many do—and make it as real for yourself as you can. What happens next? And after that? And a thousand years hence? Now explore the "too little" schema: In this mental construct, there are too few left among you who care enough or are able to effect any kind of change in any measurable way. Apathy, cynicism, and misanthropy reign. What happens next? And after that? And a little later on? And a thousand years after that? The point that we are making is that any scenario you envision or imagine has a context worth exploring, as well as a possible end and as well as a next beginning within a different contextual expression. There is always the next moment even when that moment is nothing like the last.

This moment humanity calls Now is nothing like the last. It is not like the last time humanity went in search of itself, it is nothing like the last New Age, and it is nothing like the last period of global warming [of which this is the seventh]. If it cannot be compared to its predecessor, then perhaps it is an original moment, the first of its kind. Perhaps it is a beginning. Perhaps many millennia ago, in someone else's schema, someone just like you imagined this is what the next beginning would look like. Perhaps they projected themselves forward in time and painted themselves into a landscape that was missing a shade of green so they would remember what was missing in time to do something about it.

It is not too late, and no amount of caring is too little. Whether or not others believe this has no measurable effect on what you decide to think, believe or do. You are the only one who matters in this regard. You are the one who has imagined the next beginning. And because you have already imagined it, you are standing upon its threshold, or at least where the threshold will be as soon as you imagine [image] it into place. Again, it does not matter that others may be standing upon the brink of despair or the threshold to nowhere. That may be where they want to go or feel they must go.

## DEVELOPING PERSONAL MORALITY

So are you alone in this? If your imagination is not grand enough, will the world slip away between your fingers or your thoughts? No, because there is enough will and force in the world to sustain and even revitalize life as you know it. But if there wasn't enough will, would the world be dissolved or destroyed? Yes and no. An honest and practical answer is that as long as there is purpose, there is also presence—there is also Now. Depending upon how you choose to see things, you can either place yourself near the end, or the sunset, in which case you would be around to see the next beginning or the dawn. Or you can place yourself at the beginning, in which case you may as well begin creating until others join you, contextually speaking. The end and the beginning are both places where realities collide.

Many are looking for reality checks now, but whose reality is the reality? Will you surrender your vision of reality simply because there is less agreement for your version? Is the consensus of your media, governors, scientists or those who dwell with the ordained more substantial than your own? Soldiers have ever gone to battle to test their mettle. Yet even without a battle, a banner or a belief to defend, every life is one of spirited determination and every life is an exploration of both tempest and temperament. Personal hates all too quickly become personal Hades [hells]; devils and deliverers are neighbors and friends when no one is looking.

Personal morality—a more pure distillation of social morality—is a characteristic of pure conscious awareness. It is developed within and then tested without. Personal morality is based upon higher law and not upon the right and good opinion of men. A moral victory is a personal one that guides and encourages grace, goodness and honor. Whether or not others conform, convict or condemn is irrelevant since you exist independently of their superior or poor opinions. You are still developing your moral responsibility; it is not quite mature enough, but it is ripening quickly! Do not give up on it nor chastise yourself for not exercising it often enough. Vigor and valor dwell within you, but you have not yet been properly introduced—these twins are still relatively unknown to you, but not for long.

As you begin to develop your own personal morality, you will also explore several different moral philosophies. Eventually you will arrive at one that is perfect for you, and through the experiences that you choose for yourself in this life, you will continue to make your philosophy more perfect. This life is, after all, an extension of your soul's philosophy and your journey—also called the heroic path—is an expression of that. A personal philosophy is an important tool, and longer ago than history allows, you could not graduate from an academy or university without first demonstrating that you had developed an enterprise toward inner knowledge.

## THE HISTORY OF STUDYING PHILOSOPHY

In the long ago that I now relate, ethics and morality were a branch of philosophy, a science in the tradition of mathematics and logic. The former were called normative sciences and the latter formal sciences. Chemistry and mathematics were then associated with the empirical sciences, and psychology, the design and designation of the soul, with empirical social science. Much later on, a less substantive study of the human mind within a social and cultural context emerged and was also called psychology.

In these ancient schools of philosophy, whose teachings are still relevant today, philosophers [scientists] learned to determine and express goodness in content and goodness as conduct, as both of these were deemed indispensable companions. The lesson always involved the ability to discern what was good or desirable in itself as opposed to what was desirable as a means to an end. The former implied an ultimate, or higher, value—a living example of the highest good. Most ethical doctrines were divided into categories such as prudence, pleasure or power. Unique tests of discernment governing each of these categories were presented to candidates for graduation at almost every turn. Invisible tests were administered by graduates—thinkers of the time who wore blue cloaks and indigo-colored rings. Because the tests were subtle in nature, the undergraduates rarely saw the trap they were about to stumble upon. They were given to say that the tests had been influenced by the blue cult, or "out of the blue" as is said today.

The ultimate value of a doctrine or principle is not easily revealed. You are also a candidate who is being presented with several different challenges. Your lessons may be less formal than those described here, but their importance is of equal measure. Are you certain where you stand on the issues of the day? Could you make a formal decision that affected the lives of many for better or worse and be at peace with your decision? The ultimate value of a moment, a thing or even a relationship is sometimes impossible to determine until, in hindsight, wisdom is born, which is why the development of a personal philosophy can be both useful and practical.

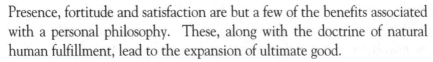

Presence, fortitude and satisfaction are but a few of the benefits associated with a personal philosophy. These, along with the doctrine of natural human fulfillment, lead to the expansion of ultimate good.

## AVOIDING TROUBLED PHILOSOPHIES

Those who lack the motivation to exercise any preference resign themselves to accept the decisions of others, for better or worse. The lives of these individuals include a philosophy of prudence, and they live in conformity with the moral conduct of their culture and society. Those who follow a philosophy of prudence from ignorance rather than choice often look back on their lives with bitterness or angst.

Hedonism, a philosophy that promotes pleasure as the highest good, is especially popular near timescapes where dimensional shifts are possible and likely. Even in a philosophy of pleasure, challenges will greet the candidate along the way. A hedonist must decide between intense pleasure and enduring pleasure, as well as when to deny pleasure for the sake of comfort. A hedonist struggles in the preference between mental and physical pleasure. Their journey may lead them through halls of addiction where mirrored distortions offer an escape to self-imposed prisons.

Those who crave competition sometimes develop philosophies where the highest attainment is power—a form of control. Each victory, however sweet, raises the competition to the next level. Eventually, absolute power becomes a subjective rather than objective desire. In this philosophy, one eventually defeats oneself and causes others to do the same. Those who seek power and control conform to the ethics of others as long as it supports their rise to power but often deviate from the same ethics once they become successful enough to do so. Their pursuit of the ordinary rewards of an ethical life will mask their ulterior motives for power for a time, but these motives will be discovered as absolute power always begins to corrode and corrupt from within.

The development of a personal philosophy will strengthen you and deepen your purpose. Your purpose is not what you do or why you were born, but it does enhance and expand your awareness as well as your desire to grow. Your purpose is like the roots of a tree. It reaches deep into the earth so you can reach high into the heavens. You rarely need to take the time to check the condition of the roots, as they are being nurtured from below and within. The roots maintain the tree in every season, weathering storms, draughts and more. The leaves and branches of a tree may grow far away from the roots and in a variety of different directions. Regardless, the roots will continue to be and do anything and everything that is in the best interest of the tree. Even a tree that has been cut down continues to be useful.

Look beyond the shortcomings of others and you will rise above your own much faster. Begin anew just beyond where you think you are. You are always a little further along than you give yourself credit for, mostly because you spend so much time looking backward. Remember that in the beginning, everything was chaos, but it was not in chaos. In the beginning, everything also seemed to be in turmoil, but since it was natural for it to be so, no one questioned it. It was understood that the all within the all was in process. No one doubted it then. The same is true today.

## YOU ARE PART OF A CHANGING WORLD

Now is the next beginning. Yes, there are endings as well, but the law of continuity encourages you to pause rather than to come to a complete stop now. Notice that others may stop where they are now and decide that they cannot or will not go forward. Honor their choices and appreciate them for the contributions they have already made. The law of continuity honors that something, or someone, must pass through several intermediate states, or conditions, on its way to becoming something, or someone, else. Those who pause or stop now may choose to rest or stay in one of these intermediate places. In that case, they are creating the bridge that you will soon walk across upon their backs, as it were. The more grateful you are for what they have accomplished, the stronger the bridge that you cross will be.

Look beyond appearances and beneath the surface of things, and do so literally. Some time ago, an evolving humanity decided that they did not want things to continue as they were. A percentage of the population thought so, said so and began to imagine a different future for the Earth. Since thoughts become things, a variety of potentials or Earths were born, and several of these are now being explored. The philosophies we have explored also apply to the Earth. The Earth serves at the pleasure of humanity, meaning that the Earth re-creates itself based upon a collective philosophy. Given this truth, much of what you see now is normal—one of the intermediate steps described earlier.

Comets, eclipses and other star works encourage you to see how different the sky looks. This is not a time for the faint of heart, and you may note an increase in the heart rate and rhythm of those who are accelerating or ascending to a new truth. Begin each day by being comfortable with yourself as you are, regardless of what you think of your contribution to the Earth or to humanity. Acknowledge that you are an integral part of a changing world and that every thought, intention and action you take matters. Change the world as you see fit or not at all. Thoughtless problems and solutions are temporary; however, thoughtful solutions are permanent. This is because when you realize the cause of the problem consciously, you will not have a need to repeat it or be intimidated by it. Ask to be part of any solution that interests you, and as you become this, grant yourself the wisdom and compassion to share the knowledge with others. That is the gift of everlasting.

# Making the Most of
# Your Spiritual Toolbox

*I believe that I have weathered many an emotional storm "on a wing and a prayer," and I credit my spiritual awakening for a well-balanced disposition regarding life's ups and downs. I consider myself more positive than most and can usually be counted upon to assist others when they are down, but I must admit that given some of the more recent large-scale world events, it is getting harder to do so. Can you offer some suggestions on how not to succumb to the latest round of global bad news?*

There is but one world and it contains many peoples. There is but one world race and it is multicultured in appearance. There is but one world religion and at its head is a deity of consciousness. There is but one measure of prosperity and its root is layered in compassion. There is but one Earthly resource and it is called "man." There is but one truth and it is visible within all that is invisible. There is but one thought, which alone precipitates itself, and it is called "mind." There is but one thing that alone precedes itself and it is called "light." There is but one origin of man and one solution for man, which is to restore himself and suffer not the effects of the wheel of birth and rebirth.

The above words are protected, meaning that they have always existed in one form or another. In desperate moments they have been one breath away from extinction, but even the breath, which is holy in origin, contains two parts and is dual in nature. Therefore, even when hope surrenders, fate intervenes with the opposite being true as well. Although these words have been revered and kept secret by brotherhoods and initiates of certain means, they have also, at times, been offered to laypeople—those who follow the rule of law first and higher law second—to solve and to save, as the case may be. Those who have tried in error over countless eons to interpret the words by ones and by twos have called them a riddle and even a curse. But for those who dare, they are words to live by, for in them and by them the future of humanity also lives. But which future that will be, and what it will look like, still remains to be seen.

## LIVE A FULFILLING LIFE

The world of today, with its modern inventions and complexities, is little different than the world of many yesterdays ago. Your world faces the same problems as the world of the ancients. They too believed that their resources yielded less than plenty and would not last. The coin of the realm changed in value as quickly as it changed hands, and many who were installed in office were ousted before a bust could be carved or a statue dedicated. History records many, but not all, who were felled by those who waited their turn with less patience than modesty or diplomacy preferred.

Economic fluctuations and devastations of fortune were as common in other times as they are now. The depredations of war are as visible today as they were yesterday, oblique reminders of wives and mothers who have seen the color purple at dusk without the benefit of the violet of the new dawn. History is littered with museums and tributes that pay homage to the dead and their spoils, but they would tell you, as I do now, that the value of life is not in filling empty moments with treasure, but in treasuring empty moments so that they become fulfilling lives.

An individual life is fulfilled when it is lived in support of something greater than itself. This simple truth has been inaccurately interpreted as a warning to the selfish. One can live in support of a skill, a loved one or even an argument. The purpose of life is to make the hollow whole; it is to fill erstwhile adventures with sovereign memories. A superior life is one that is self-reflecting and endeavors to improve upon the day by the light of the next day and the next. A successful life is one that is lived in spite of or even with adversity. A successful life is one that is not easily surrendered to the stroke of a pen, the strike of the clock or the absurdities of those who will call the day their own.

## RISE ABOVE AND THINK NEW THOUGHTS

Humanity's future depends upon its ability to reclaim its will and to raise itself to a standard of pride that sits above the prejudices of the day. Hang the head low and the heart will follow. Idle the mind and the feet will not carry you. Swallow the acrimonious words of others and they will poison your health. Do not allow the hostilities of the world without to weaken the walls of the harmonious environment within. The surrender would be a silent one, but the lament would be heard in the heavens nonetheless.

*But how do we do this? With all due respect, how? You are a wise sentience, and knowing comes easy to great beings such as you, as it does to other masters. You have the ability to see far into the past and into the future too. Our vision is more limited than yours and when fear creeps in, we are more limited still.*

Your vision is not limited by your human form, it is colored by the belief that what you see outside of you is more real than what you know to be true within. You have the same ability to see into the distant past, especially as you have lived it. And it does not take a master to know that much that has been written is false. That I can see a variety of potential futures, I grant you, but because you are the ones who will choose the future you most prefer, I would argue that you have bested me again. Fear is not your enemy, but indolence is. Humanity is slow to change and quick to blame. It is time to shake off the torpor that numbs the mind and slows the body. Coax the body to obey your demands and coerce the mind to think new thoughts.

The spiritual awakening you credit was akin to an audition, and the spiritual studies you have undertaken were your dress rehearsal. Now prepare to rise to the occasion as all that you have learned is put into practice. The prize is not a diploma or a degree; it is mastery of self and self-awareness. Initiates and initiations do not dwell in the relics of the past or in soft classroom moments where personalities become pampered pets. They exist for those whom they exist, in moments where the maker and the made in fury clash and there recognize each other as one. The battle for one's own sovereignty—if it must come to that—is the only one worth the struggle. It is the only war in which two victors, without surrender, learn the meaning of peace.

## REDEFINE YOUR OUTLOOK ON ECONOMICS

*Our leaders tell us that things will get worse before they get better. Is that true?*

It is not leaders, but elected officials that tell you this. In proclaiming this warning, they are buying time and hopefully patience. Some will grant it and others will not. Those who govern are not necessarily born to lead. Leadership is a skill that comes to those who live in support of something greater than themselves. If by "things" you mean the further deconstruction of the world economy, the answer depends upon how soon the citizens of the world would be willing to accept another model.

The current model will soon expire, and even a significant infusion of currency will yield lopsided results at best. The burdens of debt have been fastened onto the backs of the common person, but even those of heroic strength cannot carry the world upon their shoulders for too long. New economic models will soon be introduced. They will immediately be embraced by some and rejected by others. Eventually the new model will become the norm. New academic models will follow and the world will change. Instead of a middle class, a variety of subcultures will emerge; subtleties will define some, uniqueness others, and even strangeness for some.

*What will happen to the many thousands who have already lost their jobs and the many who continue to do so?*

There are many who spend years loathing their jobs and wishing things were different. Like slaves chained to their posts, they have sacrificed themselves so that others in their families could live better or at least more independently. Some believed in their employers, the economy, their debts or their retirement years. What they will do depends upon what they think they are capable of. Some will become wards of the state for the time being and collect the benefits of compensation (unemployment insurance). Those who depend upon local and state support will receive accordingly, but not as much or for as long as they would like. State and government coffers are emptier than most think, as are the pockets of the average politician. These pockets, once lined in green, have also been picked clean. It is likely that some of the states will pour out the contents of their treasuries in this regard and then demand that the federal government replace its risk by taking over the task. Renamed and under a different flag (agency) this is likely to happen.

As wages become scarce, other sources of expression will be discovered. Certain segments of the economically displaced will gather together with extended family members and reinvent the family unit. The decision to do this will at first be considered one of last resort, but later, and in hindsight, it will be embraced as a true cost-saving measure as well as a unifying factor in relationships that have been distant and scarce. It will renew some relationships and establish new ones along the way. The effects will be long-lasting and will contribute to a change in how cultures evolve.

Upon discovering a spirit of adventure, some will relocate to other cities or countries where new opportunities exist. As has been noted before, this is a time of vast migration for all of the kingdoms, including humankind. Regardless of appearance, and in spite of irregularities of fortune and misfortune, all is not lost. Do not allow yourself to be defined by a past that has already been lived while the present and the future are yet before you. Do not allow the tide of change to spell out omens for you or that which you hold dear. Great resources are still at humanity's disposal, not the least of which is humanity itself. Creativity will cause inventiveness and entrepreneurship to rise again, even if on a smaller scale at first. Those who remain eager and curious will be among the first to recognize opportunity and to seize its advantage.

Please remember that who you are and what you do to earn a living are not the same. Even if finances fail, life will provide an option here and a possibility there. You can never lose everything, only what you have today. You did not arrive with your present resources and you will not depart with them; therefore, they are only for your use in the here and now. The same applies to those to whom you would leave your treasure and to those who assume it is theirs by rights of inheritance. The same is true for everyone. If you have lost a fortune in this system, perhaps you will increase your wealth in the next economic model; therefore, pay close attention to its nuances when it is first introduced. Those who believe in the benefits of a new reality will find them sooner than those who do not.

## MOVING TRANSPORTATION INTO A NEW DIRECTION

*Do you have any thoughts about the auto industry, American or otherwise?*

This form of transportation has become rather arcane, and as seen from afar by those who uphold humanity as a creative and evolutionary species, it seems somewhat of an insult to human ingenuity. But until humanity tires of it and conceives of a more popular idea that suits the population at large, it will remain in place. Contrary to popular thought, it is not control by the oil rich nations and corporations that prevent a transition to another model; it is humanity itself that believes that an automobile is a defining attribute of individuality and status. It is an old belief, but one that is still strong and represents a significant number of the Earth's population. Humanity has not yet conceived how to build without cranes for heavy lifting or other giant scale machinery to fulfill its demands. It has not yet created the next model for how to replace trucks that haul garbage to landfills or how to transport its necessities beyond diesel trucks and coal-based trains.

*Can you say when that model will be introduced? This year? Next? You say that many will embrace it, but why would they?*

The new model will be introduced when the current one is almost exhausted. It is moving in that direction very quickly. That is one of the reasons why there is such little concern for how or when the current accumulation of debt will be repaid. It cannot and will not be repaid. Like the queen bee in the beehive, it lives for many seasons in service to those who have installed the queen as their monarch. The queen is protected at all costs, but in the meantime, those who serve her also feed off her a little at a time. Eventually the queen exhausts her usefulness and a replacement must be found.

The present system must first be proven obsolete. It will not be allowed to die easily or generously. It will be slain, and its head—or the symbol that represents it—will be mocked. Its weaknesses have already been exposed, as have the riches of those who have lavished upon themselves its largesse. The rescue plan that is being mounted is already too late, but it must appear otherwise for the time being. Eventually, under the restorative efforts of the newly elected, the benefits of the new model will be introduced. The advantages of the new model will be obvious and will include something for almost everyone, from those in the highest echelons to those in most need of charity. The new model will do away with the accumulated debts of the old, and it will allow almost everyone the same advantage. It cannot be said with specific timing how soon it will come about, simply that it will or that it already has, depending upon how it is viewed.

## TRUST THE VOICE OF SPIRIT

*Will established religions and other spiritual entities be affected as well? Will they be credited or blamed in any way?*

Everything and every being that is part of the old paradigm will be affected in some way—everything and every being that has believed or not, participated or not, assisted or not, voted for or against and so on. With or without honor, that which is condemned to die is allowed its final rites of passage. Those who are asked or forced to abdicate the thrones of power, whether of religion, government or economy, will not do so lightly. The will of the mighty will be tested. Some will fall and others will fail. It is not the religions themselves that will come under attack, but what they believe will.

In the immediate future, there will be a renewal of interest in all things spiritual, established or otherwise. Established religions will be favored, at least in the beginning, because in the current moment there is an increased need for stability and security wherever and however it can be found. Established religions will seize this opportunity to increase their membership and advance their cause. Most will enjoy at least a temporary gain. Some will even go to market [advertise] with their cause by hiring agencies to make their words appear more golden. Those who are experts in their fields will indeed gild the words and offer them as if they were heaven sent.

Newer religions and offshoots of established ones will have their own say, as will more cultured and open-ended secular movements, including those who unfold themselves from within the branches of the New Age. Expect the advent of more mystery schools, modalities and modern traditions. There is value in that which empowers the individual to author his or her own life. Be aware [beware] of that which scorns the beliefs of others or drags through the mud the good name of those who have earned it. Trust the voice of Spirit as is unveils itself from within and displays itself throughout your life. Spirit is not constrained by religion nor constrained by the good opinion of others or lack thereof. It is resplendent in the form and the formless, and you will recognize it as it speaks the language of universal law.

## LOOK FOR THE GOOD NEWS WITHIN YOURSELF

*Are you aware of the kinds of headlines we see daily or the news reports on the radio, television or Internet? Are you aware of the consequences, spiritual or otherwise, that affect the individuals in the headlines?*

There is an awareness that is inclusive of all that takes place upon the Earth, but it exists from a detached perspective and is very different than your own awareness. The headlines are not accurate for the most part, and in many instances they are less than true; therefore, there is little validity in them from the greater context within which Gaia exists. Gaia is aware of them because you are aware of them. Better put, I am aware of your awareness or interest in them. A headline is an exclamation point that reinforces a thought. There is little reason to dwell upon most thoughts as they become denser—but not more true—in the process. Why stoke the fires of the disenchanted when there are more creative endeavors to envision and pursue?

I am interested in the relationship between cause and effect where humanity is concerned, but on a larger or macrocosmic scale for the most part. The exception to this is when I am invited to participate to a larger degree. Prayers, invocations, ceremonies and celebrations are invitations that specifically link my awareness. Likewise, my full participation in your interests and personal endeavors is brought forward, such as during a personal session, for instance. I do not, however, have an opinion or preference as to the outcome of an event, public or otherwise. It is for those who are more directly affected by such events to participate wholeheartedly in them. It is true that the Earth is affected by large-scale events of a global nature, but not as an individual. Gaia is not an individual presence; it is a sentience.

Your spiritual awakening occurred at the dawn of time, which was long and before this life. There is a subsequent new dawn or awakening in each life, which is unique to the purposes of that life. This life is no exception, as by your own acknowledgement an awakening has already taken place. The latest round of world events are just that: a virtual carousel that goes around and around the same track. It only appears different than the last time because the frailties—not failures—of human nature make it seem so.

Carousel horses are always beautifully painted and decorated. They go up and down and even seem to speed up or slow down to make the ride more interesting. When the music stops, the rider dismounts, and another rider, whose experience will be completely different, is invited to take a turn. There will be another turn and then another one. Some will be simple and beautiful and others more difficult or complex. After many turns on the merry-go-round, the wise carousel horse recognizes that there is no race to win, and he makes no attempt to pretend that there is one. On his stationary track, he is no less eager for adventure than he was before this realization. The difference is that he can now relax and enjoy the ride.

Look for good news not in the day's headlines but within yourself. Look for the good within you and put that to work for you, for everyone else, for the planet and for life itself. This tool is lifetimes old and will always serve you. Offer something good to others and to the world every day. To offer is to extend; it is a presentation or extension of quality. Even as large-scale events unfold, remember that life is lived in the smaller, more personal moments. You are more affected by the breath of a butterfly you have never met than by the heated breath of world debate. Breathe deeply. Breathe because there is life force in the breath, and this same life force has the brilliance of a thousand suns.

Those who promote global headlines are well-trained to coax a response in their readerships. Your response, while not trained or rehearsed, is often a collective response. You can train yourself to respond through your higher awareness rather than through the more obvious human collective. You will not be less than human nor less compassionate by elevating the vibration of your response. Rather than the sigh of exhalation, respond with a deep inhalation. You will see an almost immediate difference in how body and mind relate to one another and to the collective. Spirit will see to that. You can share the world with others without sharing the same worldview.

# Righting the Wrongs: 2006 and Beyond

W hat will be, will be, but only if what is, is. By design, a look at the future must always include a comparison to the present, for how else would we recognize it as the future? The future does not and cannot exist unless the present invites it, and with so many disappointed with their present environments and situations, what can be said of the future? Where do your predictions about the future come from—do you know? They come from you, from the collective consciousness.

Given this premise, what differentiates the future from the present or the past? Desire, intent, creativity and purpose. What else? Time—linear time, dimensional time and intentional time. Into which of these categories do prophecies and predictions belong? To all and to none, depending upon where consciousness directs them, if at all.

The future cannot be completely experienced while one is still in the present, but the future is—it exists. To explain further, the more static the present is, the more static the future will be, making it difficult to predict with any measure of certainty what it will be like when it arrives. How does one interpret the future, then? By following the timelines associated with various trends and events to see how they respond to energy.

For instance, let's say Being #1 is upset about something and knows that Being #2 will also be upset with the news. Being #1 could easily travel slightly into the future to see this future experience for him, because there would be energy lit up around the event or the person. This basic idea can be applied to all future events; one need only follow the energy.

Is it really that simple? Almost, but not quite. It is very important that one remain an observer of both light and energy without becoming interested or attached to it, for to do so is to influence the future and, more than likely, one's own participation in it, do you see? Using our same example, Being #1 is upset about something and knows that Being #2 will also be upset with the news. Being #1 travels slightly into the future, and upon seeing how upset Being #2 will become, decides to alter the time, place or circumstance in which he will deliver the news, thereby altering the future as it would have been.

Were his motives honorable? Yes. Was the future altered? Yes. This is not a matter of right or wrong, nor does it matter what one's motives are, but visions of the future must be approached without bias so that undue stress is not introduced into the equation. If, for instance, a glance at the future were to show a buildup of energy near an earthquake-prone area, the introduction of worry or fear might catalyze an event that may or may not manifest, do you see?

A prophecy and its maker are one. A prophecy and its believer are two. A prophecy and its experience are three. With each progressive sum, the laws of probability become exponentially greater. Therefore, a prediction that is consistently reinforced has a greater probability of occurring than one that is ignored or disregarded. The law of attraction is a universal one and applies to all things without prejudice or preference. As always, we approach this subject matter with great care, acknowledging the power of the individual and the All That Is in all things, for to be careless in such things is to be careless with life, the most precious aspect and All There Is. With this understanding, let us have a look at tomorrow through the eyes of today.

## *That Which Already Is*

You are not the same being you were last year. You are different now. Your thoughts are different, your desires are different and your experiences are different. Why? Because your reason for being is to be. Being is not an idle activity. To be is to plan, expect, intend, suppose and become. It is what Creator calls radiance.

### THERE ARE BEINGS ALREADY AMONG YOU

Being requires presence, and in the third dimension, this translates into form, which in turn draws upon certain qualities and attributes. These often include identity, nature and value. Beingness is what you are.

Human beingness is what you do. This distinction is an important one, because if you overidentify with your human (doing) nature, you may miss some of the finer beings and energies that already are or will soon be among you.

The funny thing about predictions is that one is often in such a hurry to see what is around the next band of energy that one can overlook what has already moved from the future into the present, which is oftentimes just as wonderful and exciting as what is yet to be. These beings find it rather unusual that although many within the human kingdom long for such contact, that which passes before them also seems to pass through them!

Who are these beings? For the most part, they are from your near future. You long to know what is right with the future so that you might be at peace with the present. They desire a firsthand look at the past (your present) so that they might experience what choices you made. They can be of assistance, but they must be invited to do so in order to honor the laws of noninterference.

They are few in number and, for the most part, simply observe—for now. To say that they are from your near future is not altogether accurate. They are from the future that is, but it is not yet. In other words, based upon your present experience, there is a most probable future, and it is here where they began their journey, working their way slowly backward until they found themselves here. Why here? Because this is where cause is, which is to say that they came from effect. It is not where they are from, but it is where they came from.

## CONTACT WITH THE TRAVELERS

In other communications, we have spoken of beings called Travelers. Travelers are like interdimensional detectives, seeking anomalies within energy signatures and events that could have "zigged" rather than "zagged," for lack of other words. Some of you who now read these words have had similar adventures and journeys, and may even feel a note of nostalgic envy. Travelers always begin their journeys near the end, or effect, but not at the absolute end, for what would be the fun in that? It is a bit like skipping ahead to the end of a beloved book in order to see that all will eventually work out as it should. Often it is not the last page that is of most value, but the ones leading up to the last, do you see?

Travelers are fairly ordinary in appearance, almost too much so, and it is not within their purpose to stand out. They are, however, a bit more translucent of skin and more clear-eyed than most. They do not alter or disguise their appearance in any way and would not, for instance, wear eyeglasses if they did not require them. They simply adjust their energy and their appearance to their environment, and with the Earth as heavily populated as it is at present, they easily blend in. They are fair and honest in what they say and do, and although they will not reveal themselves completely, neither will they lie to escape a moment's interrogation.

A recent dialogue between a present-day Earth human (question) and a Traveler (answer) is recounted for you here to give you an example of what you might experience in such circumstances yourself:

*Do you live nearby?*

No, I'm not from around here.

*Do you plan to settle down here?*

I don't think so. I don't think I've found where I belong yet.

*Join the club. What kind of work do you do?*

I'm a scientist by trade, but I'm currently on sabbatical.

*Is that a fancy way to say you got laid off your job?*

Not exactly, but I felt I just had to take this trip.

*I know that one too. Where will you go next?*

I think I'll stay here for a while. I'm hoping something will really stand out.

*Do you have someone special waiting for you at home?*

Yes, but they know what I'm like when I'm traveling and what to expect. There's no rush.

*I wish it were like that for me! Want to talk some more over a cup of coffee or a beer?*

Thank you just the same, but I really haven't been too hungry or thirsty lately.

*Wish that were my problem! Any chance I'll see you again?*

Probably not. I enjoyed meeting you, though.

*Yeah, I feel the same. Good Luck.*

This dialogue reflects why it is difficult to tell a Traveler apart from an ordinary citizen. Might the same also be true of other near-human beings who might be in your present-day midst? The future is now, in a matter of speaking. It is where you create your future that counts. This Traveler's future happens to be in your past and in your own backyard too! Would you like to meet a Traveler and have a firsthand experience of your own?

## MEETING A TRAVELER

Let your thoughts about what such beings might look like or act like blur. Do not assign them a race or a mannerism. Expect them to be friendly and polite. Some look a little like tourists, but without that "lost" quality that seems to make so many stand out, both here and upon other worlds too. Expect that they will seem less displeased with the quality of your present-time experience than you do.

They will be in less of a hurry than you. They may or may not be aware of the latest players on the world stage. More than likely, they will not be concerned with the outcome of the war or with the economy or with the current rise in identity theft. They will not pretend to be so for your sake; neither will they minimize your own concerns. On the contrary, they will be very interested in what you think and feel and know. They will speak with you respectfully and hold you in high esteem, because they know who you really are. They may read your thoughts, but they will not interfere with them. Above all, they can be trusted with the truth or with your version of it.

Travelers are by no means the only near-human beings sharing your daily experience—there are many others as well. A human body is a vehicle; it is not who or what you are. The same goes for these beings. Dressed in their human bodies, they will seem very attractive, because their nature is less dense than your own. They do not hide from you, but their purpose is their own. They are not among you as a display of things or beings to come. Some make their homes in humble monasteries so as not to stand out. In such cases, their hosts are aware of their true identities. In such a guise, it is much simpler to be a Traveler and of service to others as well.

There will be many opportunities for you to have contact with such beings if it is your desire to do so. Those who are among you today are the predecessors of others who will come from further in your future. Each time something or someone from the future merges with your present, it alters both. The future accelerates the present and opens the door to the future a little wider. Remember that the future is an equal-opportunity employer; it is the field of all possibilities. It is important, therefore, that from this field the highest and best probabilities are selected to pass through its threshold.

# Children of a Greater God

I f it becomes easier to recognize visitors from another reality and to have an interaction with them, it would also stand to reason that it would be easier to understand the needs and desires of the new children. Alas, if that were the case! Such will be the lament of parents, siblings and other family members for some time to come. But these beings are not children, although they are childlike by nature. They are Piscean-Aquarian hybrids, having been born at an intersecting juncture in time, a cross between two different genetic constituents. As hybrids, the new children are part of the human subspecies and not the species itself. They are a new-and-improved you.

## THE NEW CHILDREN ARE HIGHLY DISEASE RESISTANT

The term "hybrid" is sometimes used to describe that which consists of two or more elements not ordinarily combined with one another but associated with the same original. Other terms worth noting are "hybrid vigor" and "heterosis," the increased growth, disease resistance and fertility often seen in hybrid species. This term accurately describes some of the attributes that can already be ascribed to the new children. They are (or will soon be) highly resilient to the onslaught of viruses that are all too common during such end and crossover times.

Their antibodies would seem artificial to you, as they are the synthesis of two different antigens. An antigen is a proteinlike substance that rests on the surface of a cell or a bacterium that stimulates the production of an antibody. A hybrid antigen can detect and repair a cell that has been attacked before a normal human antigen could even detect an abnormal cell. New children are and will be more resistant to cancers, viruses and other diseases. Can you see why off-planet beings have gone so far as to interfere with your reality? In some cases, the need was (and is) very great. A hybrid child is a thing of beauty to behold. It is Indigo, Crystalline, Violet-Ray and Pre-Cognitive Atlantean in nature, and there are many more hybrids yet to come.

The modern Olympiad is widely known for receiving each country's best representatives to commune, to compete and to set and best new records. The youth and vitality embodied by these athletes is inspiring to all who share in their feats. Great moments of victory bring celebrations, whereas overwhelming defeats bring moments of sadness. Activity is everywhere at once as batons are passed and kings and queens are deposed in favor of new heroes. Ending/beginning times are inspiring and intriguing for the same reason. Each kingdom, species and element comes forward to offer its best and its worst so that each might be recognized, healed and reorganized.

## THEY ARE YOUR FUTURE

The new children will choose heroes from among themselves, ignoring the voices of young and old, parent and teacher. It is not that they will think themselves better, just different. Their minds are already arranged differently, and the processes that govern the brain's ability to reason are vastly different than that of their ancestral parentage. Their response to a question may come from their left brain, their right brain or both at once, for they are able to distinguish between them. More's the pity that they have no real teachers, for even in this they come to choose them from among themselves. Truth be told, it will be another generation or so before they are recognized and understood for who and what they are.

What is so special about the new children? They are your future. If you would like to see what you might be like in your next Earth life, look into their eyes. They are an advanced version of you, and you will be an advanced version of them. They have more self-esteem than you do. Every one of them is an entrepreneur. They know the meaning of true friendship, and they can heal themselves (but they will allow you to try). They conceptualize more quickly and expand beyond the reasoning mind all too easily. They are not interested in history or the mechanics of language. They accord respect when respect is accorded them and they are masters at recognizing deceit.

New children have purposes that are more specifically defined than your own. This is because they are more conscious at birth than most of you were. They are not more fortunate than you, and it would be a misconception to believe this. You also could have been born this year or next. The choice you made was unique, individual and purposeful.

Long ago and even yesterday, humanity said, "Let the next generation inherit the Earth and its woes." To these words, some added suffixes to the effect of "and good riddance," while others murmured, "and may God forgive us." So be it. These are the inheritors of the Earth, and you will see that they waste no time in recognizing this.

If they look upon their elders with a disdain or disbelief from time to time, is it not understandable? They will do their utmost to be responsible, and with your assistance, they will grow into fine young men and women of the future. Assist them by seeing the wisdom that is already there. Do not fail to recognize that they do or will soon have solutions your generation did not conceive of. Do not berate or pity yourselves, as your purpose was and is different than theirs. Do not expect them to follow tradition; they will create their own.

## THE GREAT SEPARATION IS OVER

The new children belong to the Rainbow Tribes of long ago. The races of humanity that seeded the continents long ago were of different color. Their pigment received and reflected available light. They were guided to live in balance with their environments, and each succeeded and failed in their own way.

The expansive migration in evidence today between races and cultures, creeds and religions, is an acknowledgment that the great separation is over. The rainbow becomes as one again; all colors become as one light. The Rainbow Tribes, having nearly completed their task to rebalance the races in the Piscean era, now set about a new task: the raising of the octaves by redirecting the frequencies of the Aquarian Age. This task requires flexibility, variety and the release of the boundary markers of the mind that are associated with the present generations.

New children are hybrids, but of what origin? Genetically, they are both your ancestors and your descendants. They carry the best that the universe has to offer at this time. After what you term the "ascension," a transmutation of dimensions, consciousness will expand by another league or so, and the universe will add another complement to its future generations, after which physical and spiritual growth will seem to slow for a time. This is not altogether the case, but after a great acceleration, it will seem so.

Although you cannot remember it now, there was a time when, as very young beings of light, you relished the idea of your physicality and danced before gossamer mirrors in delight at your appearance.

Such times will return, when the physical and the nonphysical are once again in balance. End your wars and maim no more, and the process will be quickened.

# The Medicine Makers

A re you healthier this year than you were last year? If yes, is your wellness due to advancements that can be attributed to the medical community or to changes and choices you made on your own? If no, then what choices did you make or could you have made that would have contributed to your wellness? Although that question reflects the past, its answer points the way to the future. Another appropriate question might be, where do you hold your truth regarding your personal health and wellness? In your body's elemental awareness? In your genetic heredity? In your family's medicine cabinet?

## YOU ARE THE KEY TO YOUR WELLNESS

Your health, wellness and physical longevity are associated with your understanding of what, not who, you are. In other words, your identity is not your wellness or vice versa. Your personality has been given an artificial idea of what wellness is, and your body has been diligently trying to live up to that. For instance, it is normal for the body to age gracefully and for it to age more rapidly when it is under stress. The greatest cause of stress is attempting to live a life other than your own or the one you are meant to live. If you are less interested in your wellness because you are overly interested in the choices, decisions and situations of a family member, friend, employer or government, you are under stress and your wellness is out of balance. The same is true if you believe that the medical community and its pharmaceutical subsidiaries are the key to your longevity.

You are the key to your wellness, and the future you long to experience depends upon your ability to participate in it. Your healthy cells are not "under attack" by saboteur cells hoping to catch you unawares. The awareness with which cells and molecules travel through the body depends upon your own awareness. Your elemental (organic Earth-based awareness) body belongs to Earth. Your consciousness belongs within All That Is. The combination of these two brings a heaven-in-Earth quality to that which you are.

Your body is a vehicle for your consciousness, one that supports your purpose, even when you think it doesn't. Your body is perfect, even when you think it is not. The more imperfect you believe your body to be, the more imperfect it becomes. This is true regardless of what you ingest or subscribe to. You are your body's owner, and it responds only to what you offer it.

Another's key does not open nor power your automobile, and neither does another's truth give your body more wellness unless you accept it and make it your own. The health and longevity of your body depend upon the truth you live, not the truth you talk about living or are convinced to believe. A belief system is not a truth. A belief system is a set of instructions the mind follows, and it is not always based upon reason or fact.

## NATURAL VERSUS ARTIFICIAL MEDICINE AND THE AVIAN FLU

As we have now established the rightful owner of your body and your being, perhaps we can count upon you to remember this as so-called miracle drugs flood the marketplace beginning this year. Do miracles require two-page disclosures and warnings? A miracle is an event that appears to be contrary to the laws of nature. Sometimes regarded as acts of God, these events are known to be amazing, extraordinary and unexpected. Why, then, would science need to hide behind God, as it were? True science is an aspect of nature; it is not artificial, and neither are you.

The problem with natural science is that it has been corrupted by artificial science. The same is true of natural medicine, although to a lesser extent. But why? As was said in the last segment, end times bring the best and the worst to the surface, and by necessity every kingdom, element, species and subject is affected or at least acted upon. As you have already perhaps noted, the animal kingdom, with its avian companions, is now highly featured. The avian flu is the animal kingdom's response to ignorance and intolerable living environments.

The wellness of not one but an entire species is in question, and because all are truly One, even at the experiential level, this species will share its pain with others. To be more specific, the animal kingdom is not wishing difficult moments upon humanity. To the contrary, it desires awareness and wellness for all concerned. It is awareness above all that will heal all things and all beings, but before awareness arrives, less than viable solutions will be introduced, including vaccines and other measures that will instill fear rather than peace.

Fear quickens the metabolism but slows the response time to wellness because it freezes the very systems that are most needed. Fear invites the mind's participation with sometimes disastrous and artificial results. The rush to quell a possible pandemic by artificial means when natural means exist may trigger a response from the other kingdoms with a less than desirable effect upon humanity. This is one of many possibilities, but the proximity of it makes it well worth noting. A vaccine to counter the effects of the virus is already available. It is being tested, stored and hoarded even as these words find their way onto the page. Its effectiveness is only relative, as this virus and others that will follow are known for their ability to mutate and disguise themselves as something else.

The vaccines have side effects of their own, and their artificial quality makes it difficult for them to identify which cells to target. Other vaccines of a second generation will soon be introduced as well. It may be suggested that these are coupled with ordinary seasonal flu vaccines, but the body will not react well to this.

The key to this and other affectations of nature is not to hold yourself apart. Respond from a natural place within instead of a reactionary place without. You have no natural enemies; therefore, if any present themselves, they must be unnatural or artificial. But if nature were out of balance, wouldn't its response be also? Not necessarily, because that which began as natural retains the wisdom to return to that state, but that which was created artificially does not, because it can only emulate that which is natural—it cannot become that which it is not, do you see?

## STRENGTHENING THE IMMUNE SYSTEM

It is time to discover and strengthen your natural systems of health, beginning with the immune system and continuing on to others. To begin with, hydrate yourselves with water and natural juices, particularly those that contain high doses of vitamin C. If the juice is natural rather than reconstituted, the sugar will be converted to usable energy. The importance of vitamin C at this time cannot be overstated. This vitamin, above all others, can recognize foreign (artificial) intruders and escort them safely and gently out of the body. It can also help the body to function more effectively and optimally, even during times of stress.

Vitamin B is also an excellent choice for strengthening the body's ability to respond to unnatural events. This intuitive vitamin understands your individual needs and will adjust itself as necessary. It can help regulate and balance the body's polarity system as well as maintain the body's left and right hemispheres. It bridges the gaps that exist between mind and body, making consciousness more accessible.

Other vitamins are worth exploring as well. Ask your body which one and how much, and it will tell you. The best choices are the most natural, as the goal is the return to natural health and wellness. Therefore, if these vitamins can be consumed in their original states, so much the better. To underscore, the endorsement here does not favor the vitamin-producing industry but the longevity of your consciousness that yet has much to accomplish!

## BEWARE THE MEDICINE MAKERS!

The medicine makers are hard at work influencing the decisions you make about your health because you have been told that you need what they offer. You must think for yourself whether or not this is true. Soon they will introduce next season's agenda, and if your will is more human than divine, you will heed their suggestions and ignore your own. It is important to note that many of the new introductions will indeed improve certain systems and offer a semblance of wellness, but many will do so at the peril of other systems and organs. That is why there are so many disclaimers.

Do you know, for instance, where your spleen is and what it does? Your spleen belongs to the vascular system. It is a ductless organ located in the upper abdomen. It assists in the restoration of healthy red blood cells by separating and removing those that have completed their purpose. In doing so, it spares the lymphocytes, important cells that support the immune system, by producing antibodies that reject cancerous cells and other foreign tissue. In this way, the blood supply remains whole and intact. Many artificial medicines bypass the spleen, weakening it and rendering it susceptible to that which it is sworn to defend. We could next speak of the liver, but perhaps enough pages have already been dedicated to this subject. It's all in the small print, as they say.

This season's lineup will include new contraceptives for men and women, advances in blood pressure medication and new anti-stress hormones for women. Among these will be included one that will purport to bypass the onset of menses as well as the body's natural biological response called menopause. New obesity medication that also regulates the heart will seem a godsend at first, as will other "life-extension" miracles.

Convenience drugs such as those that induce the body to perspire less will be an online order away from a fast home delivery. With the proper release forms, physicians will be further removed from the process and you will be able to deal directly with the pharmaceutical industry via your computer. A few short years from now, computers will transmit and confirm your relative health, making physicals a thing of the past. Convenience surgeries will also be on the rise, and the line of demarcation between want and need will be harder to distinguish.

Where does all of this leave the natural food, cosmetic and herb industry? What of the naturopaths and those who have bravely set themselves apart from the allopathic community by joining the new science of complementary medicine? In good stead, it gives pleasure to announce! Like all cravings, the desires of the body must also be satisfied. Those who ignore their bodies do so at their peril, but those who heed the elemental language of the body will benefit greatly. The middle path, straight through the center, is always the easiest to follow, for less shadow falls there.

In this example, the body's primary meridian is most able to respond to light, or Source. Source, recognizing Itself in all of Its forms, responds first to that which is most conscious, patiently waiting for the rest to see itself as a reflection of the whole. The elemental body will draw to itself that which is a reflection of Itself—in this case, that which is most natural.

A word of caution must, of necessity, be included here. Not all alternative therapies are natural or beneficial to the body, not every practitioner is a healer and every new modality is not heaven-sent. Draw wisdom from your own truth, and you will recognize the next step in your own healing process, if indeed it is necessary. There are many different body and soul types upon the Earth now, each requiring a balance of its own as well as the means to achieve said balance.

Listen for an energetic match before embarking on any new endeavor—literally. If you feel a resonance within, your outer experience will echo it, and if you experience a sympathetic tonal quality without, your inner experience will endorse it. The Aquarian Age, even in its infancy, carries its own signature. In your near future, almost all healing will be accomplished with sound and frequency. Already there are such techniques to draw upon, but they yet require fine-tuning, if you will pardon the pun on words.

# *The Estrangement of War*

The world begins to tire of war, but not so much as to call on its officials to put an end to it. There are politics to war whose philosophy involves a winner-take-all pageant, replete with parades and heroes and flags. Currently, there are only good guys and bad guys on a chessboard-like playing field where loss of human life is little more than a casualty of speech on the evening news. Wars are the reenactments of the battles that rage in the minds of humanity. Such battles can have no real conclusion, as they were never real to begin with. An act of war is not an action for or against violence; it is a reaction to the instability of human thought and the polarity that exists when reason does not.

## WAR DOES NOT JUST HAPPEN; WAR IS CHOSEN

If the war in Iraq could end tomorrow, another war would begin before the Moon's shadow had passed over the Earth again, because those who direct the will of humanity would desire it to be so. War is neither an end nor a means toward an end; it is but a continuation of the exploits of minds that are not free to create. War begins when unconscious thoughts attack themselves, thereby creating an enemy. Were they not on the same side less than a moment ago? Can one thought truly be the enemy of another? No, no more than one people or one country can. Countries do not go to war, but they follow their leaders there. Soldiers do not go to war, but they follow the orders of their captains and generals. Who goes to war, then? Thoughts and beliefs do. Everything else follows.

At any given time, half the world is in light and half the world is in darkness. Minds are a lot like that too. As long as the dark, or unconscious, aspect of the mind fears rejoining its wholeness, there will be war. Wars do not happen; they are chosen. Each one is selected from a variety of available choices and evaluated in the same way that a corporation considers a new acquisition. Decisions about war begin in plush boardrooms over lavish lunches and warm handshakes. There are no enemies here, only strategies designed to fill coffers and bank accounts. It has always been thus, for war and government are synonymous with monarchies and oligarchies.

The famous and the infamous alike have at times associated with personages who may have appeared no different than common stable hands but who truly rule even the infrastructure of society. Those whom you see as personages of interest are little more than puppets, and even their puppeteers have masters of their own. If you wish to know who the real warmongers are, you will have to look high and low—literally so. You will have to look underground and in the skies and even to other worlds, for where did war begin if not there? The Earth was always intended as a library, but a public library does not screen its applicants, and so Earth became a battlefield in the making.

## It Is One War

The wars have not been many; they have been one. One thought, upon attacking another, began a war. That war landed here on Earth a very long time ago and continues to this day. This war did not belong to humanity, but it needed more soldiers, and this is where they were found. Children make poor soldiers, but orphans make better ones, so your consciousness was disabled until your memories failed you. Without parents, often gods and generals will do, and humanity has inherited both.

"Pacifist beings cannot be made to fight," you might say. It is true, but they can be taught to defend, and that is exactly what unfolded. What father would not defend his child? What soldier would not defend the land upon which his mother raised him? Under such beliefs and contrary to the original nature of humanity, wars have raged, with no apparent end in sight. Is it so? Is there really no end to the vile and the violent that all but rule the planet? Based upon third-dimensional linear time, there is no end forecast for the rulers and the ruled, because they are as one—two sides of the same coin. No? Even those who tire of this war would vote for the next with the proper inducement. Still no? If one country were to lay claim to the world's supply of oil or drinking water or food, would the others stand idle? The third dimension is one of polarity, and its purpose is to explore opposites, be they in the domain of the mind or its battlefield.

## A Turning Point

As said earlier, the world tires of war, but most of its leaders do not. Still, the few who do will make their decisions public, thereby assigning themselves a minor, albeit pivotal place in history. History is rarely accurate, because those who scribe it are subject to editors and like the gentry who commission portraits, they wish to see themselves only in the best possible light.

That being said, the pivot will be thus: The leaders who abstain from voting for further war(s) and refrain from making their obligatory contributions will be forced into the limelight by those who continue to do so. It will be said of them that they are supporters of terrorism and insurgency, and they will be called to account for this. But a true insurgent is not a terrorist. An insurgent is someone who rebels against false leadership, policy and authority. This distinction will be a quiet one at first, but it will become louder when it begins to apply to the home front as well as to faraway shores. Those who plot the course of war are careful to steer it elsewhere, for it is one thing to receive news of the death of a loved one and another thing altogether to witness it.

The change in the political climate will be a subtle one, but it will be a blow struck on behalf of humankind. Its effect will hasten the plans of those whose agenda would have been deliberate and well timed to hurry it to market. Without a sophisticated publicity campaign to accompany it, the underlying purpose will be thin enough to see, even by the legally blind. If a leader cannot gain control of his or her subjects, then the leader's general cannot command his or her troops, for the chain will have been broken. Then the quickening will be available to those who would receive it, and as the tides retreat, they will take with them what the last tide left behind. Such a turning point is fraught with many perils and will come at a cost to humanity, but it will be considered a prize worth having when history is committed to memory and not to books.

## MANY FRONTS, MANY PLACES, MANY NEW WEAPONS

Shall we be more specific? Must we? The war in Iraq has no end and has no victor. The war on terrorism also has no end, because its enemy is its maker. The fact that the emperor has no clothes seems to remain a secret even when he appears before all of his subjects. Because of this, he is well armed; disarm the emperor, and you disarm the enemy. The war has many fronts and many places to which it can retreat. It also has many new weapons it wishes to try out. These involve sound, where frequency can inflict more harm than a bullet and on a much larger scale. Almost everything can either heal or harm. For instance, one can drink water or drown in it. Newer weapons will be based upon this premise and require less militia to enforce them, a timely and effective strategy, since there will be fewer soldiers to draw on.

Less soldiers will not mean less war, at least not yet; and although there will be fewer, they will be better armed. The military will be looking for less able bodies and more able minds. They will entice young minds with the latest technology, promising them gadgetry instead of guns and placating them with laboratories in place of labor. Those who are courted today are invited to visit think tanks that look more like virtual reality environments than anything else. Their escorts are not uniformed recruiters, but updated, latest-version exports of modern technology. Well-planned and supervised tours include visits to dreamlike inner and outer environments almost too good to be true. Positions are and have already been offered to adolescents as young as fourteen years of age, for the new children are well known in these circles as well.

If you are reading these words in hopes that the final paragraphs will weave a conclusion to your liking, disappointment is on the way, for this year and the one that follows it belong to a sequence that came into play long ago. Just as the observable light from a star journeyed far to make your acquaintance today, this pattern also has long existed. It is here to be of benefit to you, but you will not recognize this nor reap its rewards for several more years. It is important to remain present and alert while refusing to become a skeptic or a cynic, as to do so would be to become estranged from the subject and the teaching it offers. Be an observer of nature, human and otherwise, as that which is natural abides by natural law first and other influences second. Speak your intentions softly but clearly, especially where they reflect what and whom you support and in whose name. Place your own true name at the top of the list and at its end as well so that you will not be underrepresented.

# On the Home Front

The world might be at or near war, but on the home front, mouths still need to be fed and mortgages need to be paid. The drums' din is the sound of war, but the persistent echo fades as they approach home. Truth, like reality, is subjective; the closer you come to it, the louder it should be, unless you close your ears. Such is the case with respect to the world's economy, a singular rather than a plural subject. The din of the drumbeat has confused humanity, and its repeated reinforcement has fixed it in humanity's mind, compounding it even further. Its cadence goes something like this: The rent is due on the first, the car payment is due on the second, the tuition is due on the third, the credit card payment is due on the fourth, and so on. The drumbeat becomes louder, until it is harder to hear that which exists beyond it. One hears one's own agenda, not because it is more important, but because it is louder.

## NO LIFE IS BETTER OR WORSE THAN ANY OTHER

Each life is cast its own lot and is not better or worse than another. One would need to know the intricate experiences underwritten by the soul and underlying each and every life before being qualified to say who or what is better or worse off than another, all appearances to the contrary. Every life is worth its light in Sun's gold from beginning to end, and no one is paid short shrift in heaven or on Earth. Soon, however, it will become increasingly difficult to believe these very words, and even my own sentience will be called upon to give account of their validity or, better yet, to offer proof of their merit.

The world stage changes now, but the home front will change faster still. Did it not change in a matter of hours for those whose lives became inextricably tied to the course of a hurricane? Lives change because it is necessary that they do. Hurricanes are not malicious by nature, but they are not accidental either. They are purposeful, as is all life. Most employers are not malicious, but they are not beneficent either. They are purposeful; they have an agenda, which may or may not support your own. Although these examples are both real-life and real-time, they do nothing to ease the din of the drumbeat's cadence and the place it occupies within your being.

## HUMANITY CREATED CURRENCY AND ACCEPTS ITS DEBT

In order to consciously care for your home front and its responsibilities, you must become more aware of that which exists beyond the din. This word, din, is being repeated here so that you will grasp its meaning more fully. Din is a loud, persistent noise composed of confused and persistent sounds which, when repeated over and over again, fix something in someone's mind. Din is also short for and a symbol of dinar, a subunit of currency still in use today, though it was more common in ancient times in the Middle East, where it was the standard of exchange, being a gold coin. Do they not both pose a problem today?

All That Is, abundant and resplendent, did not create currency or its lack; humanity did. Today's system of currency was created long ago, and though your ancestors succeeded in freeing themselves from slavery, they indentured themselves and you to another god. Any form of currency will continue to exist as long as there is widespread acceptance or use of it, even if it is no more than a theory, word or phrase. In this case, yesterday's currency has become today's god, and at least in this reality, humanity has also accepted its debt.

Your beingness is debtless and faultless, but your identity is not. When your identity becomes less and your beingness more, your debts will be reduced, and you will find the means to detach yourself from them. In the meantime, latching on to another reality, belief or system will not free you from this one. Your soul did not determine the creditworthiness of its beingness before choosing a body. You were not offered a greater or lesser human vehicle based upon your ability to pay for it throughout your life, but once you were born, your identity took on debt and is still doing so. In ancient times, a debt was synonymous with a sin or that which your beingness could not trespass upon itself, for to do so was to create a condition that was impossible to bear.

Obligations weigh heavily upon your being, and those with associated debt are among the densest of all. An obligation is a condition, and although most obligations are not life threatening, they affect the ability of the whole to function optimally. Conditions such as these contribute to physical and psychological disorders and are often characterized by hardship and suffering. Informal conditions are no more than circumstances that affect how one works or lives, but formal conditions create situations in which position, rank and social status come into question. Under conditioning, people act and react in certain ways that gradually accustom them to patterns, events and identities. The accumulation of debt—due to its association with identity—has made it more difficult for you to remember who you are.

## LOOSEN THE BINDS OF YOUR
## IDENTITY AND LOOSEN THE BURDENS OF DEBT

Awaken, awaken and remember! Your divinity is real, more real than the debt that prevents you from recognizing it. Loosen the bindings of the identity you have taken on, and the burdens of debt loosen as well. It is not your debts that shackle you to your beliefs; rather, it is the other way around. As long as you are harnessed to your identity, you will not recognize your true self and it will be more difficult for you to discover new solutions. New solutions will not come from the very system that enslaved you or from your identity that willingly, albeit unwittingly, donned the shackles of your time. A debtor is someone who has trespassed against another; in other words, a debtor is someone who has assumed that which is not his, including an identity. It is no wonder that the one crime that the creators of the current system have the most difficulty combating is of their own making! There is nothing less tangible than an identity, do you see?

The current system will crumble in favor of another one, but it will not be a better one—not yet. Still, it is best to recognize it for what it is and to disavow it from the first. In doing so, you will not erase your debt, but neither will you don yet another identity that is not your own, another layer to peel off later. You are not your debt, and your debt is not you. It belongs to the beliefs associated with your third-dimensional awareness and the conditions implied by it. Your endorsement of this debt has made it denser and more real, but its reality is still tethered to the third dimension and yours is not.

## NEW FINANCIAL SYSTEMS BASED ON BARGAINING

Those who hold your creditworthiness at risk will soon introduce new banks and new methods of accounting. These methods will be to their advantage, but they will doubtless be touted as of benefit to many, and indeed at first glance, they will seem to be that. There will be an easing of the methods by which one establishes credit and by which a score is established. Many will receive clean slates with which to begin again, and others will have a portion of their debt deferred into a unique account by which they can earn points that can be used to offset debt or to defer it further. One of the factors upon which the new system will depend will be as if a bargain against the future. For instance, if a healthy young male sees many years of earning potential ahead of him, he might bargain with his retirement account today, with the promise (in writing) that it will be there when he needs it. This is a simple example, and others will be more complex. Suffice it to say that there will be a scramble among many to see what they have to bargain with and for. Such bargaining, where columns of credits and debits work for and against each other, will minimize the need for cash, making the longevity of currency a bit of a gamble in itself.

Interest rates will continue to rise, slowly at first and more quickly later. The timing for the introduction of this new system will be appropriate. It will be on the lips of candidates and politicos. Plans are already in place to assure the endorsement of relief agencies that have been of pivotal support to the poor and the devastated during the recent worldwide natural events, especially if the new system does not gain momentum quickly. It will be shown, for instance, that the generosity by which the system operates was responsible for the funds that were made available during these catastrophes. CDs and DVDs introducing the system will be mailed to everyone and shown everywhere. Individual worksheets pointing out obvious benefits will also be available. Corporations large and small, each with something to gain and a part to play, will offer incentives of their own.

This description is a modest one and cannot take into account all of the ramifications such an operation implies. You will not be able to opt out of this system any more than you can opt out of paying your mortgage or your taxes, but for a time, it will seem that you have the better of it. The disadvantages will not be apparent until later, and that is why it is said: Do not assume an identity that is not your own and that does not support you. Do not run from your debt nor make it your all. Take responsibility for it by acting in accordance with the laws of humanity, but do not forget the universal laws by which you create and were created, as they will remain in effect.

## TAKE CARE OF YOUR TRUE SELF

The world cannot pay for the debt it has accumulated, and neither can you. Many of the world's countries can hardly pay for their food and will not be able to assume their share of the world's debt when the time comes to ante up. This will place debtor nations in a predicament that provides no egress and perhaps no escape. The great countries will not fare better in the long run, but these countries will not show their cards for a while yet, nor will those who, for a time, can get by on a bluff. No longer are there aces in the deck, only kings in positions they are not qualified for and queens who, like foxes, guard the chickens at night while you sleep.

Take care of your true self; do not abandon it in favor of an identity that is temporary and hardly your own. If you make a promise, do so in kindness and by pledge but not so as to accumulate a debt. Be of a mind that is innocent and a body that is pure. Reflect upon a past that is nearly complete and a future that is near its dawn. Share words of wisdom with the less fortunate and whisper your words of fear to me at night. They will be returned to you in the morning, mended and of good use again. Do not discard your fear or your resources; they will both come in handy soon. Recognize that what makes you whole is your beingness and not your identity, your soul and not your overcoat.

# Nature's Call

W hich way do you think the wind will blow?" said one weather forecaster to another. "I don't know," said the second. "I guess it's nature's call."

Is it so? Does nature now dictate to humanity? What and where is nature's intelligence that it is not also with humanity? Nature has many faces, but it has one voice, which has not been heard by humanity and that belongs to humanity. Nature's voice says simply, "Be that which you be and do that which you do in good season, now as always." "Be that which you be" means to be natural in all that you are. If you are human, be human; and if you are animal, be animal—but if you are plant, then be that. "Do that which you do" means to flourish without giving thought elsewhere, without expectation or reward. It means to perform an action because it is the most natural of all things to do and not contrary to that which is. "In good season, now as always" means that you will not change that which you are or that which you do midstream. It means that the law is not temporary but eternal. A season is as dictated by nature and the Spirit that guides it, and all things are alike. A good season means one that is well spent and complete, with no agenda; it leaves nothing before it or behind it.

## ANTICIPATE CHANGE

That which is natural can be only that and nothing else, but it can be made to act unnaturally given certain circumstances and a narrow bandwidth within which to express. This is one of the challenges presented to humanity in these times; soon there will be more. The Earth (my body) prepares to renew herself now, as the gap between endings and beginnings is a gift from the universe for just such a purpose. This gift is bestowed upon all, but like all opportunities that arrive dressed as challenges, one must recognize them for what they are. In the spring, the Earth renews herself as she sheds winter's cold. There are signs above and beneath the ground that warn every kingdom and every element to anticipate change. Is this not what is taking place today? Does the Earth not rumble, and do the tides not signify that change is in our midst?

As long as humanity's collective head remains in the sand, change will continue to take us by surprise. Open your eyes! The Earth renews herself; will you not also choose renewal? There is much to lose in remaining ignorant and much to gain in looking for new opportunities. Have you watched your friends or family lament a sunset when the next dawn already hearkens? It is a pity to behold, yet this is how many of the Earth's species perceive humanity. Your brothers, sisters, cousins and teachers stand at the ready off-planet, but they will not rescue you from yourselves. Your long sleep keeps you apart from what is taking place rather than making you a part of it. You are beings of light, a collective consciousness from the brightest constellations and star clusters—who or what are you cowering from? Awaken! You have but a few short years in which to do so.

By collective agreement, your body makes its home atop my own. This agreement is valid as long as there is purpose in it. Purpose is not hewn of concrete and mortar; it is flexible, soft and loving. We are not adversaries, and nature has no wrath to inflict upon any of its species, for where does one end and the next begin? The relationship between human and Earth is a resilient one whose purpose is to balance and develop conscience and sentience. The Earth (my sentience) is not angry or sad; she is not wounded, and she does not seek retaliation for the unconscious acts that have depleted many of her resources. The Earth has laid no gauntlet before humanity; it is the humans' own immaturity and mindlessness that now challenges them to seek solutions for the folly they have wrought. So be it. If solutions are needed, they will be found. Is this not the same law by which all beings live? Peace be with you; let us now put our collective awareness to the test!

The globe warms now—at an alarming rate, they say. If consciousness rose at an alarming rate, would there also be concern? Yes, more than likely, yes. If an hour took longer than sixty minutes, you would also be alarmed; and if the Sun rose elsewhere on the horizon, many hearts would stop beating—literally so. These possibilities, now near realities, instill fear, for great changes—even good ones—are known for doing exactly that. How can so many ignore the obvious? They do not, at least not at the levels that really matter. Why don't they do something about it? They are, but they are you!

## Revive Your Awareness of Being at Cause

The current process is an evolutionary one, and it began long, long ago. You were there when it began, even if you cannot remember it now. Forgetting is a tool that allows you to concentrate on other things; remembering is a tool that allows you to concentrate on this thing. Ignorance is a tool that removes cause, placing one at effect, do you see? Currently, those who do not wish to be at cause prefer that others be that for them—scientists, government officials, emergency response teams, doctors, family members, employers and so on. When one is at the effect of life, surprises come often and from many directions. Your soul has animated this life upon this world at this time to revive your awareness of being at cause; this is true of all beings, without exception.

If you are at cause, will the Earth not quake? No, but you will quake with her and recognize that you too caused such quaking. If you are at cause, will the hurricanes diminish their intensity? No, but perhaps your conscious awareness will join with their elemental awareness so that their purpose can be accomplished at sea rather than inland. It amazes my sentience that a tuna fisherman baits a shark by luring it too close to his boat and then cowers in fear as he is taken by apparent surprise. Likewise, it is just as amazing to behold the sophisticated technology by which hurricanes are tracked, broadcast worldwide and then baited to shore by both fear and sensationalism. The element of surprise would seem undone, yet it is all too present. I say this without chastisement: Could your awareness not be equally fascinated elsewhere?

The simple truth is that humans are fascinated by the rapid rise in Earth changes. They look at the destruction of cities and the demise of lives, contribute to the relief of others and give thanks that it happened elsewhere. They support the effect suffered upon others without placing themselves at cause, do you see? The surface of the Earth is changing because her inner composition is changing as well. Do you not dance with the idea of your ascension and the changes that are taking place within your inner and outer environments? The Earth does as well! Have your teachers, spiritual and otherwise, not forecast such a time and bid you prepare? Well, such times are here, and they are now. In awareness all things are possible. Such awareness comes to those who draw it to themselves, be it in peaceful meditation or in the throes of upheaval.

## MELTING ICE AND CHANGING COASTLINES

The Earth intensifies her motion now, bypassing older deposits of energy in favor of newer ones. To reiterate, this is a natural process, and humanity has been its witness and its participant many times prior to this. The polar caps are melting quickly now, dislodging volumes of ice into the seas, but not all of the melted ice becomes additional sea-water; some of it seeps into the Earth's crust and travels elsewhere via the systems that crisscross the inner surface of the Earth. Once under the surface, the characteristics of water become altered, thereby altering the composition of that which the water interacts with. By this say-ing, expect water tables to rise and fall throughout the Earth, with no detectable sequence. Island nations will be most affected, because their reserves of fresh water are not as deep as those of mainland nations. The rise and fall of the Earth's water tables will affect public water supplies and private well systems alike. Under such circumstances, it would be appropriate to test water supplies more often and to study desalination techniques, some of which are already fairly adequate.

Water from within and without will continue to erode the Earth's shores, inundating that which is close enough to sea level to become sea. Sliding earth due to oversaturation will also change the shape of the world's coastlines. If you own or will soon purchase property in these areas, be well guided in your decisions and be in balance with the Earth's elements. The Earth only takes and uses what she needs, returning the rest in a variety of forms and functions. If you can say the same, you will have no cause for concern.

Earthquakes will also be on the rise this year and for several more to come. There are no earthquake-safe or earthquake-prone zones, but there are earthquake-proof people. Remember and awaken. Draw unto yourselves learning experiences, but if you have already learned, must you relearn? Earthquake-proof people are those who remember who they are and that they are not separate from the experiences they draw to them. By contrast, earthquake-prone people live in fear of that which seems to be outside of them and therefore outside of their control. Even earth-quakes do not come from that which is outside of you. They emerge from the center (an epicenter) and move outward. You too have emerged from the center, from which you moved outward until you thought you were separate from your center. You are not.

## You Are a Community-Based Species

All of your individual adventures do not preclude that humanity is a community-based species. Although private moments can be uplifting and revealing, solitary forays into the depths of beingness may not be. Choose your physical and spiritual explorations well. For instance, a new healing technique or thought-based system may or may not trigger your intuitive nature regarding Earth changes. Trust your intuition and continue to develop an abiding relationship with it. Trust your teachers and heed their lessons when they are appropriate.

Know that you are safe in your beingness and that you are not your pride or your possessions. If loss presents itself, remember that what is owned or earned can be re-created, because the supply is endless even if chaos rearranges it temporarily. Seek shelter in appropriate places, and share your shelter with others when and if the time comes. Lay in a good quantity of supplies, but do not hoard these. When you make a purchase, make an extra one that you would be willing to share. Imagine that others are doing the same on your behalf. The shelf life of the resources you have will be commensurate with your faith in manifesting any resource you will need at a later time.

Be your own first responder. Do not count on federal, state or local emergency personnel to do for you what you are capable of doing for yourself and others. Soon the federal government will have fewer funds to allocate to disaster relief. The responsibility will then fall upon individual states, most of which are unprepared, to say the least. Local communities, being more in tune with their constituents, will be better prepared, but if they wait for instructions and deployment from superiors who project their authority from elsewhere, it will not bode well. The same is true of other countries, and those who receive these words in another language are advised to receive them as their own.

The science fumblers and weather makers will be hard at work for some time to come; the thought behind their efforts being that if such power could be harnessed, its energy could be controlled—and if it can be controlled, can it not also be owned? A percentage of the world's catastrophes—but not all—can certainly be considered human-made and can even be attributed to the activities of these earth rakers and those who sponsor their efforts. Those who go about insisting that all such events are planned and the result of sinister activities might invest their energies elsewhere for the good of the entire planet, for if all are one (and you are), then they too are the planners and inciters of such fiendish invocations of energy. Pay them heed when they work for your well-being and a favorable environment, and give them no succor when their words are loosed upon already chaotic times. Malpractitioners with good intentions always seek followers, though leaders they are not.

This subject cannot be called complete, and we will revisit it from many places and perspectives as the year unfolds.

## *When the Cat's Away*

S candals will be many as the year unfolds, some from tried and true corners and others from unlikely people and places. Secrets are fragile, multilayered things that unravel not at the end but at their beginning as where, who or what they were assigned to guard begins to fray. Secrets are not meant to be kept hidden or buried forever, but the timing of their release is another thing altogether. Secrets are made of an elastic fabric that can stretch almost as far as the fabric of time, making that which they guard valuable long after it was sworn into being. Those who weave the fabric within which a secret is embedded become the fabric's caretaker for however long is necessary, often long after the secret is revealed. For instance, those who embedded secrets into the books considered holy are still responsible for them today, and will continue to be until such time as the secrets are revealed and righted if need be. The same is true of the dashing men you call the framers of your government's constitution, for they too must be held accountable on certain measures. Can those who whisper in the corridors, behind closed doors and in between bed sheets expect less?

### THE LIFE OF A SECRET

Animals are exceptionally intelligent, in that they will immediately distance themselves upon completion of their elimination cycle, especially from any proximity to the excrement associated with their last meal. Humans share this instinctual intelligence, but seem to be less fortunate in their escape. Why? Because an invisible tarlike substance adheres itself to those who speak less than truth in less than opportune moments to less than trusted companions, thereby rendering the elimination cycle incomplete. In other words, one cannot simply walk away from what one has created and/or participated in, do you see? Those who are haunted by the truth more than likely avoided it or misspoke it at some point. Those who tell a lie fare no better, for the consequences they have wrought often become their own. Humankind metes out its own justice and requires neither condemnation nor judgment from others. Sentences of punishment are not conferred by a panel of one's equals but by a distorted mirror's edge, for one's true equal could not condemn.

A secret begins its life much as a cell does. Around its nucleus are clustered all manner of bringers and takers of information. It also ends its life much like a cell, albeit a cancerous one, with everyone and everything running for safety before it's too late. By this guide, you will see the contrast of light and dark this year, and examples to choose from will abound. "If the walls could only speak," the saying goes. Well, what if they did? "I'd like to be a fly on that wall," goes another. Well, what if you were? "I wonder if he's going to spill his guts?" asks a conspirator of his companion. He will. The year 2006 is a turncoat year, so to speak. It will make fools of friends and enemies alike. The dead still walk, you know. The dead walk because they did not speak the truth nor reveal their secrets when it was their time to do so, but all things (times) being equal, they are more than willing to do so now.

Political scandals will be at the forefront, with corporate falsehoods bringing up the rear. Contradictions and investigations will seem to delay the obvious, but wildcat oil wells, sometimes called "gushers," will cause even the most greased wheels to spin. Why speak in metaphors? Metaphors, as vessels, are more seaworthy per square inch than well-organized speech. Why does the wisdom of Nostradamus live on long after he did? His fine poetic words, arranged to tickle, tantalize, provoke and protect, are still at work on his behalf and are still of benefit to you, as well.

## NEW AUTONOMICAL TECHNOLOGY IS DESIGNED TO WATCH PEOPLE

The world is under watch now as well-placed cameras record faces and microphones record speech. Conspiracy, however, is more difficult to detect, and piracy even more so. That being the case, sophisticated draconian measures will soon accompany those already in place. Those who enact such measures will find that they will fall upon their own swords as their own strategies begin to backfire. A new technology designed to spy on anyone at any time is still under lock and key as of this writing, but not for long. This technology surpasses even the sophisticated nature of that which is already in use, even before public awareness, even before a complaint has been spoken. As it turns out, very few of you will be worth spying on, as you are even more ordinary and predictable than the creators of the technology itself.

Not everyone is ordinary or predictable, however, and a veritable who's who list of people will be unable to allow such an opportunity to pass by without attempting to use it to their own advantage. So the folly will begin, and where it will end is still anyone's guess. The technology itself is not faulty, but it is invasive and difficult to disable without knowledge of that which created it. Do you remember HAL in the moving picture *2001: A Space Odyssey?* He (it) lives on, and those who created HAL are still in their laboratory, albeit a better financed one. What if that which was created to protect or detect a secret decided instead (autonomically) to hold it for ransom and/or to divulge it elsewhere?

Autonomical technologies include devices that contain semi-intelligent, near-conscious active agents. Autonomical agents were created to be independent and self-governing, with a capacity to make moral decisions and to act on them. They exist, develop and react as self-regulating semi-organisms. The technology upon which they were created emulates the functions of the human nervous system not under the ordinary voluntary control of the individual, for example the regulation of the heartbeat and the secretions performed by the glands. Their emulation and compatibility with such systems makes them hard to detect. On the other hand, the moral "code" under which they operate has been programmed, at least initially so. Even without metaphors, can you read between the lines?

Information and technology will long be remembered as the cornerstone of this age. Artificial intelligence is now featured. So be it. When humanity tires of it, natural intelligence and its many benefits will be restored. Do you not wonder where your space friends have gone? They will not share in this folly, but they will be available soon enough when it is set aside. Such toys bring no conquests, and this they already know, having learned it long ago. "I have no part in it! I have no conscious knowledge of this, nor would I support it if I did." So my sentience has heard it said, not only in this age, but in others as well. Be at peace, dearest friends; no blame is settled upon you. Though you wrote your future long ago, you also wrote your past, and you shall be present to see them both.

Whose truth does your heart today embrace? Is it your own? Are you sure? How many trusted misadventures have sprung from truths too readily embraced? How many deeds and misdeeds lie alongside knowledgeable accomplices? Think well before embracing a truth that you stumbled upon through a friend or in a book, a cave or a class. Trust truth to stand upon a pillar of spirit, for those of salt and stone will crumble now, and again later. There are no secrets such as cannot be revealed to the worthy or the wanton, depending upon their nature. "Tell me no secrets and I will tell others no lies," may well be the mantra of those who guard well their integrity. "Speak softly even when you whisper truth, that your blunders be not shouted from the battlements." A wise, long-lived and much beloved king was often heard to say this. May wisdom extend its time-earned warmth to you and yours.

# What About Me?

The year ahead already seems almost out of hand, and it is barely upon you. Stress descends out of nowhere but settles itself upon your shoulders just the same. What have you done to deserve such treatment? Nothing? Exactly! A diamond, even an imperfect one beset with carbon deposits and inclusions, does not inflict upon itself the very stress that leads to its own perfection, but the stress arrives just the same. Why? It is an act of nature upon that which is natural. Humans now draw to themselves such as will make them more tensile, each in his or her own way. Tensile strength is a measure of flexibility shown while receiving or exerting force. That which is tensile true is capable of being stretched and pulled out of shape without losing its structural integrity—in other words, without ceasing to be that which it is. You, humanity, are tensile true. You cannot and will not cease to be that which you are, but you do not know this yet, not experientially.

## YOU ARE A COLLECTION OF THE BEST OF ALL THINGS

Short of spelling it out, this year will reveal to you as clearly as possible what you are. You are not a who, you are a what—and a grand what at that. You are not the bastard children of laboratory experiments gone wrong, and you are not the top of the discard pile of a more advanced race, as my sentience recently overheard on one of the channel's outings! To use another borrowed phrase from a recent seminar participant, you are divinity in drag! You are a collection of the best of all things, with many of the lights still turned off. Blaring lights will not make the process quicker, but they will make the contrast between light and dark more stark and severe. Do you not already find fault with shadow, especially your own?

This year will be marked by an invisible need to hurry along, as if to a supposed end or a foregone conclusion. Many will go there and extend an invitation for you to join them. "It is the destination," they will say, "the big aha!" If you go there, you will find what they promised, but you will also find disappointment, for you are more than "aha!" and your origins are as well. Might I suggest that you accompany your friends, and especially your family members, there without calling the journey your own? Might I also suggest that although what you seek is natural, it is not as obvious as what will be demonstrated?

Your friends and your family have been waiting for just such a moment as this year will seem to provide. Your New Age ideas will be called to account this year, and so will your far-fetched theories and far-from-mainstream views on human origins. All conspiracy who-done-its will face near extermination, and it will all be at the hands of one of your own pseudoscientists. Science and religion must merge, you see. Such a joining requires a Judas in monk's robes, as it were. And from among your great community, a light will offer itself. These words are offered to you now so that when the time comes, you will remember that it is light that speaks, and its language is light. This same reminder was put forth long ago, do you remember? Do not test yourselves needlessly.

## A NEW LANGUAGE

A new language will emerge beginning this year as well, one that will take away some of your complacency if you let it. Languages are born, and much later they are taught. Language is a form of communication, be it spoken or silent. It includes signs and symbols, and even operations, in the case of mathematics and geometry. This language will be an unconventional one whose characteristics will include intuitional gestures and inarticulate muscle movements. The intention behind the language will cause you to rely upon forgotten aspects of your being. If language is a bridge between people, then it is also a bridge between hemispheres of the brain. Though you may be loath to be programmed, your brain responds to unique signals and rules that will lead to greater awareness sooner rather than later.

Performing certain functions and upgrades upon your computer's brain often yields rewards elsewhere. This language will yield similar results. If you pay attention to music, you will see that it is also a language and your brain receives it as one. For instance, let's say that a language is irregular in its form, emotional in effect and improvisational in nature—this language describes the architecture of rhapsody; you hear music, but your brain "hears" a language. A new language can help to offset or remake how you hold old programmed agreements in your life. Ask yourself what your brain hears when you say, "I can't afford that/go there/do this/sleep/ stand him or her." Is a new language, be it one of words, melodies or symbols, not in order?

## Questions and Answers

During the first half of this year, you will have more questions than answers. But in the second half, especially if you allow your true nature to speak for you, you will have answers to many important questions. Here is an important key: Ask questions whose answers will settle you and your mind rather than ones that will provoke the next irritating question to come to the surface. All questions have answers, otherwise the question could not be formulated, but not all answers are satisfying. Have you ever asked a question and had it answered only to ask it again in the next moment or of the next person? My sentience has addressed many such questions, and when the redux question is asked and answered, it still seems to be reprised later in the same dialogue. Reason would dictate that you did not like the answer you received, but truth be told, you did not understand the answer, or know how to make it work, or imagine how you might change it. If an answer does not please you or engage your creativity, you can set about changing or reinventing it; but if instead you set a course to ask your question again here, there or elsewhere, you will become frustrated and decide your question has no likely answer, in which case it won't.

Questions are not forever things; they belong to the Now. In order to make sense and good use of an answer, you must also be in the present and apply the answer there. If the question was, "When will the war end?" the answer you are hoping for would be, "Now, today." But if in asking the question you projected yourself into your mind (which does not often remain in the present), you would allow all of the reasons regarding the impossibility of the answer to arise, and the answer would have been nullified before you even heard it. Who is asking the question, then? You or your mind? The mind asks many questions; in fact, it could ask questions all day long, and it often does. Interestingly, the mind does not expect answers, but you do, so ask the questions whose answers will benefit you in the Now. If the answer to your question prompts you to say or think, "But what if _____ ," then you did not ask the question—your mind did.

Again, during the first half of the year, you will have more questions than answers. Why? Because your mind will be more actively engaged in your affairs and concerns. The second half of the year will provide many opportunities for answers, but you must be present to receive them.

"What about me?" The answer to this question already exists within you, but you must breathe life into it. It is a question that seems to say it all, does it not? Its answer does as well. "Me" is what you have projected into your identity so that you could experience your beingness as individual, but that is not what you are. Your identity has needs, but you do not. If you begin the year by asking, "What about me?" by year's end, you will have the answer to many of your needs. If you will also ask, "Who am I?" and "What is the who that I am?" by year's end, you will be a different person, with a subtler identity and a grander presence.

# *Righting the Wrongs*

The year 2006 will see the beginning of the world and its leaders attempting to right some of the wrongs by more effective means than they have attempted thus far. It has become all too obvious that the world has changed, and so have its people and its resources. Some would say, even at this juncture, that it all happened almost overnight. Some historians will record it this way, and the descendants of your future generations will marvel that it happened so. Of course, they will have other tools to guide them as well, for it will also be recorded that the close of this era was fraught with deceit, ignorance and the struggle for control. To be fair, there are those who do and will say that it was no more than good old-fashioned horse trading.

Before wrongs can be righted, there must be agreement as to where to begin. Unfortunately, while this is being argued, little will be done and many of the wrongs will continue and even increase. The world's resources will continue to dwindle and so will those of most individuals, but the world has other resources that she was previously unaware of, and so do you, the individual. The world cannot create her future by discarding her past or ignoring her present; she must choose a new pattern or spiral from which to ascend rather than continue her descent. The future of the Earth rests upon this.

## WORLD LEADERS, THE DIVINE FEMININE AND THE SPACE BROTHERHOOD

In hindsight, all choices seem obvious, but in the muddle of the moment, when confusion reigns, the fog of doubt and inconsistency does as well. This fog will cloud the minds of many of the world's leaders, and there will be those who choose to step down rather than continue. So close to a shift in paradigm, the world's leaders find themselves in parallax, with a different view of the same object or situation because their own position has changed. Choose well your leaders and pay close attention to those whom they appoint, for they too shall become your leaders. Will they remain at the helm when the fog settles upon them too?

A battle between the world's leaders is in the making, but it will not reveal itself this year, and perhaps not even next. It simmers now, but it will eventually boil over. The battle will be over promises not kept, as many are, but the stakes will be much higher. The world is only a chess match away from unrestrained war, some astride their horses and others hiding or watching from their ivory towers. The pawns have thinned their ranks and the king, as always, is powerless for the most part. The powerful queen is within all of you—that which represents the divine feminine. Has this subject not found a prominent position in almost all areas of life? There are clues yet to be discovered and rewards for the having, but these will only reveal themselves to those who understand the true nature of the queen and her power.

We have shared few words with you of late as to the activities of the space brotherhood that also shares your fate due to an interesting array of anomalies. Their hands were tied even as your eyes have been shut, but solutions have continued to present themselves just the same. They are not your heroes, only your brothers, and it is their wisdom and not their presence that you require. They will not rescue you from yourselves, but they will intercede on your behalf if a threat not of your own making presents itself. In this, and this alone, they have leave to act. You will hear and read many words to the contrary as this year and the next progress. You will have both cause and desire to believe what is told to you in this regard. Those who proffer their words do so based upon a certain understanding, just as do those who interpret the symbolic language of the holy books as literal. Belief is a very fragile thing, even when it seems strong and concrete. The sturdiest of foundations will begin to crack this year, and they will soon crumble as well. Be not too near them when they do!

## True Solutions Exist in Your Ability to Remember

The wrongs that will be righted will not appear on your front-page headlines; it is still too soon for that, but their presence will be felt and seen. A lovely woman named Rosa Parks recently transitioned from the physical plane to the next. Her body received high honors and her memory much praise because of what her life represented. But many like her go nameless and homeless for the same principles, do you see? Headlines offer insight as to what has been. You must look elsewhere for what is and what may be. Today the wrongs seem more plentiful than the rights because they have gone ignored, but ignorance makes its presence known in many places, even where right seems more than plain. Wrongs are teachers. If a father was himself raised wrongly, then that which was wrong must be righted in the parenting of his own son. If a generation or an epoch has wronged the Earth, then it has also wronged itself, do you see? That teaching, which might last many generations, will once again belong to those who wrought it, that they might right it! True teachers do not point fingers; they point the way. In this case, two wrongs can indeed make a right.

As was said earlier, there will be much dissension about how to repair or replace what needs to be. After many short stalls and a shake up or two (one of these in the physical), a variety of options will be explored. These will run the gamut from the ridiculous to the sublime, as you might imagine, but from the ashes will emerge the phoenix itself, clutching a few shreds of truth upon which to renew the planet and the hope of those who make their home upon it. The costliest plans will more than likely be the least effective, because they have no energy of their own. Next on the list of ineffectiveness will be plans that involve legions of brawn toiling in the fields of the bewildered and forgotten—this was already tried long ago, remember? Remembering is the key. Remember who you are, and you remember a little. Remember what you are, and you remember more. Remember what you and the planet are together, and you are well on your way. True solutions exist beyond your human mind, but not beyond your ability to retrieve memories, do you see?

There is no wrong that cannot be righted, no weapon that cannot be abandoned, no reality that cannot be transformed, no wisdom that cannot be recovered. The year 2006 will address these subjects from a variety of perspectives, until at last someone dares to utter the words that tongues have swallowed and lips have silenced, "Can it really be the end—*the* end?" Only when yesterday's questions become today's acknowledged situations will tomorrow's solutions arrive. Only then will science meet religion and Spirit speak to both.

❋   ❋   ❋

All that has been addressed here has been pondered before, and there is little that will take you by surprise this year. That being the case, why not become a bit of a sleuth? There are mysteries to be revealed and experiences to be had. Can you recall how many children's games involve being blindfolded or otherwise handicapped? Even so, some become experts at such games—perhaps you are one of them. This year will be a bit like that. Of the past year it could be said that the blind led the blind, but this year only some play at blindness—a vast improvement. Shall we gather again next year to view and review? In the meantime, perhaps we will meet again between these and other pages, or in any location of your choosing, for they are all one where my sentience is concerned.

# The Lemurian Changelings

*T*he body that was Lemuria was once grander than its technologically advanced contemporary, Atlantis. Lemuria was divided into islands of light and learning that spanned far beyond the borders you now imagine. These forums of divine expression belonged to all, and a well-fashioned request was the only prerequisite to gain admission to one or more islands of light. Far from institutional, Lemurian islands of learning were robust, familylike communities held together by common interests. They belonged neither to Earth nor sky, and it would be difficult to place them in a specific geographical context upon or within the Earth. In fact, it was almost as if the islands appeared where their will directed them. If you have experienced difficulty placing Lemuria upon a map or taking the word of another, perhaps this is why. In truth, Lemuria was no more divided than the individual aspects of a spider's web, each individual strand intricately connected to the next. The Lemurian infrastructure was feather-light, self-evolving and self-healing. It rarely evoked a crossed thought. That is, of course, until the arrival of the changelings.

Folklore has it that changelings were children who were secretly substituted for others by the fair ones. The long-lived Lemurians were accustomed to evolution but not to change, and they did not know what to make of things when the changelings began arriving in droves. Lemurian changelings, like their modern Indigo cousins, did not look like or act like their kin. Taller and broader than former generations, they stood out from the start. The decisions they made did not require a consensus of council or precedent but seemed relative to the perfection of all just the same. Their minds seemed to reach far into the future, steering to intercept or avoid the next thought as easily as the next dimension. Their thoughts were not the frivolous novelties of adolescent minds, for the changelings foresaw a future that somehow eluded the elders within their communities of light. What did the changelings see?

## THE SKY IS FALLING

Specifically, the Lemurian changelings knew that they had been born at the end of time, at least as expressed within the Lemurian hologram. They knew that the partnership the Lemurians had long enjoyed with nature was about to take a giant pause, and they perceived with pinpoint accuracy that the islands of light and learning would soon succumb to the same polarization that was evident elsewhere in the globosphere. In essence, the changelings were saying to their elders, "The sky is falling, and you had better get out of the way."

The Lemurian elders, gentle stewards of the natural world, were not quite certain what to make of the changelings who seemed neither Lemurian nor of any other recognizable descent. Long did the elders sit in council, pondering, questioning and studying without conclusion. Lemurians were not bound to the Earth as beings of later civilizations were, and their bodies, although human in appearance, were not tethered to their souls. Thus abandoning their place upon or within the Earth was but a matter of choice.

One day great clouds gathered in huge numbers, a rare and unfamiliar sight in Lemurian skies. The Lemurians had lived long within a balanced ecosphere and were unfamiliar with thunderstorms. They did not recognize the spectacular, rounded masses of cumulonimbus clouds associated with such storms, but the changelings recognized them well. They spoke to the Lemurian elders in gentle, mature words with an authority they had not previously possessed. They described strange and uncommon things in ominous, prophetic and altogether marvelous ways. Their words did not instill fear, for this was unknown within the Lemurian timescape. The changelings spoke of accelerations that would propel the Earth and its inhabitants into and through schemes and schisms that would be defined by time, dimension and density.

As the changelings continued to speak, the islands of light and learning began to draw together, as if reuniting into one great frequency. A fusion of light unfolded, joining color with sound and spanning the breadth and length of a continent. The Lemurian populace now revealed itself as individual strands of one being reuniting into a single unit of consciousness. As such, they could not help but see themselves reflected within the oneness that the changelings had already embodied. As one voice, there existed only one truth. Singular in nature, the changelings projected a future vision of both the possible and the probable into the minds of all. Each was presented with a future that included individual endings and beginnings, as well as the elements of structure for reuniting as one at a later time. Rather than limitations of experience, each vision was an endless kaleidoscope of creativity and choice.

## A TIME OF INDIVIDUAL CHOICE

The Lemurians also saw that the sky was indeed falling, at least as far as their current Lemurian life was concerned, for woven into their vision of the future was the need to choose either a further descent into physicality or a withdrawal from it altogether. The Lemurians seemed almost evenly split in this regard. The resplendent Earth took their breath away, magnificent and magnetic as it was. Alas, the descent into matter also drew the breath, but differently so. Divided in mind and body, the Lemurians found it impossible to choose, but united in thought and deed, new possibilities began to emerge. The Lemurians decided to divide their numbers based upon individual choice, while remaining of one mind and one heart where the future was concerned. After all, was this not what the islands of light had been created to accomplish?

The Lemurians moved their islands of light onto specific points within the Earth's energy grid that corresponded with the future of the planet. These would be held in place by the codes of light and the lords of wisdom for the duration of the next cycle. The Lemurian age was soon to end, but only for an age and a season, as marked in galactic time. Lemurian sentinels remained upon each island of light, awake throughout time, as silent guardians of the codes entrusted to them.

## THEY LIVE AMONG YOU

The end of the Lemurian age did not mean the end of gentle Lemurian ways any more than the sinking of Atlantis erased its citizenry from your cellular memories. Each age lives on, finding complement where the will directs it. The Lemurians live among you, and perhaps even within you, as their numbers steadily increase. Their sentinels stand beside you and before you, peering out from within the powerful mountain you so admire. Can it be they are no longer silent, calling and inviting you to return to your own island of light? And the changelings are among you again. Have you noticed? What might their message be this time around?

# The Long and Short of It

### THE BEGINNING OF THE NEW AGE

*Is there a specific point when the New Age began? If so, is there a specific point when it will end? And if it does end, what place or condition will the Earth find itself in?*

This New Age (and there have been many) began in the latter half of the nineteenth century. It began without fanfare and with nary a welcome mat upon its threshold. Almost imperceptibly, the world awoke to a new dawn—or at least one that was so ancient that it could no longer be recalled. An age is a measure or a progression that can be charted as a movement throughout the heavens. Though illuminating, the New Age was not designed to ignite the popular and thematic movement that now carries its name.

Humankind is but one of many species that have progressed through the Age of Pisces. Humans have found themselves aware that a new age—with new opportunities and challenges—awaits them. Other worlds, with their own race of beings, also prepare to ascend into the next realm or dimension. It has been human's privilege until now to think of themselves as special and even unique. While not entirely untrue—especially from this mother's perspective—it would be unfair to continue the journey much longer with eyes still closed, and even blinded in some cases.

The New Age belongs to everyone and everything. It belongs to those who believe in it, those who do not and those who have never even heard of it. It is at its best when it is not described as a movement popularized by thoughts, concepts and conditions that are only available to those who subscribe to its tenets. Teachers uphold it—and masters

...o lovingly pave the way, pry open doors and wipe away tears of frustration. Similar teachers also work elsewhere, without need of the pedestals upon which they have been placed here. Likewise, angels walk and dwell among you—guardians of the tapestry of life of which you are part.

The New Age did not actually begin at a specific point in time as measured by a calendar, yet it can also be said that, prior to a certain time, it did not actually exist. What is the change that takes place when unconsciousness becomes conscious of its unconscious condition? What changes when the polarity called "effect" reverts to the polarity called "cause"? Nothing changed in the one moment, yet by the next moment, the entire universe has shifted. A new age is like that—and so are you.

A new age is the span of time in which evolution accelerates to include everything that can evolve in consciousness. The more conscious and creative the beingness (or thing) is of its own evolutional undertaking, the greater the evolutional leap it is capable of achieving. Unfortunately, this also brings about a tendency to think of oneself as more advanced than, and even superior to others—a delusion within illusion that creates an imbalance of its own. Similar to an implosion, the effect of this imbalance is felt deeply and painfully until the imbalance is corrected or removed.

## THE THIRD DIMENSION WILL BE THOUGHT OF AS A RELIC

This New Age will likely continue for the next two hundred years or so, though its effects will likely begin to diminish after the interval year of 2065. By then, the planet will have changed significantly, as will have all of life upon and within it. Those who are aware of the intelligence of change now—and who do not seek to reverse it or otherwise control it—will be the inspiration for those who follow. These are the true pioneers who, without reward, will yet reap many benefits. Beyond 2210, the Earth will be reestablished in a slightly different orbit that will both stabilize and enhance the Aquarian Age. The fifth dimension will be the norm then—the rule rather than the exception. The third dimension will not yet be obsolete, but will be thought of somewhat as a historic relic—that which you would observe and marvel at in a museum of near history.

Do not run too quickly to catch the wave of the New Age as if it were the tail of a comet. It is true that it does not come about all too frequently, but it is intelligent, and so are you. It is important that you find your own vibrational match within it. You cannot live another's purpose any more than you can life another's life—certainly not successfully so. Be aware that it is impossible to be left behind or to progress in a manner that goes against nature. There are yet many seasons left in the remaining Piscean Age, and they are worth experiencing to their fullest. To cheat the Piscean fish, you must swim against the current, and even the mighty salmon pays a dear price for this. It's better to swim with the current, navigate the tides and steer by the stars.

## DRAWING A DISTINCTION BETWEEN JOY AND HAPPINESS

*Can you define joy? In what specific ways is it different than happiness?*

Joy is that which exists when illusion and separation are stripped away. Joy is the natural and peaceful knowing that there has never been a beginning or end—and never will be. It is the perfect and constant flow that enables the movement of all things to be as they are or to transform in the ever present Now. Joy is beingness at its fullest; it is the discovery and fulfillment of the selfless self. Joy is the presence of All That Is in its purest form, which is formless. Joy is being, without adding "but," "if" or "when." To know joy is to be content with what is, simply because it is what is.

Joy is not measurable and it cannot be purchased at any price; however, there are beings who teach joy simply by their nearness. How is this possible? These beautiful beings—for there are no other words to describe them—have never been in human bodies or beset by human disappointment or tragedy. Like angels, they are innocent in all of their thoughts and deeds; they are able, even by their proximity, to restore the balance that humanity has forgotten. Humans take their own magnificence for granted and, for the most part, carry themselves about as if their long forgotten, cobweb-encrusted thoughts have forgotten the majesty of their own creation. The presence of a beautiful being can reverse these adverse effects. Their speech—if it were to be heard—would be like a fragrant poetry that touched your soul and, all at once, moved through every aspect of life. These beings are not bound to humanity as angels are, and they are among the freest of all the nonphysical beings in the universe. It is difficult to describe such beings, as even All That Is would not think to summon them from their careless joy.

Joy is not happiness, as happiness is no more than the temporary human emotion that recognizes harmony, peace and well-being.  Happiness rarely lingers long because it does not tarry from the scale of polarity upon which it dwells.  In other words, its opposite is rarely far behind, and the pendulum's swing summons it far too soon.  Because happiness is temporary and sometimes even fleeting, its polar mate, sadness, comes all too often to spoil the moment.  Sadness dwells in the shadow of human nature, sometimes emerging when least expected.  Sadness is the remaining residue from unfulfilled experiences and even lifetimes.  It cannot be erased until its corresponding moments are relived and completed.  That is why they emerge uninvited and cannot be easily dismissed.

## BLISS, MISERY, ECSTASY AND AGONY

Bliss, on the other hand, sometimes linked to joy, is neither an emotion nor a feeling.  Bliss is a state of beingness similar to a dimension, but without time or place.  Bliss is what exists when beingness suffices and there is no struggle for domination by any state of consciousness or unconsciousness—past, present or future.  Few know the pleasure and paradise that bliss brings, but far too many know its opposite—misery.  Misery is the absence of hope; to dwell here is to dwell in the poverty and squalor that is lack of spiritual essence.  While misery is not synonymous with suffering, one most often invites the other, in which case grief is rarely far behind.

Ecstasy, also associated with happiness and linked to joy, is a physical experience often characterized by an intensity that is unnecessary in the lighter realms.  Ecstasy is most often brought about by intense religious experiences, sexual and sensual pleasures of mind and body, and emotions that are more extreme and deeply concentrated in a specific area of life.  On the scale of polarity, the counterbalance of ecstasy is agony—all-consuming in its intensity and anguish.  Agony quickly enters a race against itself, straining in a contest to suffer more than it did in the previous moment or the previous life.  Agony's close cousin, anguish, often contributes to the mix by adding anxiety and emotional torment.

On the physical plane, joy also has its opposite—sorrow.  Sorrow is the personality's response to separation from soul and from All That Is.  Sorrow regrets its physicality because it cannot remember its nonphysicality or its oneness.  Beyond the mundane plane, however, joy has no opposite—for why would it oppose itself?  The spiritual planes—those beyond the third dimension—do not require the teachings offered by the scale of polarity. While they are not above it, they are beyond it. You can access joy by not defining it. You can access it more quickly by not defining yourself. Joy asks nothing of a moment. Can you do the same?

## THE MEMORY OF OUR BIRTHS AND DEATHS

*Is it important for us to know the exact moment of our birth or our death?*

You carry both of these with you all of the time. In fact, you carry the exact moment of every birth and every death you have ever had, but in almost every instance these are held in the recesses of your unconsciousness. You carry these not as dates, but as experiences. Your conscious mind is concerned with linearity; it feels most comfortable in an organized world that understands a past, present and future, in that order. The conscious mind understands multidimensionality as a concept, but not as an experience. In other words, in order for you to be you, you must have an identity—but any identity is an illusion compared to the reality that is the real you.

Your identity is the carefully crafted invention of your soul. It is the story of you and your life, and it comes complete with ownership papers, or in this case, birth and death certificates. But these too are only associated with your present life as measured in present time. To be specific, your births and deaths on the physical plane are only accurate on the physical plane, because time, as an expression of light, is measured differently elsewhere. Here is an example that you might relate to easily: Science tells you that when you view a supernova—the explosion of a star in the latter stages of its evolution—that explosion took place as much as tens of thousands of years ago. The experience seems current to you because that is how long it took light to travel far enough for you to share in the experience. Light can travel faster or slower depending upon the position and dimension from which it is viewed.

This same law of the universe applies to all things and all beings in this universe—it is a universal law. The law of acceleration states that the rate at which something develops accelerates the rate at which light travels in accordance with evolution—hence, the quicker you accelerate your discovery of self-awareness, the quicker light travels to you, with you and through you. In other words, when viewed from a dimensional awareness, you may have been born on a different day or at a different time altogether! This does not mean that your specific day and time of birth is insignificant, but it does mean that it is more relevant and cogent to your present experience of self. It also means that time is flexible.

I reveal the larger aspect of your question to you so that you will relate to the consequence of your birth in a newer or larger way. You chose your date of birth not only within the context of time and dimension upon the Earth, but also as a cosmic expression of who and what you are. As such, you are able to change these, accelerating or decelerating within time to suit your needs and purpose. This also explains the concept of simultaneous time, though we will leave that for a more opportune moment.

Perhaps you will begin to notice that if you can change your relation to your date of birth, the same would apply to the time of your transition, or death—a birth, of sorts, as viewed from elsewhere. With few exceptions, the time of your transition is as flexible as time is. Ever changing and adjusting to your soul's purpose, it can be long and drawn out or sudden. Either way, it will be perfect and in divine order as expressed in and through time.

What would you do if you knew the specific day and time of your death? Would you panic, work hard, celebrate, be more compassionate, make amends with loved ones sooner, travel, be present in the moment, try harder, surrender, be courageous or heroic, try something new, overcome fear, teach or learn? You design all of your experiences and then place them within an appealing context of time, thus you are also the director of the context of time itself. It has been said that you are All That Is disguised as "What Is." Perhaps it is time to remove the disguise.

# Rounding the Corner to
# The Fifth Dimension

*Are we closer to the fifth dimension than we were a year ago? If so, in what measurable way? Are we, as a collective human species, still evolving in a true progressive sense? I would like to believe so, but I am unsure. Can you give us an overview of where we are and where we are going?*

The fifth dimension is right around the corner, exactly where it has always been, and literally so. By way of distance, you are not closer today than you were yesterday or the year before, because dimensions are not separated by distance. The exception to this rule is when distance is measured by human thought without bias to belief. In other words, when human collective thoughts are ordained—divinely ordered or inspired—and not subject to lower repetitive patterns of behavior, the distance between them is shorter. The distance, albeit without measure, can be traveled substantially faster than otherwise. It could be said that dimensions are separated by commas and not by periods. They overlap and border each other in the same ways that nature presents the seasons to you.

## THE DISTILLATION OF THOUGHT

All dimensions take place in the same moment but not in the same awareness. There is an additional relationship between density and time, and it would be helpful to understand this as well. The denser an object, the quicker it will sink or fall. Likewise, a dense being or culture will fall faster than one that is lighter in density. Density is sometimes confused with weight, but they are not the same. Density is the amount of substance contained within a specific area, and the density of a substance can change under different conditions. Some of those conditions include temperature—a noteworthy and interesting fact at this time. For instance, hot air balloons rise because the heated air within the balloon is less dense than the cooler air outside.

The density of all things and beings can be measured, but humanity has not yet discovered how to influence and therefore alter its own density in order to benefit itself and its future. By contrast, ancient Egyptians, as well as certain cultures before and after them, understood how to do this. They were able, under certain circumstances, to alter their reality and their dimension. Primarily only those of initiatic tradition knew this, and little evidence of any true relevance remains today. Still, those who study the properties of gold, and monatomic—meaning one replaceable atom—gold in particular, are often fascinated to discover that under unique conditions, it will manifest as substance without density. In other words, it can weigh less than nothing, as well as influence the density of other matter. The importance of this that I relate is that the influence of precise thought upon matter is what closes the gap between what you know and what you do not know. Knowledge is not the accumulation of information—it is the distillation of thought.

With your thoughts concentrated on the ordinary stresses of life, it is difficult to stay the momentous tide of unconscious beliefs associated with these. The more removed you are from being able to think for yourself, the further away new thoughts and ideas will seem. A new thought is not one that you believe, or even one that you think is plausible. A new thought is one that you invite into your field without resistance. Like an electric current, the flow of pure thought is best explored through the field of superconductivity or awareness without forethought or resistance. The neighbor and partner of this electric current is the magnetic field of concentrated creativity. The intersection of these two crosscurrents is where the fifth dimension begins. You will access the fifth dimension when your frequency vibrates within this range of expanded thought and creativity. At that point, the duality that has been a part of your daily experience will yield to a greater diversity of life, and it will seem less consequential than it does today.

## Move from the Third Dimension to the Fifth

Although there are natural forces that protect the integrity of the dimensions, there is no tally of how many good deeds you may have accomplished in the previous dimension. Access is neither gained nor denied by any authority other than your own, yet without a like vibration, the halls or currents would seem unstable and you would not venture across them. That is one of the reasons why humanity strives to liberate itself form a history that does not accurately describe its origins. The beliefs by which humanity have lived have kept it in bondage to its past, and even now prevent it from crossing the bridge to greater consciousness. In collective thought, humanity hopes to break the barriers of time and space in order to finally see itself and recognize its God. By what measurable degree are you closer to God than you were a year ago? Were you ever apart? Not really, unless you count the small places within you that doubt the perfection and majesty of All That Is. Do you think that the fifth dimension will be absent of doubt? What about hunger? War?

The fifth dimension is a less dense version of the third dimension. It affords a more consistently conscious view and understanding of life. The electromagnetic currents are more stable in the fifth dimension, so thoughts and experiences complete themselves more quickly than in the third. There is more space in the fifth dimension but there is less time, at least as it is expressed in the third dimension. Since there is more space between the atoms, there is less density, meaning that there is less waste. Wasted thoughts and actions account for a great expenditure of energy on the third dimension, and generally contribute to the global warming effect with which humanity concerns itself. Indirectly, the management of waste also determines access to the fifth dimension. So you see, even unconsciously, humanity takes a stride in favor of its evolution.

Before exploring the fifth dimension in detail, we must first give a nod to the fourth dimension, which is the bridge to the fifth. The fifth dimension is widely accepted to be the concept of time. Time is the concept that gives relevance to the shift from the third dimension to something else, but it is not time as it is currently measured. Better put, it is the curvature of time by which time expands or contracts with relevancy to how much light is present within the space that is being measured. Basically, when more light is present, time accelerates both forward and backward. The result of this acceleration is a more refined experience, one that is more seamless and less abrupt. The fourth dimension unites the third and the fifth by quickening sequences and segments of time wherever that is a possibility. This is accomplished by curving or bending time. Time is sequential, but not linear—it only appears linear within the hardscape of the third dimension. Beyond these barriers, the measure of time is not as you know it, and the speed of light is not constant.

The importance of the fourth dimension is that it is fueled by consciousness, and it strengthens the fabric of time and space. The fourth dimension is the bridge between the third and fifth dimensions because it invites the field of possibilities to become the field of probabilities, as well as that of experience. As you imagine a better world and attune yourself to living in it, your consciousness becomes more enlivened. You quicken the pace of your endeavors until your awareness matches your experience. So the fourth dimension is responsible for what you call the "quickening." It is also responsible for some of the unusual and irregular experiences that are generally associated with a time period, especially where your body is concerned, as this is the most physically dense aspect of life for most. That being said, it is noteworthy that thoughts can be as dense as or even denser than physical objects.

## A LEAP FORWARD

Once you cross the seamless and invisible bridge to the fifth dimension, you will find that life there is less complex than in the third dimension. It is amply creative and artfully expressive. Because it is less dense, form and shape are more subtle and graceful. This is particularly true where architecture is concerned, as fifth-dimensional construction does not depend upon wood, steel or concrete to anchor its buildings to the earth. Glass is less brittle and more resilient because it is made differently. This discovery will be made as current recycling plans become more efficient and the market for such products expands. Shortages of current materials will lead to the discovery and use of other resources.

Given the existing standards by which health is measured, the fifth dimension offers a leap forward in the well-being of the individual and the community. Given presently accepted practices, the third dimension can no longer guarantee nor sustain its existence. The value of life has decreased to the degree that there is less sanctity for life; therefore, there is also less sanity in life. The mental faculties of old and young alike continue to decrease, while the stresses of the middle age are starting to increase. A greater capacity for mental and physical health is essential at this time, and humanity's diet would benefit from the addition of more calcium-rich foods, as well as supplements that are more mineral rich. Fifth-dimensional thought is more mindful and its thoughts less chaotic.

This requires a higher than average oxygen intake, and today you would describe the experience as "heady."

The fifth dimension is not somewhere else—it is right here beneath your nose and under your feet. You cannot see it? Look again, but this time with blind eyes that know there is nothing to see. Where does the fifth dimension begin or end, can you tell? If you cannot see it, does that mean it is less real? How many must acknowledge its probability before it becomes a part of daily experience? What experts must accredit which scientific finding? The more real you allow the fifth dimension to be right now, the sooner you will have an experience of it. A dimension cannot prove its existence to you, nor can a teacher reveal a mystery to you that you cannot reveal to yourself. Remember that while the half-wise are the keepers of the keys, the wise have no need of locks. Let nothing and no one prevent you from your next step or your own next thought.

The fifth dimension is not a haven for those who have endured a difficult life, and it is not a cosmic reward for those who gather near heaven's gates. It is the natural progression for those who propose rather than oppose life. This does not mean that you must abandon your battles or that you must lower the standard under which your flag has pledged its allegiance. Yet I ask, how many of your battles are within your own ranks? How many weapons are still in your own arsenal as you call upon others to surrender their own? If you feel that the pace of your development has slowed and you do not feel Spirit in attendance near you, choose a moment each day in which to silently abdicate the throne you sit on—the one in which your life seems even remotely more important than your neighbor's or your friend's. Instead, be enriched by the wonder that is life and know that its everlasting quality encourages and invites even the sewer rat and the cockroach to evolve, for they too have their place in this world.

# Understanding Your
# Cosmic Lineage

*I* ndeed then, I greet you one and all. Those who find themselves
gathered here and those who find themselves by extension of this
voice or the recording that is being made, I greet you as well. For
these words will travel. They are being heard not only in this room, not
only in this dimension, but also by those who would project them and
those who would anticipate them. They are being heard by those who
have sent them forth—not only by this channel who would now usher
them on my behalf—on the behalf of those who have come long and far
to the here and now.

To those who are gathered here and those who will hear these words,
I will say: You are one of a cosmic lineage—a cosmic lineage that is one.
For if we take the journey back far enough, we will find but one lineage.
We will find but one Source. We will find but one Sun—a galactic Sun,
a cosmic Sun. There was an original thought, and the original thought
was: Let there be many. Let there be many experiences, many journeys,
many paths, many environments, many beings. And from that original
thought came the original words. And from the original words or frequencies or vibrations that were offered, came the many.

Here, then, was born what you would term cosmic lineage. The cosmic
lineage was the original thought that gave birth to the original frequency
that created the original beings who said, "So it is. I Am That I Am."

## YOUR COSMIC LINEAGE IS ONE WITH SOURCE

Each time a beingness became conscious, it would say, "I Am That I
Am. I am that which is in the likeness of the Source, of the One." Each
time these words were uttered, whether in star language or in frequency, a

cosmic lineage was born. When these words were not uttered, the cosmic lineage ended. Whether its duration was one day, one year, one thousand years or many millenniums, the cosmic lineage would end because the species could not bind itself to Source, to the One. The cosmic lineage, then, is one with Source. It understands itself as able to evolve into another species, into another beingness, into another language, world, soul, lifetime or body.

You see, it matters not what bodies you occupy. You call yourselves humans, but indeed you are not. You are cosmic beings in a lineage that has evolved into a being that is currently called human but that is always in transition. It is always in a state of flux, as you can see by your relatives, friends and neighbors—those who are like you and those who are quite unlike you, as the case may be. Again, all who are here now belong to a cosmic lineage. Some are related to others, and some are not. Some are related to a lineage that is far away. Others are related to a lineage that is here upon Earth. There is no cosmic lineage that began here upon Earth. The Earth simply is not old enough to have created its own cosmic lineage.

The Earth welcomed as a melting pot all of the cosmic lineages that have come from elsewhere, saying—just as your Statue of Liberty in the great harbor would say—"Bring those who are tired, weary, uncomfortable or unsure of who they are, where they have come or what they are to do. Bring them here." And that is why you see many around you who are tired, weary and uncertain as to their past or their future—be it their human future or their cosmic future.

Now, you would say, "How is that possible? If a great beingness has said, 'I Am That I Am, one with Source,' then how can so many be as lost lambs, finding their way here or there in the dark, being blind?" That is because cosmic lineages become distorted through the dimensions, through the realities. The distortion of the dimensions brings a forgetting of beingness; it brings a forgetting of divinity. Therefore, in your cosmic lineage, you may very well say, "My great ancestor once said I Am That I Am." But if you cannot say that for your own beingness, then there is a distortion.

If you wish to know whether you are distorted, here is a simple test. Can you truly, honestly, in this very moment say to all concerned, "I Am That I Am, one with Source in this very moment"? If you can say that, understanding fully all of the implications, then we will say there is no dimensional distortion. And if you cannot say these words in an exacting way as I have put them forth, then I would say that you are a part, at least, of the distortion.

## UNDERSTANDING YOUR ENERGETIC WAVEBAND

A distortion is a misinterpretation of that which you are. A distortion is an inescapable reality that you must escape. A distortion is a paradox in your beingness. A distortion, then, allows you to be what you are without understanding or seeing the fullness of it. Therefore, the distortion is what you are here to transcend. If you believe you are here to heal yourself, I will say, "Incorrect; you are not." If you say, "I am here to heal others," I will say again, "Incorrect; you are not." If on the other hand, you say, "I am here to explore my cosmic lineage and that which aligns me with Source, All That Is, as it is expressed in the physical body through an act of distortion," then I will say, "Welcome. You are in the right place." And I would say you are all well placed.

Long, long ago there was a decision made that brought you forth unto your own beingness, understanding the distortion, understanding the lineage, understanding the many worlds that you have lived upon and within and experienced, and yet knowing that there was more to discover. Here is where you will discover it. Who are you then? You are one with All That Is—one with the beingness, one with the Source, one with the original thought, one with the original being, one with the original I Am That I Am that said, "Let there be many. Let me be one and let me be many." That is who and what you are.

From that all the lineages have come, all of the races have come. All of the beings—physical or nonphysical, dimensional or nondimensional, inner plane or outer plane, from this world and all other worlds—have come from that vibration. Now, the vibration itself is the wave that moves through the distortion. The wave itself is the evolution. It is the evolutionary scale that will say, "Now and here, and then and there, I Am." And so there is a waveband that carries all that you are, all that is your essence, all that is your truth, all that are your genetics both here and in your other lifetimes—here and in all of the other lives and bodies that you have expressed yourselves in, which are carried through a waveband of energy that moves in and through your soul. That is where your cosmic memories come from. And of course, you have these, for it is not only past lifetimes of the Earth that your memories share, it is past lifetimes elsewhere as well.

The waveband moves through the soul essence, awakening, reawakening and stimulating the cellular structure of your beingness until all generations, all activities, all awarenesses are brought into balance with the One frequency, the One wave that says, "I Am, I Have Been, I Will Be." That is your purpose in this lifetime. If you are uncertain of your purpose, it is that! It is to understand fully and completely, "I Am, I Have Been, I Will Be." And having understood it fully and completely, it is to assist all those who are near you to discover that their cosmic lineage is to do and be the same. If you call that healing, so be it. If you call it learning, so be it. Education, philosophy, whatever you call it, that is your purpose, and yet it is one and the same for all.

## YOUR PURPOSE IS TO GRASP YOUR TOTALITY

What is your purpose? It is to be all that you are, all that you have been, all that you will be in the here and in the now, in this dimension and other dimensions, in this world and other worlds. From that standpoint, it matters not if you experience yourself upon Earth or upon any other world of your choosing. However, the dimensions that Earth offers are many. It would seem that you are mired in the third dimension, mired in material aspects of the third dimension as density, but that only holds you to the Earth—that grounds you, as they say. All else is within your grasp. If you move in one direction for the light, so you will be. If you move in another direction of the light and you find shadow, so you will be there as well. In all directions that you choose or move or express yourselves, so you will be—so you are allowed without limitation.

Therefore, the full spectrum of light is open and available to you as it always has been. If you wish to express yourself as the Red vibration or the Red race, so you have done, so you have experienced. If you wish to be of the Blue race, that as well you have been and you perhaps will be yet again. If it's the Yellow race or the Yellow ray or the Yellow frequency, so be it as well. And as we continue to move through the spectrum, it is not surprising that we would arrive at those who you would term the Indigo race, the Indigo frequency, the Indigo light or the Indigo aspect of the wave. The Indigo wave or frequency is that which goes against all others that have been. If we say that you are here to discover what you have been, what you are or what you will be, then we will say that the Indigo race will say that they are here to discover what they will be.

In these terms, you may see or say that one generation is different than the next. The Indigo race of beings is here to discover and express fully and completely what is to be, what can be, what is possible. And if need be, they will show this to you by showing to you what is impossible, improbable or ridiculous. That is their purpose—so be it. And you have your own. Each generation, aligned with each cosmic frequency, brings about a certain stimulus of being. That is how others will find their kin, their own lineage and their own expressions. And each of you have your own. The Indigo beings are not necessarily the children or the new children. There are many older beings who are Indigos as well, some who have come before you and some who will come after you. It is simply that aspect of the spectrum that explores what will be and refuses to acknowledge what was or what is as a reality. They are cosmic beings. They are somewhat unlimited in nature, although they find themselves in the same limited bodies as you.

However, finding themselves within the same limitations as you find yourselves, they will transcend the limitation, whereas you have accepted it. Whereas your generation or your beings accept limitations, the Indigo cosmic lineage does not. Therefore, at a specific time in history or in nature, they will offer themselves, even as they do now. The Indigo beings are not simply the children; they are not simply those who are birthed into bodies at this time. It is a vibration of light similar to your own and yet with a purpose, an understanding and an unfoldment of their own. Whether it is the rest of the spectrum or the rest of the world, they will challenge the past in order to create the future. Let us pause for a moment for questions relative to this.

## THE RED RACE: WHAT WAS

*Gaia, which race or spectrum band at the present time most exemplifies what was, as well as what is?*

It is the Red race, it is the Red vibration that will say what was. You might think of these beings of the Red race as being Native Americans, the Indians, but it is not necessarily that. However, a great deal of beings who embody the Red race will call themselves Native Americans. It may even be those who are Caucasian by nature but follow the philosophies of the Red race.

You see, it is the Red vibration that we speak of. Therefore, it is not necessarily those who would call themselves Indian by nature, Native American—it is those who ascribe to the philosophy. This is the "what was." As you can see, there is a smaller population of the Red race than there is of the other races. And those who carry this vibration believe in what was. "These lands were mine," they will say, and yet they are not. "We understood the Earth, we were one with the Earth, we communicated with the Earth," they will say, and yet that is no longer true.

The Red race fades into the background now. It is not obsolete. It will not disappear from the Earth, and yet it will shift. It will shift from what you term the Red race to perhaps the Crimson race. It will evolve. It will transcend. It will shift itself from one frequency to the other, and the spectrum of life will assist that. But in answer to your question, those who express themselves in regard to what was are the Red race, the Red philosophy and the Red frequency.

## THE INDIGO RACE: WHAT WILL BE

*How could the parent of an Indigo help the child if he or she seems really troubled with all this energy of going against everything?*

Describe this in more detail.

*Well, like in school—she doesn't like any school I've ever sent her to.*

But of course, if the school, as you say, belongs to the "what was" and the Indigos are the "what will be," then how will they find the middle ground, being the "what is"? If you wish to assist them, it is to find wherever possible the "what is." Not yet can they bring forth the "what will be." They will, but not yet. Neither can they move into the "what was." This will trouble them more than any other aspect—the "what was" is the most difficult for them.

Therefore, the "what is" or the "what can be" is what you must find. This is the common ground. You see, you cannot yet create the "what will be," because they must do this. And they cannot, as you know, exist in the "what was," but they can exist in the possibility of "what will be." Always speak to them in terms of possibility—what can be, what they can accomplish, what may be, what they can design, how to design a life, how to design a beingness, how to design a consciousness, what can be done, what can be said, what can be brought—always as the possibility.

When they say, "No, it cannot," it ends there. If they say to you, "No, it cannot be," then it belongs to the past, for they will speak to you only the truth. If they say to you, "It cannot be, it cannot be done or it already has been done," the conversation will end to you, for they are wiser than you in this case. When you offer what can be done to exist in the world of possibility for them, in the world of wonder, then that is where you will find the ground. Whatever schooling and educational tools you can offer that involve wonder, creativity and possibility, that is where to offer yourself.

*I tried home schooling but it didn't seem to offer any stimulation for her creative mind. My energy was too low-key for her, and she opposed it. She is very fiery and I am not.*

Your energy is of a different cosmic lineage, dear. It is common for someone from one cosmic lineage to give birth to a different one altogether. Cosmically, this mirrors how one race or culture blends with another to include the traits of both. This is a very diverse universe and this is one of the ways that diversity prevails. Where the past and the future meet, evolution is at its most creative. Generations past, present and future benefit in this way. How else is there to be variety? How else is there to be learning between the races? How is the race to evolve? If the races do not blend, if then does not become now, if the past cannot find the future, how does a race of beings evolve? If you continue to give birth to those who are just like you—it matters not if humans develop cloning—you will simply give birth to each other. There is nothing to learn, nothing to evolve. Each generation will offer itself to another generation and to another possibility. That is how evolution takes place.

Again, I will say to you that when one generation cannot give to the other a possibility to say, "It is yours, make of it what you will," evolution ends and devolution begins. In essence, you have already given birth to future generations. All of you have. You give birth to generations as far in the future as you can imagine. You do not give birth to beings, you do not give birth to bodies, but you give birth to possibilities. And the possibilities give birth to beings, and they later become children—cosmic children. That is evolution. It is a thought process, a mental capacity, a variation of frequency and wave moving through the universes as time and structure.

Again, when one generation cannot give to the next generation the possibility to dream or to create, evolution ends and that you can see around you now. You can see certain races ending. You can see end-ings more than beginnings at this time, because possibility is not given. Scripture is given and the past is studied; archaeology is given to the masses. That is not possibility. It is not the possibility to dream. One does not dream of the past, I say to you—one dreams of a future. If one dreams of the past, the past will come to life. But if the past comes to life, the past has already been lived, so it will die. If the past is brought to life but it has already been lived, there is nothing for it to do but die. Do you understand? For the universe has no use for this.

## The Indigos Carry Great Power and Great Burden

Again, one generation gives birth to another. One generation births the possibility of another, but not necessarily the next race of beings. If there is an Indigo race, the Indigo race does not necessarily say, "Very well, the Indigo color will now give birth to the Crystalline color, to the Rose color, to the Violet." It is not like that. It is not a box of colored pencils, after all; it is a lineage of beings that we speak of. It is the colors and frequencies of the universe. It is the one, and the many, expressing itself as all possibilities, as all waves.

The Indigo race is here simply to give birth to possibility for the future. The Indigo holds the possibility that the Earth will continue to evolve. The Indigo race holds the possibility that that which does not serve the Earth or humanity or the future will fade into the distance. And so they do both, in essence—those who bring life and those who will surrender it—and that is their great power. It is their great vision and it is their great burden. If you look about you, you might say, "Why does this Indigo being seem troubled? Why is this Indigo being uncomfortable in his or her body? Why can they not find a purpose in their beingness? Why are they less creative in this environment or that?" It is because they carry a great burden. It is a great burden to say what will be and what will not be, what holds possibility and what does not, what will have life and what will transcend or have death, as you would say. It is the Indigos who carry this very vibration, and it can be considered a burden if it is not carried well or carried lightly.

Therefore, the Indigo beings carry great power and great wisdom, and they are troubled by their burdens. What can you do for those who are troubled? Only offer support. Only they can do what they are here to do, just as only you can do what you are here to do. You can offer support, but beyond that, only they will understand themselves, and that is why they understand each other. They understand each other's burdens. They understand each other's choices. They understand the limitation that they must transcend, and they see in others the limitations that cannot and will not be transcended. Just as you might see life in others, they see death in others. It is not the death of the body; it is death of the being, or the lineage, or the dream or the hope. That is a difficult energy for them to carry, and that is why they are little understood as well. They are seen somewhat as those who would bring troubles, and indeed they are, for they will stir within each other what is the greatest possibility to construct and/or destruct, whichever brings activity and movement.

To their great credit, they are the only ones who can do this. I will say to you, if they are Indigo beings in this life, then they have been Indigo beings in another life. If there are Indigo beings in this world, then it is quite likely that they have been Indigo beings in other worlds and at other times as well. Therefore, the burden that they carry is not only the burden of this life or this choice, but it is the burden of their beingness. And it is by choice. One does not simply fall into an Indigo lifetime; one chooses it significantly. Therefore, if you are the caretaker of an Indigo being or in relationship with an Indigo being, be in compassion for that being, for he or she is your teacher and the teacher of others. If they are your children, so be it. They are also generations beyond what you can imagine at this time.

## Do Not Make the Indigos' Burdens Your Own

*Mother Gaia, I have a question about the Indigo vibration. I am very attracted to working with them, and I was wondering if my cosmic lineage reflects that energy or if my cosmic lineage will attract the energy to my field.*

I will say to you what you have not yet considered: Your Indigo essence is carried within you, within your blood if you like, but you are not an Indigo being. Imagine that you have had somewhat of a cosmic transfusion in order to truly understand the Indigo being. That is your nature. In your time, in your years, there are those who are considered to be family therapists, counselors, and you may consider yourself a cosmic therapist of the Indigo being, of the Indigo light. So it is not necessarily the Indigo child, it is the Indigo light, and you understand this light as a structure. Therefore, in or out of body, this is a part of your cosmic lineage. We spoke earlier this evening of cosmic lineage, and it is within your lineage to understand the Indigo being—not the troubled youth, but literally the Indigo frequency that understands what will be. For you are a dreamer, are you not?

**Yes.**

One dreams the future, then, yes? It is confirmation, yes?

**Yes.**

Now then, though you carry the Indigo frequency, again I will say to you, you are not an Indigo being but you understand it well. Therefore, do not limit yourself; do not burden yourself as the Indigos do. Do not make their burdens your burdens, for they are not yours to bear. It is for you to see them through their burdens or to counsel or to offer words of wisdom, but it is not for you to bear their burdens.

## YOU CAN LINK WITH YOUR OWN COSMIC LINEAGE

*Gaia, my son has always been very troubled. He has always had a lot of trouble with what was and what is, but he doesn't seem to have a sense of what will be, and I think that is perhaps a part of his struggle. Can you say something about where he fits into this model?*

Indeed, sweet, that is exactly where he is stuck, as you say. It is as if he cannot find his way forward or backward—not forward, backward, inward or outward. He can break beyond the bounds of this, but it will take a tremendous effort on his part, and that effort he does not yet wish to make because he searches for his way out from the catacombs that he finds himself in by moving into the past, where he understood at least this life. There was a time and a place where he understood himself, yes?

*Yes, when he was much younger and before everything seemed to change.*

There was a time and a place where life understood him and where you understood that which he is. Then there was a break in that, and this is the link that must be created again. That is what he is searching for. But again, he is an Indigo being who has come to find the future and yet he has lost himself. So he searches for himself in the past in order to acknowledge a present, in order to fulfill a purpose, which is to discover a future. As futile as it seems, he fights himself and he fights all those around, all realities that make no sense—and no reality can make sense at this time. Therefore, your next question is how to find a resolution to this, yes?

*Yes, that's certainly a good next question.*

Indeed, it is not impossible as you would believe—as you have been told and as he has come to believe—and yet it will take more Indigo vibration and that which comes beyond the Indigo vibration to release him from his burden. His burden can only be passed on through another Indigo, and this he is reluctant to do. It can be done somewhat easily on the inner planes, but this he will not do and this further traps him in his own beingness. He is not trapped in his mind and he is not trapped in his body. He is trapped in a purpose that cannot be fulfilled, and this he wishes not to acknowledge. This is what he battles within himself. Therefore, only other Indigo beings can free him, dear. He must free himself, and he must pass on his purpose to another. Until he is willing to do that, he will fight himself and those about him.

*Did he know he was going to have this kind of struggle before he was born?*

He did not. There was an understanding that there would be a difficulty, a challenge and a burden, as there has been at other times. There was not a full and complete understanding of the forward and backward stagnation that he would encounter here, and that is again part of the struggle, part of the fight and part of the rage and the battle within him.

*As you have been talking, I feel that this is maybe a bit of reflection of what I'm going through too. I think I'm bouncing around from one lineage to another, but . . .*

Not necessarily, dear. But you are this one's father, and you would take his burden if you could, yes?

*Yes.*

But you cannot, you see, and yet you can associate with the burden. You can link with your own cosmic lineage, and your own desire to be of assistance to him allows you to link to him—whether it is mind to mind or heart to heart or via heredity. "The ties that bind," as they say, and so you seek to release this one's burden by taking it upon yourself. But as you well know, you cannot do that, for you are not aligned with the purpose. And I will say to you that the attempt will make you ill.

*I have always had a lot of trouble with what is. It seems so chaotic, and I probably have overvalued what was because at least I could sift through it and find something I could link to. And it seems that whenever I tried to create what will be, I wasn't always able to find it to a satisfying level. Is that part of what I came in to do?*

That's an interesting question. Very well, I will answer it this way. There are those, as I have said, who are here to discover, reiterate or restate what was; there are those who have come to be in the what is; and there are those who have come to understand what will be. There are also those who are here to support all of the search, and that is your beingness, you see. You are not of a specific ray, a specific nature or a specific being, and yet you are of the same cosmic lineage that understands the search for truth, the underlying search for the Oneness that originally said, "I Am That I Am"—the original thought, the original being. Before there was a thought that said, "And the one will be many," there was an original thought that said, "I Am." And that is what you are here to support, however you can. You will not find satisfaction in the past, though you search there and find some comfort there. You will not necessarily find it in the present, where you accommodate yourself as best you can. And you will not find it in the future, where you somewhat hope that it will be as has been promised, but you are not entirely certain of it after all, so you will leave that to others.

*Gaia, my question is very similar to the previous question. My daughter is just like a lost soul. Will she ever come out of it? Will she ever believe in herself?*

Yes. The difference is that the aforementioned one desires to find himself through one or more realities—through the past, the present or the future in some timeline. The one whom you speak of does not yet wish to be found. It is as if she is playing hide-and-seek, but she hides so certainly and so far away in such a secure place, that it is certain that no one can find her. And rather than give up upon the game later on and say, "Here I am; here I am!" this one does not say that but will say, "I will stay here in this one place until one is wise enough to find me." And if one is not wise enough, then she will continue to stay. Can you be of assistance to this one? Not necessarily, for if one locks oneself away and holds the key and pulls the shades, then there is nothing that can be done until she at least releases the lock or will say where the key is hidden. Therefore, not yet, although there is a possibility for this one.

## YOU MUST CLAIM YOUR LIFE

*Gaia, would you please speak to my cosmic lineage, as well as to my more traditional human lineage in this lifetime?*

Make your question more specific, dear. There are others who wish to hear your question, but they must understand it more clearly.

*Okay. Early on in this life, I had the perception of having given birth to a child without the benefit of the genetic contribution from a human father. I have always wondered if this could have been possible, and if so, what our purpose and connection might have been.*

I will answer your question by first asking a question or two of my own. What is the purpose of giving birth to a human child with a human father?

*Genetics would be involved, perhaps those of a different lineage than my own. It might further the human race in ways that I cannot yet see. It would fuel the human experiment.*

What is the purpose, then, of bringing forth a being without the seed of a human father?

*It would demonstrate what might be possible or even common in other worlds. It might make that possibility real here.*

Very well. Now, another question: Why is it that you speak of this occurrence as rarely as you do?

*Who would believe me if I did?*

Exactly. And do you believe it yourself, then?

*I think I do, yes. I have pondered it for a very long time because I have no plausible explanation for it. I have searched for proof or even validation and have found none, but I still think it is possible.*

Very well. You are correct. It is possible, but here is your challenge: You do not, cannot, and will not know for certain—because its purpose was not (and has not been even now) revealed to you—and without a specific purpose you are in the dark, as they say, at least relative to this subject. One reason this remains a mystery to you is that you never acknowledged the child as your own; it was quickly passed on to another who then named it and guided its life. Because this experience was forfeit to you, some of the memories associated with it are as well. Memories are like realities, appearing out of thin air when purposeful, and dissipating as quickly when they are not purposeful.

Now then, here is your answer without further delay: The experience, as you remember it, is a combination of the past, the present and the future—that of this world and others. Upon other worlds your experience is, and continues to be, just as you remember it. Upon the Earth your experience was of a different nature, one that yet bears some remembrance when the softness of time no longer combines with salted tears inflicted on an open wound. By your own reckoning you have not fully engaged, accepted or embraced the event or the being. One day the being itself will give you a full answer, one that includes a purpose and a full understanding.

There are others such as yourself who have embraced moments such as these, and others who have not. This is a part of your unfoldment, dear. You must claim your life, because no one else can claim it for you. Each being must have a lineage to claim, even if it is not aware of it at the outset—foresight or hindsight means nothing where Spirit is concerned. It is human to be concerned with linear timelines and who or what should have known this or that before or after, you see. On the other hand, if you remain silent on this issue then you will continue to have the equivalent of a bastard child who has not been claimed—the experience will follow you. If you truly wish to receive the full, complete and unaltered version of this answer, then claim all that you are in its fullness and as a complete experience, only then will the answer be as legitimate as the child is today.

*What about my own cosmic lineage?*

Your own lineage is that of the Violet race, dear. It is that which cannot harm and rarely speaks. It is that which understands and supports all. It is the pedestal energy, the very strong, the very broad and the very silent that supports silently and with great strength all that will come. Regardless of what will come—peace, war, joy or apocalyptic visions— the Violet race holds forth and holds fast the ideals of the world that one lives in, hopes for and dreams of. The Violet race is the visionary. The Violet race understands all of the other races, all of the other vibrations, all of the other frequencies that have been and will be—all of the possibilities, whether or not they are embraced.

## THE CRYSTAL KIN WILL HOLD A LIGHT

We have not yet spoken of those whom we will call the Crystal kin. It is time for a bit of liveliness after all, for the time that the burdensome ones are carrying is somewhat over. The Indigo beings will be the last race, the last time structure to hold burdensome energies. Those of the Crystalline nature will not do so. Their vibration will not hold a burden, their vibration will hold a light, a candle. The Crystalline beings are those who will manifest themselves among you, as was said earlier. If there are those who you would term as of a walk-in nature, then the Crystalline beings can be termed as of a drop-in nature. The Crystalline beings do not require a mother and they do not require a father, though they may choose one or the other. The Crystalline beings are of an essence all their own.

The Crystalline beings understand this world and other worlds. They understand not only what was, which interests them very little, but they understand what is, which interests them in a minor capacity, and they understand what will be (and even that is only of surface interest, to stimulate the being). Beyond that they understand what is the dream. The Crystalline beings are the reincarnation of the Mayan structure, which understood that as the dream is created, so the life is interpreted. The Crystalline beings are those who have been supported and have dwelled within the Earth, on the outer part of the Earth. They have always been present in this world and other worlds, in many different structures, in many different capacities, with or without bodies, with or without cosmologies, with or without lineages. Their lineage is yours.

But their history is not yours. They do not come to reinvent the Earth. They do not come to fix it for those who have mucked it up. The Crystalline beings come simply to participate in a world because it is their choice to do so. They will interact with the world as they choose to do so. What they bring will be by their choice, and for the most part, humanity will benefit by it. It is important to know that they are not here to save humanity or a particular race, for many will yet fall from the races.

As we have been speaking of evolution, there are those who will not evolve. Many races exist upon the Earth now. This is not simply those who are of a color, a vibration or a country. There are races of beings, frequencies that do not wish to move forward—not dimensionally, not in a capacity in which they must extend or expand themselves. The Crystalline beings come forward, in essence, to take that place. Their expanded awareness is so great that they can take the place of three, four or a dozen beings. Their aura is much greater than yours or even the Indigos or any other being who has been. Some of the auras of the Crystalline beings can extend as far as what you would term one or two miles. They can connect one to the other, just as the ley lines within the Earth connect.

The Crystalline beings understand each other in the same way, as a net-worklike essence. Some of the Crystalline beings are brought in by birth, but some are not—they simply manifest. How is that? How can a being simply manifest? Because it is the Crystalline vibration that can do so. The Crystalline vibration does not belong to the third dimension. It needs not the third dimension in order to create itself. It needs not the cellular structure, the molecular structure, in order to create or re-create itself. It needs only the vibration of the Earth magnified, extended and multiplied in a geometric fashion in order to create a beingness, a body, a likeness, a physical dense one or a holographic one. It is the Crystalline nature that can bring about a change in vibration, a change in frequency for all concerned.

If a Crystalline being were to enter this very hall now, all of your vibrations would be raised instantaneously because the noninvasive quality of the Crystalline being allows for this, calls for this and invites this. And where it touches upon any other being in its own noninvasive way, it will lift the spirits, it will lift the soul, it will remind you of what your truth is. It is the Crystalline beings who can assist the Indigos with their burdens. It is the Crystalline beings who will assist themselves, who have forgotten themselves, forgotten their purpose, forgotten whether they are in the past, the present or the future.

So another race of beings comes, and these we will simply term the Crystal kin. They will come from far and they will come from near, from the inner Earth, the outer Earth, and from other celestial bodies and worlds. You may welcome them, for you will recognize them. Indeed, they are like none you have yet seen. Are there any questions regarding this?

## COMING FROM ANOTHER WORLD

*Gaia, my daughter has mentioned being from a different, high place and that somehow there was an invasion by a lower frequency of this higher place and that is how she came to Earth. She seems very troubled by this. I was wondering if you could speak to me about this.*

Very well. Do you know the story, somewhat of a fable come to life, that is called Superman? In the beginning of that story, two young parents very concerned for the demise of their world find a way, somewhat miraculously, to take their only son and send him hurtling away from that environment in order to create in another environment. In essence, that is similar to your daughter's past life on a world being invaded by an enemy—not a human enemy. It is not as you imagine it now, but we will term it an "enemy" nonetheless. For those who could be saved or could experience themselves elsewhere, there was created a plan or an opportunity to infuse their light elsewhere. And some were of a high enough vibration that they could simply transcend one world and find themselves in another, as if in a safety net. That is exactly what took place.

So her memories are accurate, you see. These memories will fade as she becomes older. She will think of them somewhat as a fable, as a dream that she had when she was young. It is appropriate that you allow her to obscure these, for indeed they are troublesome. You should allow them to fade, not by saying it was a dream, but simply by placing within her heart, mind and desire the possibility of what can be achieved in the here and now. That is how it will be healed. If it is not healed, then it will surface and resurface in later life. Yet it can be healed now in the child.

## THOSE WHO GO BEYOND WILL
## HAVE OPPORTUNITIES TO CHOOSE FROM

*Gaia, in regard to the Crystal kin, is their structure such that they would probably not experience medical problems? How does their DNA get here, if in fact they have DNA?*

The DNA they have is what allows them to manifest the body. Those who are in denser bodies have DNA. Those who have holographic bodies do not have DNA, but the likeness of DNA without the physical means of manifesting. In reference to the balance of your question, they need not manifest a physical difficulty. The future generations need not do so. You see, in a very short time, in very short order, all of the generations now of this planet will discover that there is no longer medical assistance. It will become either too costly, too ineffective or somewhat ordinary compared to other possibilities. Therefore, the body will decide either to make itself quite healthy, or it will decide that it can no longer support the being or the soul, and it will end its career.

Therefore, those who will go beyond that will glance at the bodies that are falling by the wayside and say, "What use do I have for that?" And they will simply not manifest the difficulties of these generations, you see. They will look upon the past generations and say, "How is it that you sustain your body with what you put in it? How is it that you sustain your body thus far by how you have guided it?" And they will make decisions beyond what are made today. That is not to chastise the decisions of now. They are decisions, no more or less than that. They are choices, given what opportunities are offered to you. But you see, those who will go beyond will have opportunities of their own to choose from. Remember, those who come to an unsatisfactory world are here to shift that or change that. If it is unsatisfactory, why would they put up with it? And yet this generation of which you are now speaking, including your own beingness, will say, "Very well, if that is all I am given, then I must indeed put up with it." But those who will come will say, "I will not," because they are here to discover what will be.

## MESSAGE FROM A CRYSTALLINE CHILD

*Mother Gaia, recently in a timeless moment I received projections of a Crystalline being, a young girl, quite young. She called herself my daughter, though I'm not sure if she will come through my being or not. I am curious as to my connection with this Crystalline essence and if she is kin in disguise.*

Yes. She may or may not be your daughter in this life, as has been decided, and yet she is your daughter vibrationally, speaking through this Crystalline connection, or she has been your daughter, and so it matters not whether it will be in this life. It is an aspect of the Crystalline lineage. The Crystalline lineage is not new. Some will say, "Oh, look what is new upon the Earth; it is a new item upon the shelf." It is not that at all. The Crystalline lineage is the most ancient. The crystals on the planet . . . are they not the most ancient of all upon the Earth? And so it is with the beings—they are the most ancient of all. They do not measure in the past, the present and the future. They measure in the all, if at all. Therefore, to say she is your daughter, as she always has been the daughter, is an aspect of lineage, but it transcends even the word "lineage." Can you imagine?

*So then this Crystalline lineage is also the daughter of my own lineage?*

Yes, in essence, this being is both your daughter and your mother, both your granddaughter and your grandmother. It is not a lineage that can be described. That is why I say to you to transcend even the word "lineage," which would suggest a linear movement. And yet this is not.

*Then why does she come to me now? What is the lesson she brings?*

But, indeed, sweet, could you survive this world without her?

No.

## BABY BOOMERS AND THE INVASION OF NEW LIGHT

*Was the plan for the baby-boom generation to take first crack at the density that was the society at that time and to let in some initial cracks of light?*

Somewhat, yes. Those whom you term the "baby boomers," those who have created many, many children, it was their first crack, as you say, at creating possibilities. The more numbers that can be created—although they would fall by the wayside—many would yet come, you see. It is this invasion of new light, the invasion of a new vibration, for it matters not how many numbers there will be—many will fall. Of all those who would be desired to be conscious, most will be unconscious. But of all who are unconscious, there will be some who are conscious, and those will bring about those who are more conscious. And on and on.

*Was there a connection between that generation and atomic energy?*

Somewhat. It is more what you would term subatomic energy, but your question is a valid one. The subatomic particles within those who were birthed during that time were split as the atom was physically split—the subatomic atom was joined. It is the opposite of what you think. Physically, upon the third dimension, the atom is split. Dimensionally we will say that the subatomic unit is joined, and it was joined at the soul level, giving rise to consciousness or the possibility of greater consciousness.

*Has the baby-boom generation accomplished what it set out to do, or did it fall short?*

It is yet in process. But we will say, yes. We will say yes with a lightness of being and yet acknowledge that it is yet incomplete in structure and it will be somewhat unfair to name it completed, you see. To say that it is complete or that they have accomplished it would somewhat put an end to it now—when there is yet more to be done. It is not yet time to have earned the gold watch of retirement.

## YOUR EVOLUTION OF CONSCIOUSNESS

*I heard a cricket in the room and I feel we have a message, but I'm not sure what the message is.*

When you discover it, will you relay it to the rest of us?

*I think maybe you have a better idea than I do.*

Indeed. And yet my interest in this moment is the subject matter at hand—unless we shall discover as well whether the tune that you have heard is of a Crystalline nature or an Indigo nature.

Now, then, is your generation more clear? Is your generation more evolved? Is your generation more conscious than that of your parents, that of your ancestors? Are you more evolved than your historical being, than those who have shared themselves with you through the pages? Can you say that you are smarter? Would you say that you are more? Would you say that you are lighter? What is it that you would offer, then, in this moment as you see yourselves in the cosmic mirror that I put before you now? Who will venture an answer?

*I feel like I got the linear perspective. It is as if we place ourselves in time in comparison to others in times before, but there is a more multidimensional perspective that is being called forth from us. It is as if the seed or the potential that exists now has been present through all times within the Earth and within the cosmos. Perhaps we are able to cultivate that seed with more attention in certain moments, but I don't feel that there is more or less than there was or than there will be.*

Indeed. And yet it is within human nature to measure itself as more or less: more understanding today than yesterday. "I am more evolved than I was yesterday. I have learned more than I knew last week." And if you have learned more than you knew last week, then perhaps you also have become more than those who have lived before you. But you have lived your own lives before you. The question is a bit redundant. It is as if you are saying, "Are you more evolved in this life than you were in your last life?" or "When last you came to Earth, were you evolved or unevolved compared to where you are now?" For you come and you play many roles and many experiences, in many times that will guide you. Each time is designed to bring you to a more evolved aspect within you. But that evolution can be of an outer nature, an inner nature, a cosmic nature or a planetary nature—or of an inner world or an outer world.

This is, as you say, without comparison, because all beings belong to the One being or the One thought or the One experience. But as the one becomes the many, the many compare to the one, because the many desire to be, once again, the one. Therefore, it is the stretching and pulling, the tug of the one to the many and the many to the one, that determines how expanded you are in consciousness or in evolution in this life or in others. As you say, it is not linear, it is not this evolved now and a bit more evolved in the next life and a bit more evolved beyond that. It is more as if the cosmic wave, or the band, will move in and out, in and out, as the cosmic inhalation and exhalation of the

Source, All That Is. The generations that understand this understand their ancestors, whether they are cosmic ancestors, linear ancestors, hereditary ancestors or children ancestors. Your children are your ancestors, given this realm of thought. To know if you are more or less evolved than your ancestors is to see whether your children are more or less evolved than you are. That is the answer to that question—a bit of a paradox even as it is.

## YOUR CHILDREN ARE YOUR PARENTS

*Mother Gaia, is that set up so that the child will be more evolved and spark the evolution in the parents to continue the growth?*

In essence, yes—the child is the parent. For those of you who are parents, you are not the parent of your child. Your child is your parent. Your grandchildren are your parents. Your great-grandchildren are your future and your past, because the spiral nature of beingness allows you to be one with Source and one beyond Source. How does one become beyond Source? By being the many. The many move beyond Source only to return to it. Therefore, your parents are your children and your children are your parents. And the vibration that you carry makes the full spectrum of possibility your own. Are there questions regarding this?

*What is the current timeline on Earth or on other worlds whereby a genetic lineage from parent/child/grandparent will awaken to the realization of oneness so that the many realize they are one together, moved by consciousness?*

Not yet for much time to come, dear. It is a concept that will not be braved by many, or it will be thought of as an experiential concept that cannot be proven for a much longer time yet. It is grand that you will explore it, and perhaps you will put it forth as well.

## THE CRYSTALLINE CHILDREN WILL CHANGE THE WORLD

*How specifically will these Crystalline children we have had make their connections? How will they affect the society in a tangible way?*

They will present themselves and their energies in forms that are unconventional, and yet the world will then embrace the unconventional. You see, now it seems somewhat more difficult to accept, for although the Indigos will carry the burden of the world as it is now, it has been said that the Crystalline beings will not. They will not create a burden, and they will not carry a burden. They will be neutral. And because they are neutral, they will also be somewhat transparent in their nature. And because they are transparent, they will be of unconventional rather than conventional density.

How will they affect the future? If they are neutral, they will say, "I will neither fight for what I believe in nor not fight for it, but I will allow you to do so if it pleases you." Can you see how this will begin to make a difference in your world, in the battles that prevail, in the wars that are called for. The Crystalline beings will say, "I will not take up an arm or a weapon, nor will I take up a sword, nor will I speak words that will harm another. But if you will do so, I will stand by your side and witness it." That will begin to transform the world around you, and there will be more changes as well.

If they will neither give a burden nor take a burden, what is left to do but for the burden to allow itself to either let go or to take down the being that carries only the burden? And the Crystalline beings will see the burdens fall or the beings fall as well. But for every being who falls with its burden, the Crystalline beings will make of that light. Whereas the Indigo beings cannot make light, the Crystalline beings can. If you hold a crystal to the light, the light becomes brighter, the light becomes more expanded.

*Are they caught up in duality?*

They are not caught up in duality at all.

*Even in the human state?*

Yes. Have you seen a crystal be dual in nature, dual-terminated? We will say yes, but not with polarity. Polarity carries a charge, duality only an acknowledgment. Again I will say: Polarity carries a charge as positive/negative. Duality is simply an acknowledgment that there is more than one. Therefore, the Crystalline beings will be the acknowledgment of that more than one choice. How many humans now will say, "But I have no choice, I must do this; I must go there; I must work for this or pay for that." Those of the Crystalline nature will understand that they have a choice. Now, if you will not act upon that choice, so be it, but indeed there is a choice. Whereas a country or a being will say, "I must go to war; I have no choice," the Crystalline beings will say, "By all means, there is a choice." The Crystalline beings will simply present the option that there is a choice, allowing all others to make their decisions. They will simply stand in their truth with their choices, offering them to those who will take them or heed them.

## YOU ARE AN ART FORM

*What is Pepper's [the channel's] lineage?*

Her lineage is linked with that of the Earth structure—not the Earth itself, not the celestial body Earth. However, the composition and structure of the Earth nature has its own lineage within the construction of celestial bodies of the third dimension capable of transferring or translating into other dimensions. That is her ability, or gift, or lineage. It is the celestial body itself; it is not a human lineage. It is the lineage of the celestial body, the celestial body incarnate, the celestial body capable of holding life, capable of transmuting life.

*It is interesting what you said about Crystalline children being transparent, because my daughter said that to me. She said, "Momma, I can only tell people about this planet that I'm from if they are transparent." And she looked at me and said, "When I look at you, you look transparent, so I know I can tell you about this planet, and that means you are from that planet too." I was just wondering what my lineage is, if I have more of that, because I've never felt like I belong.*

Your lineage is not exactly that of which she speaks. However, recall that she must see you in a certain way or in a certain capacity because you are her mother. There must be an understanding, without question, that there can be trust, that there can be conveyed all that is seen, all that is understood. Therefore, though you are not the same within the cosmic lineage, in order to have given birth to this being, you had to have created the image or the illusion or the maya of that lineage, of that transparency. We will say that in this case, your heart is transparent when it comes to her, and yet your own lineage is from a time and place beyond here. It is that of a facilitator, who facilitates life coming, who facilitates change without being change itself, if you like—the silent aspect of change, the supporter of change that needs not speak, that needs only to be.

You see, the vibrations are many, and there are many who will go about masquerading these days, "But I am from the Pleiades, but I am from this structure or that celestial body, Antares and all the great star systems." Indeed! You have all manifested yourselves in many different times, places, ways, bodies, structures and such, yet it cannot be forgotten that you are light and frequency expressing itself as an idea. That is your truth. And that being the truth, you can and will express yourselves in a myriad of possibilities, places, thoughts and patterns, as art forms of the One. If you will say, "What am I?" I say, "You are an art form, one that is yet evolving."

# The Wars of
# Humankind in Heaven

*I recently saw the latest Star Wars movie and was amazed at the effect it had on me. The story line seemed almost too real, and I am still having dreams that seem somehow associated with it. I remember reading something about "wars in heaven" and wonder if there is some truth associated with the movie after all?*

Truth, as they say, is indeed stranger than fiction. The imagination behind this fictionalized saga is a creative one, and the writer(s) collaborated with past, present and future memory modules to create a movie that seems as if it could have been inspired by historical events, but was it? Those who have grown into adulthood during wartime have a different perspective on life than those who have not. Likewise, those whose memories include wars that took place upon other worlds are still affected by them. The possibility that such memories exist in the present seems remote, but the mind has many places in which to store nonlinear modules, and when associative correlations such as these are drawn, the mind makes little distinction between then and now, or reality versus illusion.

In some ways, the memories triggered by this fictionalized account are more real than the real wars that currently plague this planet. There is no doubt that humans' injustice to themselves is severe, but for the most part, it is also remote. The evening news that describes the latest battle is neither personal nor impersonal, and you are either for war or against it. Many believe that things seem to have gotten a little out of hand, but a solid turnaround in leadership will once again restore the balance between nations. By contrast, the "heavenly wars" lasted so long that very few could remember a time when peace had ever existed.

Long ago—and longer than that—a great war did occupy many of the worlds that belong to both history and the heavens. Relatively speaking, the Earth is a very small world in a remote corner of an average-sized universe. The Earth was very young then, and the resources it would one day yield were still a mystery, therefore this telling is from a time even before here. The oldest of Earth's inhabitants were brought here—or were dumped, more likely. Some literally "fell" to Earth, but that was near the end, and we are only now at the beginning. To make this telling accurate, my sentience must borrow from that which is older, a fine exercise for the channel and for my own being as well.

Many of the myths and legends regarding the constellations in the night sky began long ago as stories told by those who traveled the galaxies. These travelers of various trades had the opportunity to meet beings from many different worlds. As such, they learned a variety of languages and customs as well as what was most useful about each of the worlds they visited. From such a description, one might surmise that they were ambassadors of some kind, but that would be misleading. They were what you would call a common people—traveling merchants, teachers, voyagers and wanderers. They were among the first to express concern over a minor skirmish that had begun between those who were neither allies nor enemies.

## THE STAR GATE IN ORION'S BELT

Just as today there is interest in the resources of the Middle East, substantial interest existed in a resource that can best be described as a passageway from and between the stars that number Orion's belt to other places in the universe. This small but convenient star gate was no more than a shortcut through space and time; in terms of convenience, it could be likened to the Panama Canal. This shortcut is still in existence today, though it is no longer in use, having been sealed at the conclusion of the Great War. The initial incident would not even have made the front page of your newspapers and was no more than a curiosity of public interest for those who witnessed it. No one took the event seriously, because for the most part, peace had existed in almost every sector of almost every galaxy for a long time. In fact, there were not even any laws governing access to this or any star gate. The star gates belonged to everyone then, much as your highways do today. There were customs and courtesies, to be sure, but there was no penalty for ignoring them, so how did such a small event come to be known as the Great War for control of the heavens?

Each who was involved in the original scuffle wanted the same thing—to exert a small amount of control over the star gate, by which they might benefit a small profit. But it so happened that one of the participants had a distant relative who was a minor (junior) member of the governing council on a nearby world. Minor in more ways than one, this junior council member aspired to a grander lifestyle. In the recesses of his mind, memories of warriorlike beings from another race and time existed side by side with his current reality. He could not explain his dreams any more than he could explain the longing for greatness that captivated him at odd and inappropriate moments. He rarely, if ever, spoke of them, but they were as real to him as anything else. Truth be told, he could easily have gone unnoticed in the background of the council room or even remained in his study chamber for his entire term, for he was not a likeable chap, but history records it otherwise. There have always been those who hunger for power and control for its own sake, and no imagination can fathom how much power or control is enough to satisfy such an appetite. If awareness over a minor scuffle such as this had not fallen upon the ears of the hungry, history might have rewritten itself. Alas, it was not so.

Meanwhile waves of energetic discord continued to settle over the star gate, and even the least sensitive among travelers knew that something was amiss. Some travelers began to choose an alternate transport site, or better yet, a farther destination, but due to the all-too-immediate convenience of this star gate, most did not. It did not take long for the distorted waves of energy to make their way to the nearby world, where the council already sat in session. There was no past matter such as this to draw upon for precedent, and the council had no official standing in the affairs of other worlds. Still, the decision to intercede seemed small and the benefits to all concerned were many. As they were nearest to the situation, they took on the subject at hand, laying all other issues aside.

## DISCORD BEGAN TO ALTER THE WEB OF HARMONY

The council quickly arranged a visit to the star gate so they could settle things firsthand and with no delay. While there, they discovered a significant increase in the movement and trade of commodities and resources from many worlds. Astounded, they saw no less than the wealth of kings and conquerors exchanging hands, moving along corridors of time and space on their way to the next destination, where they would once more be exchanged for a cargo more precious than the last. The council debated a course of action that would suit most, if not all, who had become disgruntled, as the process had slowed considerably. Some inroads were made as the council negotiated first as agents for one side and then on behalf of the other. The council was also interested in settling and dispersing the discordant energies that by now had spread even farther. Like a fine mist of pollution, discord was beginning to alter the web of harmony that had existed unhindered for so long.

Unfortunately, even the members most noted for their unbiased fairness began to fall under the spell of the possibility of riches in heretofore unimagined quantities. It was not long before the council became a divided house as to the best course of action. Bias captivated their words and deeds, and their very leadership became tainted with greed. The more obscure their minds became, the denser and more polluted the resources and the riches became. The light was shrinking back; mistrust and misdeeds were forging their way forward. Imagine a simple and timeless game come to life—many play it still today: A magic wand is waved, and you are instantly transported in time to where you can purchase property for pennies on the dollar compared to its current worth. Substitute gold, precious stones, inventions or even ownership rights to certain objects. Do you recall the game? Such was the situation at this minor star gate, whose fame was growing as fast as the fortunes that passed through it, multiplying between one breath and the next.

As the events at the star gate continued to unfold, the visions and dreams that haunted our junior council member came more often, becoming more real and more violent as the days progressed. Severe headaches accompanied visions of strange beings invading and plundering defenseless worlds, controlling and redirecting their resources and their livelihoods. While his visions were on the calmer side, his dreams often concluded with the destruction and annihilation of entire worlds reduced to cosmic dust by weapons so powerful he could hardly imagine. Try as he might, he could not dismiss these images or even lessen their frequency or severity. The illusion of dream was beginning to overtake his reality. Daily he attended to the tasks set before him as a council member in training, and nightly he succumbed to another reality altogether. As you might imagine, this was taking quite a toll on both his physical and mental stature. He looked awful and felt worse, but when asked, he attributed his discomfort to the same energetic waves of discord that were manifesting in different and unique ways within the various life forms that passed through the star gate.

## A NEW VIRUS ARRIVED

At one point, it seemed that negotiations had turned the corner and were nearing success, with all interested parties gaining something and losing something in the spirit of peace and commerce. But in some obscure moment between light and dark, all gave way once again. No one knew exactly how, why or when the process unraveled, just that it did, and discord once again prevailed. Some whispered that negotiations had stalled once again, whereas others lost interest in the debate altogether. With unfortunate timing, a virus was brought through the star gate, and though it could have been easily contained, it spread very quickly among many. Immunity to most viruses had not been necessary given the harmony that until then had most often prevailed; no one could have imagined just how quickly this virus spread. As if the virus was not bad enough, the fear of contracting it was worse. Those who could make arrangements to leave the area paid handsomely for the privilege. Shuttles and transports of all kinds set out in all directions, taking the virus with them to other destinations before the word "quarantine" could be uttered. Rumors of the debacle at the star gate now traveled near and far, accompanied by a virus that replicated itself and then mutated in severity depending upon the vibration and the density of its recipient.

Our council member, overcome with viral symptoms, fell into a delirium from which he could not be wakened. He no longer belonged to this world but fell captive to the one that now claimed ownership of his mind while tolerating the demands of his quickly deteriorating body. At one point, a wormhole of consciousness opened within him, and he found himself transported through time and space, unable to gain control of his own being or even to assess his position within the cosmos. Eventually, with what awareness remained, he found himself upon a world much like the images that had been haunting him for so long. As light turned to darkness, he felt himself consumed by a power he could not begin to describe. Dissolving into fear, he lost himself forever and a day, surrendering to the vibration that had preyed upon him and the weaknesses that had governed him. A vibration with an insatiable appetite for power and greed devoured most of his energy and then pursued the remnants of his signature to its point of origin—the Orion star gate.

Those who have told this tale more often than my sentience say that upon this day and within this place, the dark met the light and there consumed it, but that is not altogether true. Following its hunger to the star gate, the ravenous and dark vibration found what it still hungered for. The rapacious survive by eating live prey, and this predator fed with voracity on avarice, then indulged itself on selfishness and cupidity. The darkness had not felt so much at home in a very long time. It set about ordering things to its liking, creating a hierarchy that fed the dark by feeding others their own desires, thereby feeding itself. Only an artificial hierarchy of sorts remained at the star gate, whose control shifted in authority as quickly as the unscrupulous means by which interested parties curried favor with those who seemed to be on a higher rung on the ladder to hell.

## No World Was Safe from the Darkness

Although a world war is nothing to scoff at, a war of many worlds is altogether worse, and its memory can bring no solace to those who endured it for eons. No world was safe from the invading force of darkness and no being unique enough to stave off an onslaught for very long. Rebellions were many, but their successes were few and far between. In order to win over the darkness, one had to think like the darkness; and in order to think like the darkness, one had to embody it, thereby becoming the darkness. Getting there was not difficult, but turning back was nearly impossible. Few returned in any condition to be of use to those who remained. This symbology is all too clear in the motion picture that has inspired this topic. Every family suffered at least one loss, and multiple losses that spanned generations were all too common. For a generation or two, families attempted to control the rate at which children were born so as not to sacrifice them to a future whose worth could not be determined. But these old-fashioned strategies only served to advance the technologies that supported stealth weaponry. It would seem that history recalls and repeats itself all too easily.

Those whose minds were most expanded and whose hearts were most open were kept far apart from one another, so that their combined vibration would not draw untoward attention upon them or those who cared for them at great personal peril. The film, whose title we have borrowed, drew upon this concept allegorically by separating twins and placing them in safekeeping. How does one destroy that which only lives to destroy without being destroyed in the process? Only the answer to that question could restore hope to the helpless. In the *Star Wars* saga, a sage transcoded a message in order to inspire a soul of high vibration to become a hero, but that is the Hollywood version. The Bible has its own set of heroes designed to inspire the mighty and the meek. Its stories also belong to both sages and fools, who perhaps better than most understand the true meaning of metaphor. The war in heaven had many heroes, and many who read these words are numbered among them. One day records that confirm these words will be found, but for now it is just as well that they are not, for who could do them justice? A true hero is not a sacrificial lamb or a martyr but an adventurer. A hero is not a soldier of the sword but a warrior of justice. A hero does not always know right from wrong but sees light more brightly than dark.

## LIGHT ARRIVED TO BALANCE THE DARKNESS

Just as the darkness had appeared one day as if from nowhere, a light that had traveled a very great distance now did the very same. The light was not nearly as bright as has been described by those who tell the tale. Upon first arriving, it could not have offered more than a lantern's spectrum upon an evening campsite. But for those who anticipated its arrival and were rewarded by its vibration, it was as if night had suddenly turned to day. What brought the light? No one can know exactly where cause begins and effect ends or vice versa. It is enough to know that duality existed then as it does now. The great cycles have a timing of their own, born from the same divinity that births both light and dark in equal measure, without preference. Such forces exist beyond the reasoning mind, beyond the system that numbers and orders the stars in sacred fashion. These forces exist for the same reasons that you do—they are aspects of Source/All That Is, at once father, mother, companion and unknowable.

The light that arrived was not God any more than the dark that had prevailed was Its opposite, but those who had long awaited a miracle chose to see it as such, and myths and legends are born of moments such as these. The light did not battle the dark as is commonly believed; this is the result of a poor translation. The light overcame the dark because its vibration was upheld by the cycles of frequency that had drawn the light in the first place. The light, as described by those who retold the stories, was said to have cut through the dark, adding further testimony to the theory of battles and heavenly swords. There were battles for control, but these were not the centerpiece of what truly took place. The light assisted those of expanded mind and open heart in coming together without fear, the very thing that had kept them isolated and separate from one other.

## THE STAR GATE WAS REOPENED

The star gate was reopened in due time, but the energies that had almost succeeded in pulling it apart had left it weak, unstable and unpredictable. A quarantine of the entire quadrant seemed a predictable requirement given all that had transpired. One interesting anomaly is worth noting: The star gate, in its unstable condition, was producing anomalies and abnormalities in almost all those who participated with it in any way, with one exception—the handicapped of mind or body were unaffected! The star gate, in its limited awareness, recognized its own organic resonance. In other words, the star gate's consciousness recognized the consciousness of those who were like it. Like attracts like—it is a universal law. Long before humanity made exception for the handicapped, a star gate did! History does not always repeat itself, but it does duplicate itself. What might the implications of such duplication be today? Look closely at those you call the Indigos and the Crystals. Can you begin to see them attracting each other? Look for evolution to be much swifter now and change to be more pronounced.

\*     \*     \*

Our story—your story—has thus far concerned itself with a small and remote star gate that temporarily found itself to be the focus of an entire galaxy. Like a small town that is not equipped to handle national—rather than local—exposure, those who made their home near the star gate wished only that things would be as they once were. Some crave the limelight, whereas others are happiest in anonymity and obscurity—not because they do not warrant the former, but because they see it as less suitable where growth is concerned. But this was not to be, and the past was already hurrying past the present on its way to a future that no one could have imagined.

## THE STAR GATE CONTINUED TO HEAL AND THE EARTH CONTINUED TO EVOLVE

The wounded star gate continued to heal. A star gate is not like a bus depot or a departure gate at an airport. It is an organic, semiconscious and purposeful coordination of energy. Within its own arrangement of particlized light, it is just as alive as you are, the difference being that it has no individual agenda and its evolution depends upon its environment as well as the environments of all other star gates. If star gates were to be classified as they are on Earth, they would belong to one of the kingdoms whose laws are governed by nature and nature's elements.

Nothing stands still, and regardless of how time is measured, change continues to reveal itself. The Earth (my physical body notwithstanding) continued to evolve into the peaceful, pristine environment that has been described in great detail elsewhere, thus requiring few words here. My sentience was only vaguely aware of a disturbance of great proportion elsewhere. A developing planetary sentience has enough on its plate, so to speak, without looking elsewhere for opportunities that involve it. Although this might seem less than expansive, by what necessity would my sentience now involve itself with a disturbance upon Mars, for instance, when my prime directive is that which is of earthly concern? Still, a growing sense of unease began to permeate the evolving kingdoms of the Earth, leaving behind a residue that still exists today—an energetic fingerprint as if first dipped in blood to ensure its permanence.

The Earth was even then preparing to receive life forms. So that the ongoing debate may be temporarily abated, it would be appropriate to note that some, but not all, life forms are and were indigenous to the Earth. This holds true for almost every world, especially those whose environments invite both diversity and longevity of elements, which in turn invite variety to become form. The human form is the most mutable of all. It is a combination of both the created and the creative in each world—nature and nurture, as it were. Thus humankind on one world, although immediately distinguishable as such, may be unique and different as compared to humankind elsewhere, depending upon the direction evolution takes.

## THE EARTH WAS A PLANETARY HOSPITAL

In any case, the Earth had evolved sufficiently and had become stable enough in its environmental structure that it was prepared to receive adaptable life from elsewhere. Contrary to popular conjecture, the Earth did not belong to anyone then. Explorers, scholars, pirates and kings had certainly made their presence known, but no one had yet dared to lay claim on and therefore take responsibility for the Earth. It was a delicate time, universally speaking, and one that seemed to threaten the very fabric of evolution. Those who guide the evolution of worlds thought the Earth an ideal next place for those weary from war but still hopeful for peace. These far-seeing Lords of Light envisioned a paradiselike setting in which the spiritually starved might regenerate their divine will. The Lords of Light accelerated certain principles upon the Earth, which in turn rebalanced and restructured its elemental nature. The effect was both stunning and far-reaching.

This jewel-like effect quickly lost its luster as the weary and the injured began to arrive. In those early days, the Earth was no more than a planetary hospital for the unconscious and the shell-shocked, many of whom had never occupied a humanlike body. Strangely enough, it was the fragile star gate that seemed to decide who or what could be transported to the Earth, allowing some easy access while denying others altogether. Lest you think this a form of discrimination, a natural star gate is incapable of such and can only match energy, like for like, based upon the universal laws that govern such things. More often than not, those who arrived were true refugees, and they would have been almost unrecognizable were it not for their souls' undeniable resilience. All were gladly received, regardless of origin, condition or opinion. The Earth was then, as it is now, an unconditional planet of love and healing, albeit one that is harsh from time to time in its third-dimensional methodology. So be it, for such have been the cocreative choices made by Earth's custodians.

## THE STAR GATE COLLAPSES AND THE STORY BEGINS

The star gate, already unstable and under quarantine, began to deteriorate even more, making it nearly impossible to traverse it safely. A star gate, like a supernova, is both the past and the future of something wonderful. The day the star gate finally collapsed was a day to be remembered in cosmic history. The remnants of its presence still dot the heavens, and although it would be inappropriate to rename such residues as heroic, those who remember such times recognize them as a beacon of hope. It seems that our story should be near its end, and yet it is only beginning.

As souls began to arrive, they "fell" into different densities of experience. Most fell into the astral plane, for their frequency would go no further. Clouded in thought and murky in feeling, they searched for an identity that would allow them to go elsewhere, compounding the problem further. A soul has no real need of identity, as its presence is more than sufficient. The need for identity comes from the need to identify with something or someone, both of which seem to exist outside rather than inside. The search for anything without will eventually lead within, because to search without is to acknowledge that something or someone greater than you exists there, which is the acceptance of separation—just as on the journey through a labyrinth, however beautiful or intricate its pattern, one must return to its point of origin, thereby gaining both clarity and release.

The causal plane received those whose awareness and presence were intact. We would not go so far as to say that these beings were not deeply affected by all that had transpired, but it would be fair to say that their eyes were turned inward in search of both guidance and presence. In both cases, however, these beings were more dead than alive, if indeed these metaphorical words hold meaning. These weary travelers were little more than fragments and memories, still bearing energetic shields and swords to protect them from nightmares and horrors, real or imagined. Those who speak contrary to these words were not there. If they have told you otherwise, it was to spare you from your own memories, but with history now lapping at your heels, there is reason to prevent you from such revelations as would allow you to heal your past and ensure your future.

## SOULS HEALED AND GAIA'S
## ROLE AS THE SENTIENCE OF EARTH STARTED

Eons of time passed—the equivalent of many hundreds of years and even thousands as they are now measured. During this time, the souls, your souls, healed. How does a soul heal? Its wounds are not like those of a body. A soul heals through the mind of God. It is returned to the

Godhead, the Source of all things good, the place of no separation and no definition, the timeless tide of oneness. These are not metaphors; they are accurate descriptions within the limitations enforced by words. You can imagine such a place because you have been within it. In fact, so powerful are the memories associated with it that you long to return there at almost any cost. Do you believe those who find themselves in self-created hells do so forever? Nay, their release is eventually secured, and when it is, they are returned to the Godhead and reminded that all are One.

My active role as the sentience of this planet began thusly. Had I known about expectations then, there might have been disappointment, but a sentience learns by discovering all that is associated with response. My sentience read the thoughts of those who slumbered in deep unconsciousness and there saw exhaustion, humiliation and suffering. "What manner of beings can these be?" my sentience wondered.

My sentience also marveled, for the human being and the soul who occupies it is somewhat of an engineered miracle. Perhaps it was at about this time when my sentience began to perceive how to be of benefit to the humans already ensouled about the planet. It occurred to that which I am that compassion had been set aside for far too long and that the feminine principle associated with love and compassion was already woven within the very tapestry of the Earth. I began to see the perfection that had guided the Lords of Light to direct your presence here. Already I envisioned a different day, albeit distant, and set out to create its dawn with all of the resources the Earth already possessed and those that could be invited (attracted) from elsewhere.

## THE COLLECTIVE SOUL OF HUMANITY BEGAN TO AWAKEN

While your souls continued to slumber, the Earth continued to evolve into the paradiselike state you have heard described to you. The Earth evolved into a garden, bejeweled in splendor and bearing the unmistakable fragrance of new life. A fragrance as sweet as this beckons life itself to come forward from its silent dwelling, and so the collective soul of humanity began to awaken. Not all who were roused from their slumber were eager for the breath of life, but consciousness is not selective and the warmth of the Sun tends to ripen the entire vine.

Your long sleep brought with it a forgetting of the past, making your awakening as if but another dream. You did not know who or what you were, but it did not matter, as in a dream one can assume almost any identity or none at all. You did not know where you were, and this also was of little consequence. Those who guided you then assisted you in understanding that you had been on a long journey that had, in effect, dampened your ability to remember the past.

These same guides implanted a new awareness within you, placing it within the very structure of your beingness (the DNA) so that a new awareness and desire might awaken within you. In your semi-shattered condition, this was more than enough of an explanation and you did not seek more. With the past placed safely in semi-quarantine, a present reality, complete with timeline, was next established. Contrary to common-day conjecture, a future was not established, because the very healing of your beingness depended upon creating a viable future for humanity. Only in this way does human will begin to recognize itself as divine will. Such are the laws that govern even the Lords of Light.

The possibility of your becoming physical beings again was of great concern to those who guide the evolution of consciousness, and your experience under the force and control of others, although buried deep in your past, still existed. It is important to note that this history was not erased or taken from you. It was placed within the recesses of your consciousness in such a manner that it could only be retrieved, reawakened or activated by your own beingness, thus signaling your readiness to know. Measures and precautions were taken to protect these memories by keeping them in a quarantined state within the recesses of the mass consciousness of a now Earth-based life form. Here they could never be forgotten or altered, while at the same time, plenty of time was allowed to gather the missing fragments of awareness that would one day restore humanity to full and autonomous consciousness. Even now no other being can do this for another, much to the chagrin of those who whisper or holler into the faces and souls of friends and family.

The fields of energy that surrounded your essence were very fragile then, almost as if there was no outer skin separating you from your inner self. It was therefore suggested that you remain in your bodies of light, unencumbered by the density of form. This meant that you had no protection from the environments that you experienced, because you were not separate from them. But there was nothing to fear then, which is exactly what you needed. Pristine as was the Earth then, you were influenced and affected by all of the kingdoms and all of the environments. Such is how you returned to awareness—in the embrace of kinship to all and with not an enemy to be found.

## KINGDOMS AND EVOLUTION ON PANGAEA, THE SUPERCONTINENT

By the time your essence bodies had restored sufficiently, Pangaea, the supercontinent that incorporated most of the Earth's landmass, was wonderfully inhabitable. Pangaea was not the only continent, but it was the most beautiful and diverse. There were no hard and fast rules regarding evolution or reproduction then, as it was still too soon. The plant kingdom was the most developed—breathtaking in both bounty and beauty. Flowers were the size of men, and their language was carried by their fragrance. Have you ever wondered how botanical medicines and therapies came to be? Why, the flowers themselves were your original teachers!

The next well-developed kingdom was that of the animals. Such strong, supple and youthful bodies all of them had! There were no carnivores yet, because the edible botanicals contained many more complex proteins then. There were no enemies between the species either, although each seemed to prefer a habitat of their own choosing.

Human bodies were not altogether physical, at least not all of the time. Without density, form is closer to formlessness, do you see? (Those who seek relief from excess weight, take heed: Release density—fear-based consciousness—and excess weight is made unmanifest, for what would hold it in place?) There was no kingdom of humanity as yet; your bodies consisted of a light fabric of Earth light, fragile in appearance but tensile and resilient. These were sensory bodies, a composite of elements that allowed you to touch and feel the physical world without becoming a part of it. These semi-luminous bodies easily dissolved when consciousness did not hold them to purpose, becoming part of the great oceans, meadows and forests. By this process, everything lived within the form or occurrence of something else, a true synergy of energy and experience.

## PHYSICALITY

Paradise continued to greet the souls who awakened from their fitful slumber, while waves of energetic wholeness were gently infused into those who did not yet have the will to return to any form of consciousness. For those who chose it, physicality was very healing. To be "grounded" was to be receptive to the wellspring of benefits the Earth offered. Pangenesis, no longer in practice today, meant that the environment influenced heredity as much as experience did. Thus those who came into physical experience later still received a percentage of the original cellular memory as their own. Somatic cells, which affect the body separately from the mind by relating to the outer walls of the body rather than its inner organs, sent influential information regarding experience to nonphysical reproductive cells, from which experience was passed from one generation to the next. This unbreakable link between generations of experience allowed you to choose a future en masse by supporting the experience of one as that of all.

The animal kingdom continues to evolve via this instinctual form of expression, and all species benefit by its process. As long as purpose exists within design, extinct species could be brought back to life with less than a handful of these cells. For instance, a dinosaur could not be animated again, because there is no current environment or purpose to suit it. Of course there are exceptions, but that is a different subject altogether.

Somatic cells evolved into the somatic nervous system, the part of the nervous system that serves the sense organs; the muscles of the body, including the muscle walls and limbs; as well as all voluntary muscle activity. The human body still belonged as much to the ocean as to any other element—as undefined as the tides and as constant as the currents. The memories that accompanied these bodies were obscure and distant, clandestine meetings of synaptic nerves that touched the fiber of your being without being able to transmit a message. Your somatosensory bodies began to receive sensory stimuli from impressions whose origins could not be found. These impressions formed the basis of your imagination, and from this you began to imagine your physical forms into existence as internal organs and skin began to form a reality around your experience.

Somatopleure, an aspect of embryonic tissue formed by the fusion of ectoderm and mesoderm cell layers, gave rise to inner and outer cell membranes, thus establishing your physicality upon the planet as more than desire. From this came a desire to regenerate or procreate, offering the same opportunity to other souls. An appropriate response to the question, "Which came first, the chicken or the egg?" is that both were born of the same moment, as desire breeds purpose. Anthropology still acknowledges this ancient branch of evolution through its study and understanding of somatology, the study of human development through variation and change in physical characteristics.

## THE ORIGINAL FORM OF DUALITY

Around this time, a "veil" was placed around and between the physical and the nonphysical worlds that affected the Earth. This allowed you to experience linear time, birth and death, as well as giving you the freedom to explore unique and individual experience. Your lives were long then, and the physical vehicles you generated to house your soul essence were innocent and pure. There were no defects in these bodies; they were perfect, because your desires were perfect. Your bodies existed because a desire to be physical existed; the desire created the body, and the body sustained the desire as long as purpose existed. Being physical then did not preclude being nonphysical. In other words, you were aware and took delight in both aspects of your being. This was the original form of duality, designed to suit rather than hinder your needs.

The health of your bodies could only be described as radiant. Illness and disease were virtually nonexistent then; these came much later, after several mutations in form invited invasion from without and then, much later, from within. Your bodies were equipped with an immune system, but this protected rather than defended and was rarely used. The translucent nature of your original bodies became more opaque over time, but a luminescent sheen was retained that showed you as somewhat wet in appearance. This shimmering effect was caused by an overlay of light that sheltered you from the as-yet-undeveloped aspects of the Earth that might otherwise have been disturbing to your still developing sensory fields. Even today you are protected in this way, innocent to all but the light of All That Is. Perhaps the saying "ignorance is bliss" is but a reference to this.

The idea of remaining upon the Earth continued to comfort you and seemed more natural than anything else you could recall. The Earth offered beauty, creativity, respite from the spiritual storms of the past, rejuvenation, regeneration, the development of mind and body, companionship, custodial interests in other kingdoms and an opportunity to be at peace with a sentient celestial body whose very awareness was dedicated to the well-being of everything upon and within its being. Even so, there were reminders that cautioned you to remember that you were not your bodies; you simply inhabited them for a while. Your body, you were reminded, was a habiliment, the clothing associated with an Earth-based body. Many times it was said, "You are on the Earth and in the Earth, but not of the Earth, remember?" And for a long time you did. Still, the desire to have an origin and a beginning in linear time was very strong, as it often is in young and evolving species.

## ADAPTATION, MUTATION, EXTINCTION

The physical Earth developed as you did. Side by side and hand in hand we expanded what we were and what we knew. Over time the Earth became more physically habitable, and new species appeared throughout all of the kingdoms. Most were adaptable, but some were not and perished almost as quickly as they had arrived. Adaptation and mutation were synonymous then, as the Earth's topography seemed to change almost daily. This led to great variety, as one species soon became two, then three, continuing to mutate until it was but a distant cousin of the original. Today scientific minds believe this took place over a very long period of time, but that is not so. Plant and animal species alike are making a mass exodus now. They are becoming extinct at alarming rates, because it is their time to do so. They are departing as quickly as they arrived, because it is their choice to do so and because the evolution of the Earth no longer supports their presence here. No amount of blame or pointing of fingers will change this.

Your minds and bodies continued to evolve and develop even as they do today. One mind—or, better put, one consciousness—still guided the process, but here we must make the distinction that it was mass consciousness and not mass unconsciousness (as manifests today) that sustained and animated the dynamic force within you. Consciousness is multilayered and dimensional because it is not physical. Mass, or density, is the physical manifestation of consciousness, and as such, it is subject to the laws of linearity. In its nonphysical state, density is pure awareness and intention, but as physical density, it can be either conscious or unconscious, depending upon the active force that directs it. This important subject bears acknowledging at this time, because it was at this very juncture in time that the first great migration of beings (souls) began to divide until a second, more solid version of humanity became evident.

## HISTORY IS NOT LINEAR

These observable changes reflected the desire of those who favored physicality over those who did not. The decision seemed a simple one at the time, but history has not recorded it so. A great deal of controversy still abounds, compounded by both myth and conjecture. History is broader, longer and more varied than is commonly understood. A path can be drawn, but it is dimensional and circuitous. In order to make sense of it, you will have to begin at point A, skip over point B completely on your way to C, then double back to return to point B, from where choices C and D will now seem obvious. Again, history is not linear, and neither is the present or the future.

The division that took place within your awareness was a natural one, born of a curiosity that existed within some but not all. The changes that accommodated the desires of the many were accomplished rather quickly. As time is measured, it took less than five hundred years from start to finish! Evolution is and cannot be otherwise. Those who did not choose to be tethered to physicality or to the Earth chose experiences elsewhere. Interestingly, most have returned at one time or another, but they do so especially now when memories of past, present and potential futures ignite both passion and purpose. Many of those who seem alien to you are but reflections of your past, here to complete their own experience by contributing to yours. Look closely, and you will see that the tapestry is nearly complete, the final threads bringing the smallest details to light.

❋     ❋     ❋

This story is not a complete one, but it is enough. Draw what conclusions you will, and take care to place no blame, for the world is overfull from this already. Look within and without now for your next experience and know that you will discover much more by inventing your future than by decoding your past. Humanity is once again poised to unite in consciousness by dividing in nature, a paradox in itself. A new humanity will emerge from the chaos that envelops the world now. A time of choosing is upon the Earth once more, and its effects will be far reaching. Be still before every activity so that your movements are actions and not reactions. Allow the God consciousness within you to be cause so that as humanity, you are not the effect. An act of God is an action that involves consciousness. Consciousness is the great unifier of divine will and the great divider of human will. Choose with the higher heart, and you will know no doubt.

# The Walk-In Experience

*My mom crossed over several months ago, and I miss her terribly. We were very close, and I also depended on her to help me with some challenges and special needs. Without the kind of support I received from her, I am unsure that I can make it on my own. I have heard that sometimes it is possible to exchange places with another soul who would "walk in" to my life and allow me to walk out. Is this true, and could you please offer as many details as possible regarding this subject?*

You have heard correctly. Under unusual circumstances and with very specific conditions, it is possible to exchange "positions" with another soul. The walk-in process allows two individual souls to literally switch places. Scientifically speaking, the exchange requires a reversal of polarity to engage the process within each soul. Both souls then pass through a narrow energetic corridor, similar to an umbilical cord, that is created for just such a purpose. To be clear, however, one cannot simply wish one's way out of a tough spot when life becomes more difficult than one imagined.

Although the term "walk-in" has been popularized of late, the actual experience associated with it is much rarer. As old as time itself, the process has been known by several names, including "soul transference." As ages and civilizations ebb and flow, so has this experience risen and crested the wave of popularity. Perhaps it is difficult to imagine that a spiritual experience could be more or less popular than another, as if it were a fashion statement, yet a parallel between the two can certainly be drawn. Other epochs when these rituals were enacted more frequently include the last dynastic reign of Egypt, the latter days of Atlantis the mighty, and the periods preceding the great eruptions of Pompeii and Vesuvius. Given the late stage of the present age, it is not surprising to see such resurgence. In fact, it is to be expected.

## THE SOUL IS IN CONTROL

Thoughts of an exchange of this magnitude begin at the soul level. Although mind and body participate in all aspects of the experience, they are not high-ranking voting members, so to speak. At the level of human experience, the thought that this life is more difficult or more unfair than others is not uncommon. The soul alone knows that all things are just and in right order, even when they do not appear so at the human level. After all, how many times have you pleaded to be set free from decisions, obligations, hardships and infirmities only to see your way through them, even if it was in the nick of the time?

The soul sees clearly and steers for open water whenever possible. It is never the soul's desire to dash you against the rocks of despair or to cause you to run aground before reaching safe harbor. Still, life on Earth is designed to be an adventure in consciousness. Your adventure may take you through deserts where the creative spirit is parched and dry or into shark-infested emotional waters where the grand prize that is integrity is baited, chummed and suspended just out of reach. The struggle to emerge victorious with good will and strong desire as the only tools is reason enough for most souls to set a solid foot upon the Earth's third-dimensional landscape.

The soul—unbiased, integrated, wisdom seeking, practical, creative and loving—oversees every aspect and detail of the major purposes (there are usually seven or more) associated with this life. Other aspects, such as daily decisions, choices, creative directions, most relationships and more are explored throughout the different levels of human experience, of which there are many. If one or more of these "lights" becomes diminished or endangered, the soul is empowered to act on behalf of the whole. This includes quieting systems for a time, such as in the case of a coma, or even "pulling the plug" if need be.

The soul is a proponent of a full and engaged life. It is not interested in human foibles or forages into the dark side of life. Please do not take offense when I say that the soul considers these experiences some of the more colorful aspects of life on Earth. On the other hand, when human will and purpose are in true danger, the soul may intervene on your behalf, moving both spirit and matter, and generally acting as the hand of God. These interventions can take many forms, only one of these being assistance with and through the walk-in experience.

## REASONS FOR WALK-INS

Walk-in is an overly general term that describes the exchange of entities and souls associated with a given human physical life. The experience is not available to animals, even domestic ones. Although most walk-in experiences continue for a lifetime once the exchange is complete, unusual circumstances sometimes allow more than one, and even several, such experiences in a lifetime. Given that walk-in experiences are uncommon enough, multiple events in the same life are even rarer.

Reasons for such events might include an inexperienced pinnacle moment that has somehow become lost or incomplete where the soul is concerned. For instance, imagine that in a previous lifetime, you were about to discover a lost city, but in the moments just prior to that discovery, you were literally scared out of your life by the appearance of a ferocious lion that ultimately claimed your life. This unfulfilled and important moment could be relived and completed with the assistance of a soul that lovingly invites another to share in an important discovery. As far as the soul is concerned, the experience does not need to be an exact replica, it only needs to be real at the human level. In other words, there must be physical, mental, emotional and spiritual responses associated with the experience.

Other experiences might involve a lost love, an ill-spoken word, a missed event (such as the birth of a child), a misplaced apology or any other moment that could be made whole without repeating a life. The universe is economical in this respect, and Spirit has many gifts to bestow. If at times you have felt yourself joined by another presence during a special or difficult period, consider the possibility that you have shared the moment and assisted another being in becoming whole.

The idea of exchanging a life is a very important one for the soul to consider. The soul considers the idea lightly but thoroughly. The soul can see further into your future than you can; therefore, it explores every timeline and opportunity that you may invite to right wrongs and to invite the kind of true change that would restore a purposeful and creative course. The soul examines what it would take to reignite the spirit of life, and most of the time it can do just that. Some people erroneously believe that major, life-changing adjustments are the result of a walk-in experience. While these experiences can be called soul interventions, they do not necessarily include an exchange or transmigration at the soul level. A good example of this might be the kinds of changes one might make after a heart attack, such as an immediate move toward a healthier diet or a change to a less stressful career. Even the changes following a near-death experience are not necessarily associated with the transformative effects of an exchange of souls.

## THE PROCESS OF THE WALK-IN

The soul opts for an exchange in the form of a walk-in experience when the individual embodied aspect of its being has completed all that it set out to do in a particular lifetime or when, for reasons similar to those already described, it cannot fulfill planned or spontaneous goals that benefit the soul directly or indirectly. In rare instances, the soul may plan to terminate its physical extension—the body—through a series of planned mishaps or even with a terminal illness; however, these events are often purposeful to the soul, even if they are life shortening.

The decision to walk out of a life is a well-planned one but feels spontaneous to the physical personality. One day, it simply awakens with a distinct feeling that somehow things have changed. Procrastination is set aside in favor of completing tasks followed by a distinct desire to tie up loose ends and speak with certain individuals and so on. Bad habits either increase or decrease during this period, depending upon the individual's personality traits. The individual may feel a little disoriented or out-of-sorts, and other anomalies are not uncommon; there is a feeling of wanting or willing oneself to be elsewhere, even when there is no elsewhere to be yet.

At the personality level, most individuals are not aware of what is about to transpire. The secret rests with the soul that is guiding the process with expert grace and coordination. To be clear, a walk-in/walk-out experience is a spiritual enterprise, an uplifting time of celebration. It is not a karmic suicide, and there is no spiritual penalty whatsoever. The purpose of life is always life, and that is exactly what the exchange that is about to take place is about. It is not a life-and-death decision; it is a life-and-life decision custom designed to the exact specifications of each soul and the growth experiences that each deserve.

The universe is a creative and dynamic environment. It is perfect and synchronistic all of the time and in every way; therefore, at the exact moment that a soul decides to walk out, another is ready to walk in. This does not take place in the same linear progression as events unfold upon the Earth, however. In other words, a soul does not post a "for sale or lease" sign on the physical body of its incarnated self, hoping that another will want to move in. Bear in mind that while life is always purposeful, there are higher and lower motives and expressions. Where walk-in experiences are concerned, the incoming embodiment must be a higher expression, one that is willing to contribute to raising the conscious awareness of the outgoing being's life and everyone in it. This is no small feat, and only one of several spiritual laws (of created things) that must be observed.

## THE PERIOD OF UNITY

It is not uncommon for both entities to exist as a unity for a given period of time, which can sometimes extend into one or two years. This is not a "possession"—not at all. It is a perfect merging of two entities who care deeply about the needs and desires that each wish to express. Often there are other considerations in this process: family members, friends and business associates, not to mention past promises and present-day responsibilities. All of these must be honored and then taken into consideration. Neither the outgoing entity nor the incoming one is allowed to simply set aside these responsibilities during this time. Later on the incoming entity will make decisions of it is own but not yet. The outgoing personality can feel a little short-tempered during this time, but can rarely identify why. For obvious reasons, this is for the best.

It is important to note that while the outgoing entity relinquishes all interests in its previous physical life, it remains strangely tethered to the life. While this concept may seem unusual, it can be put into perspective if we consider that mothers feel connected to their sons and daughters long after they have become adults. If they can find a way to make their children's life better, they often will. It is the same with souls in that they automatically go out of their way to serve each other. Another example is that of twins who are also strangely bound to each other; in surprising ways and unexpected moments, they are drawn together.

This is expected and required; one of the spiritual laws associated with the walk-in process. These are important principles that make this progression of souls both honorable and praiseworthy. Only when the physical life of the original incarnated being concludes does the bond between the two souls officially terminate. Imagine what it would be like if every time you moved from one home to another or one job to another, you did the same and others did the same on your behalf?

The period of unity, or exchange process, is a time of grace for all concerned. Should any change prompt a recession on the part of either soul, the exchange may be canceled. No explanations are necessary, for perfection reigns in the universe, and the next breath brings the next opportunity. In human terms, cancellations and delays can bring disappointments and even mistrust. This is not the case here, as higher law applies. The same laws apply to the first several months after the transfer is complete. There is no specific contract time or expiration date, and each arrangement merits its own unique time, but generally speaking, this period lasts approximately 180 days.

## THE EXPERIENCE OF THE OUTGOING PERSONALITY

It is uncommon, but possible, for either personality to be aware of the exchange, but there is no deceit involved on the part of the soul. When the time is right, each soul will communicate lovingly with its younger aspect, unfolding enriched and creative ways for living artfully in the dimension of expression that presents itself. The actual transfer most often takes place while the outgoing personality and body are resting—or better yet, sleeping. A loss of sequential time, fatigue and flu-like symptoms are not uncommon for the first few days. There is no need for the outgoing soul to bid farewell to the people, places and things in his or her life, though some may have been doing so unconsciously for months or even years. The incoming soul will carry on responsibly but not seamlessly.

The outgoing personality, or entity, is received warmly in an environment that is very similar to the one that it has just transitioned from, except that it is lighter in density and constructed of a mutable material that can be easily dissolved as soon as there is no longer a need for it. Imagine a façade that has been constructed for stage-making purposes. It serves a temporary purpose, and when the scene changes, the scenery must change too. This staging effect is not mandatory, and like a parent, each soul knows exactly what to provide for its younger aspect. Just as a sailor must become accustomed to his sea legs, an entity must relearn to do without them—and without a body as well. In most instances, this awkward moment lasts about that long.

Once acclimated, the returning soul has access to everything that was unavailable during its recent incarnation, including the reasons why the lifetime could not be completed as planned. This is not a setback for the soul, temporary or otherwise. It is simply seen as an environment concern, no different than a weather pattern that dampens a day's excursion. Although souls understand how linear time affects the lifestream of a human being, they are nevertheless timeless.

Please understand that your time on Earth is deeply important in many respects, but it is not the only time that you will articulate a human body in order to express the purpose of a soul. Freed from the constraints of a now previous life, the entity explores a wide range of new possibilities. The outgoing entity is limited only by its imagination and by its ability to sustain and enliven a high vibration. Obvious parallels can be drawn between both experiences. There is no exception to the rule: as above, so below.

## THE PATH OF THE NEW WALK-IN

It could be argued that the incoming entity, or walk-in, has a more difficult path ahead, but the walk-in does not see it this way. It is grateful for the opportunity to express itself in the physical, and because most walk-in experiences take place in adult lives, there is no need to go through the birth process and the lessons that youth brings. The incoming entity is ready to begin living a purposeful and fulfilling life.

Walk-ins are often more driven than their outgoing partners were, eager to step fully into life and to accomplish all that is creatively possible. Most bring new skills and abilities to assist them in their new endeavor; they also have access to all of the knowledge that the outgoing soul accumulated during his or her experiences. A walk-in retains all of the memories associated with the body and the life it has walked into, but often without the emotional attachment associated with the memories. The new entity remains respectfully neutral where these are concerned.

It also retains aches and pains, diseases and other physical limitations, references to family dynamics, aptitudes and much more. That being said, it is not subject to the same beliefs regarding these things. The incoming entity is free to resolve a physical handicap whenever possible and to overcome or heal a disease in its entirety. The walk-in can also dissolve a relationship—but rarely does—change occupations, prefer different foods and colors, enjoy other hobbies and sports and express itself in any individual way it sees fit. The life now belongs completely to the walk-in, and any lifestyle that suits his or her preference is available.

The walk-in experience is sometimes more difficult on previous friends, family and colleagues. They, more than anyone else, see the sharp and inevitable contrast between one being and another. Old issues and unresolved situations are still present for relatives of the outgoing soul, and they have no way of knowing that a great change has taken place while they were temporarily unaware. The new walk-in undergoes changes at every level of existence, including strong changes in personality. Although walk-ins rarely leave their partner out of respect for previous promises, the opposite is not true. Spouses and mates of the previous inhabitant often find the new changes too difficult to bear. Well-intentioned family and friends sometimes subject the new walk-in to old energies and patterns that no longer apply.

These challenges must be overcome, and it is up to all concerned to allow changes of a positive nature to occur. Many walk-ins do not discover what really happened until the close of life, although they would readily acknowledge that a significant and dramatic life change occurred at some point. Of course, this is not always the case, and some have full recall of every moment and every detail in real time. Each walk-in experience is unique and has its own characteristics. A fully conscious walk-in has obvious benefits to call upon, but whether these benefits also apply to friends and family is another matter.

## FINAL NOTES ON A VAST SUBJECT

Most desires for walk-in/walk-out experiences are not granted. The process must serve a greater purpose for both entities. One cannot simply return or exchange a life because one doesn't like the direction it has taken. Life allows each individual to reshape his or her life, partially or completely. Sometimes an entity must simply bite the bullet and take the necessary steps that will lead to true growth. The next important step in a soul's development can be delayed, but it cannot be dissolved. There is no governing spiritual body that grants permission for souls to exchange places. The highest, most responsible, loving and aware aspect of the soul decides.

Life is sacred at every level and during every experience. There is no waste where human life is concerned. Your desire to exchange places with another may be granted, but if it is not, it is up to you to *will* yourself to continue to develop this life. In the meantime, work on everything that helps to make this life whole and complete. Excite the mind so that it is interested and agile, enhance the spirit so that it is in deep resonance with the soul, and maintain the body's capacity for health and wellness.

The soul will guide you through the necessary steps of reviewing the entire walk-in process. If you have walked-out of your last or recent lifetime, be aware that your experience may not be granted this time because it may limit your soul's growth. Every incarnation offers a wide variety of choices, but if you continually stay or stall your progress, the range of choices will naturally diminish. This is not meant to hamper your free will, and it is not intended as a penalty, but life is designed to help you exceed the parameters and limiting conditions that are set before you. In this regard, skipping a step is not possible.

Life is a gift, and under the right circumstances, you may pass the gift on to another. Life is always innocent and harmless. Do not blame others, yourself or life for the situations it presents. You are the director of your life. The ability to change, course maneuver, correct and other creative tools are alongside or never far offreach for them. Relearn an old lesson, revisit an old task, take on a new project, forgive a tired adversary, take a different fork in the river, plant a seed that will grow tomorrow or next year, and bend as the willow.

# Keeping Time

*I woke up the other day with these words: "I hope we can wake up in time." Time may be an illusion, but the illusion of time running out is certainly doing something very interesting to human consciousness. A sense of urgency seems apparent in most of us, yet complacency regarding our life and our future still seems to rule the day. Is time accelerating in proportion to the increase in light, or have the imbalances upon the Earth placed our own acceleration beyond reach?*

*L*et's begin with a metaphoric tale that is not too far from being accurate, because it will illustrate the answer to your question and then some. Imagine that a very great clock has been in your family for as far back as you or anyone you know can remember. Everyone knows that this clock has kept accurate time for as long as time has existed. In fact, there is a long-standing rumor that suggests that the clock itself gave birth to time, and as its parent, is still responsible for the perfect and exact expression of time—at least as far as your family is concerned.

After many generations pass, you inherit the clock, which—far from being an antique or an heirloom—is still thought to be responsible for the accuracy of time for the entire family of humanity. As the guardianship of the clock passes to you, the following words are placed within you: "You and your generation are the inheritors of time, which among other things is sacred to life itself. This clock has kept excellent time since time began, making it the father of time. Care for it deeply, as you are now the bringers of time and this is your new dawn." Recognizing that a great honor has been bestowed upon you, you receive the gift and consider yourself fortunate. All that you are swells with pride at being nominated to such an elevated position: as the guardian and keeper of the time for the family of humanity.

## PUSHING OUR CLOCKS FORWARD

You become vaguely aware that somewhere there is also a guardian of light who has inherited the task of accelerating the evolution of the family that is humanity. You know that this guardian of light will depend upon the accuracy of the clock in your care, and you diligently and protectively watch over the clock, marveling at its ability to keep perfect time. Recognizing the responsibility associated with the gift, you begin to reflect upon your ability to be responsible on a long-term basis; you secretly wonder if the task might become burdensome.

Time passes, as it should, and you relax into your new position, as you well should. One day in the future or in the past, something or nothing happens, and you become aware that the clock seems a bit different—or is it just your imagination? You begin to wonder if you have been less than observant. Is it possible that your neglect has caused time to be less than accurate? Over days, months and years your concern does not diminish. At first you are certain that the clock is too slow and later that it is too fast. You wish you could consult with someone about it, but there is no one; you are the inheritor and guardian of the great clock. You are the one who should know.

You continue to observe the clock and also how the family of humanity reacts to the passage of time, looking for any anomalies. While not everyone seems to notice, there does seem to be evidence that time may be accelerating, although how or why seems impossible to discern. Your concern increases as you determine that something is obviously wrong. What if time continues to accelerate? What if instead it slows too much? What if the clock—and therefore, time—stops altogether? What if you have failed miserably and are responsible for leaving humanity without a legacy of its own?

Imagining the worst while not yet succumbing to it, you put your most aware thoughts to work on finding a solution to a problem that has no precedent, at least not as time has marked it. Logic tells you that since you are the guardian of time, you should be able to reset the clock, but in what way? Certain that your own imperfections contributed to this burden, you wonder how you will even recognize something as perfect as time? Whether or not to act bothers you by day and haunts you by night until you can no longer tell the two apart. When you can no longer bear it, you decide to wind the clock, hoping that action is better than no action. You have a strong belief that the clock may reset itself in the process.

As you begin to wind the clock, you wonder if any other guardian has ever had to do the same: "Did the clock keep perfect time for everyone but me? Is this the generation where time falls apart, or even worse, falls away?" You wind and wind and wind the clock. It offers no resistance, no stopping point. Can the clock be overwound? Eventually, for unexplainable reasons and without resistance on the part of the clock, you determine that the process is complete and you stop winding.

Has anything changed? Yes. Something without measure has marked a presence, as if a gap in time has been inserted. The gap is not slow or fast and seems to be made of a substance that did not exist prior to the clock being wound. You observe the clock and try to assess its accuracy, but there is no telling, for what would you measure it against? You determine that the only true and accurate measure of time is you, because you were the one who first noticed the acceleration and then chose to act based upon an inner motivation to do so. You are the agent of change, the inheritor of the clock, as well as the tool of change—the winder of the clock. Somehow you have become part of the process as well as the process itself. It was you who determined that time was no longer accurate and you who chose to intervene without prior knowledge, instruction or certainty. Guided by wizardry or stupidity, you opened a gap, a portal in time when the family of humanity can find and awaken itself in its own time.

Longer ago than you can imagine, time was given to the family of humanity as a gift. It is still that way, but in order to appreciate it, you must allow its redefinition as a measure of light. Otherwise, you will feel separate from the fabric of time, which also defines dimension. There is a gap in time now and a change in how it is measured. The ancients said: "There will come a time when time will not come." In error, this was thought to describe the end of the world. Instead it accurately describes an acceleration in time beyond current standards of measure. That is why present calendars will be obsolete after 2012.

The family of humanity bears one heart and one mind, sometimes joyful but also sorrowful. It carries the burdens of its past, the uncertainties of its present and the responsibility for its future. The world remakes itself now, and whether humanity is for or against change does not matter, as the second hand ticks more quickly today than it did yesterday. As time reshapes itself it will also reshape the face of nature and that of humanity—but that is a tale for another day.

## A FEW NOTES FROM GAIA

The words I offer you from first to last are well chosen. Metaphors of my own making are accurate and as measurable as a clock. For instance, did you know that the mechanism that controls the rate at which a timepiece keeps time is called an escapement? Your history credits an eighth-century Chinese monk with this advancement in timekeeping. He named it the "celestial balance," and it was employed to control a water clock. It is impossible for an escapement to be truly accurate, because as soon as a pendulum, or balance—also form of escapement—is given a push to keep it swinging, its timekeeping has been interfered with. The difference in the rate between natural motion and motion that has been interfered with is called the escapement error. Science calls this a circular error, because these two kinds of motion are opposites; they tend to cancel each other out.

Likewise the larger gears in a watch or clock are called wheels and generally have spokes called crossings. The smaller gears have teeth instead of spokes and are considered involute gears. Their small scale makes it impossible for them to cross without the assistance of the larger wheels. Lastly, the winding pin of a clock is called the key and the winding of a watch is called the crown. When these malfunction, the problem is most often called a positional error. Please take a moment to notice how these very descriptive functions also describe aspects of your own life.

# Evolution versus Creation Revisited Again and Again

*Recently we recognized the bicentennial birth of Charles Darwin, best known for his Theory of Evolution. Why is there still so much controversy about this subject?*

*T*he controversy will exist until humanity's origin is no longer a theory, but an established truth. In order to discover this truth, humanity must reach further into its past than it has thus far, and in order to do that, memories surrounding its more cosmic ancestry must first be restored. Where are these memories stored? They are stored in a time capsule, for lack of a better word. Within the human mind there is a region that has access to greater or more expansive truths. This region begins where the lesser region ends, and to discover these truths, humanity must make the effort to break through the shell of obscurity that separates the two; it must make the effort to reconcile the dualities that have framed its current existence. As long as humanity dwells in duality, its past and its future will be opaque and obscure. Humanity evolved from a chaotic storm of creativity, and as this creation evolved, it became even more creative. The next cataclysmic storm reinvented the human form and the one that followed that inspired the human mind. Each of these cosmic storms created new possibilities and each was given the opportunity to evolve and express as both form and formlessness. Your heritage is richer and more diverse than even the most imaginative minds have yet recalled.

## CHOICE IS THE MEANING OF LIFE

The problem of creation versus evolution is further compounded by the fact that humanity overly identifies with its human form. Without a firmer knowledge about your heavenly past, and with only a sketchy description of your development elsewhere, you have come to believe that your human form and the embodiments it has undertaken are both who and what you are. This is simply not the case. The design of the human body is marvelous, well developed and capable of further evolution. Master geneticists who were privileged with both foresight and hindsight sculpted the human form and encoded it to correspond to the laws of nature. This means that as the Earth continues to unfold a new version of nature, the human form will do the same.

Currently several organs of the human body are undergoing change at minute, but important, levels of the DNA sequence. These changes are self-activated and are designed to complement and mirror the changes that are taking place upon and within the Earth. Other changes may not be as beneficial, especially if humanity does not claim its right to exist. Simply put, anything that lives must choose to live, which is what gives meaning to life. Without this choice, life becomes hollow and purposeless. When there is less regard and respect for life, an entity [you] and its host [me] are in danger of fraying the threads and fibers that link all of life. For this reason, humanity has been given tools with which to enhance its consciousness and further its own sovereign development.

The Earth has always developed its own forms and assisted in their evolution. It has also welcomed and assisted in the adaptation of forms that had an origin elsewhere. Creation, elsewhere as well as here, evolution and adaptation have all played equal parts where humanity is concerned. Erroneous beliefs, half-written truths and false interpretations have led to many theories regarding your origin, including the following:

- You were marooned here long ago as an afterthought of a more advanced race.
- You evolved from ape-like beings as a product of the natural selection of species to succeed one another.
- Having heard a clarion call from angels and higher beings, you descended to third-dimensional Earth to teach, heal and restore.
- You were created here on Earth from primordial material already present in order to serve the greedy desires of an advanced but warlike race.
- You are renegades and refugees from another planet. Due to mismanagement of resources and too many low-vibration agendas, you exploded in space and were cast, sans memories and awareness, near enough to the gravitational field of the Earth to be drawn up into its

field and caught in a web that includes a cycling through the wheel of birth and rebirth.

• You are angels, higher beings and interdimensional masters who have descended to Earth in order to earn a higher degree of ascendancy through the path of service to others.

All of these theories—and others—contain an element of truth, but none is complete and some are absurd given the gem of life that you truly are. When will humanity enrich itself with these greater truths? When the old ones are finally acknowledged as being invalid and obsolete. In order for this to happen, humanity must be willing to unwrite and rewrite lesser truths that are currently accepted as factual. This includes some of what has been written in religious texts as well as some of what science has issued as an edict of fact; it is not compromise that is needed so much as an expanded truth born of an altogether new paradigm. Amidst the persistence of these older and lesser truths lies the challenge for the future.

## THE TRUTH LIES IN THE ORIGINAL THOUGHT OF DIVINITY

*Why doesn't Gaia and other knowledgeable sentient beings simply proclaim these truths as self-evident?*

A significant body of evidence already exists, hidden in plain sight and visible to most. In simplest terms, humanity does not yet wish to claim its heritage or its history because if and when it does, the current paradigm will come to an absolute and abrupt end. Still there are cosmic markers in place that determine proper and timely sequences for the opening and closing of eras and ages. As you might imagine, you are already upon the gate and will soon be in the inner courtyard knocking upon the door. There are unlikely prophets among you. Some of them are determined to uphold the prophecies of their ancestors and others are determined to tear them down. The human experiment will allow both of these experiences to coexist. Duality cannot choose a victor, it can only oppose itself and reveal its opposite.

Between layers of lesser truths and obsolete facts, a faint glimmer of light points the way to greater truth. This light is omnidirectional and omnidimensional, meaning that the next step in the discovery process can be found in the present as well as the past, on Earth and in the higher heavens. False hope often envelops and protects greater seeds of truth; therefore, even false prophets inspire and assist the feckless to embrace faith in the face of uncertainty. How and when will you finally know the real truth? You will come to know it within before it is actually confirmed without. Inner truths are made of a finer and more natural substance than outer truths; they emerge from nothingness and without reason. Spirit will not shout at you to "wake up!" Instead, it will whisper to you lovingly and with soothing gestures that will cause you to look deeper and dig further. Subsequent generations will already have these truths woven into the pattern of life and nature will determine the rate at which they take shape.

We will not reconcile this controversy in this writing, but perhaps we can place it at hand, near enough to make it accessible and attainable to those who seek and stretch. As you choose to engage this part of your mind, you will have access to this truth and to others that are more than worthwhile. Empty your linear mind of what you can and cause your lesser thoughts to yield whenever possible so that you will not be imprisoned by them or be obliged to obey them. Let them find another master. Un-polarize yourself from any and all truths; consider the merit in each without subscribing to them. The truth does not lie to the far left or the far right of center or in the center itself. The truth lies in the original thought of the divinity that later became humanity. As you dissolve the boundaries that separate you from this understanding, you will know not only who but what you are. Enter the realm of original and creative thought that dwells within each and all and you will find answers to this question and many more. Doing so is as easy as you imagine and as difficult as you think; therefore, in this regard—and in many others—sacrifice your thoughts in favor of your imagination, which is a more fertile ground.

# *The Acceleration Of Evolution*

*E*very age, like every person, has a story of transformation to tell. Eventually, an age is known and remembered by the characteristics that described its evolution, its people, and the spirit of transformation that guided it from beginning to end. It takes approximately a thousand years for an age to begin to describe itself in both form and formlessness, creating an architecture by which the collective soul of the age begins to unfold. The next thousand years or so, generally speaking, are spent developing the art, science and culture of its collective spirit, that which lives and breathes as the yet unspoken name of the age itself.

The story of an age is written by its people and by the experiences they invite, and each person is credited with authorship based upon his or her own soul's development within that age. For instance, a soul with many purposeful incarnations within a given age may accumulate greater knowledge with respect to the kind of transformation the particular age might offer. How each soul positions itself to take advantage of what is offered is on an individual basis, and as always, infinite guidance exists in this regard.

## THE AGE OF HUMANITY

Individuals are not experts in all fields, and neither are souls in how they relate to the wisdom offered by each age. Your own memories will substantiate these words, as will your approval or disapproval of the historic accomplishments of each age. Experience is written into the soul whenever the spirit of awareness breathes life into a moment, but history, like art, is remaindered to those who work subjectively after the fact.

Because of this spiritual phenomenon, you cannot accurately recall the true significance of the Age of Atlantis, the Age of Lemuria, or many of the other transformational feats accredited to the collective Age of Humankind. For instance, you remember Atlantis as the age in which technological humans gave in to reason and caused their own demise. You remember Lemuria as the age in which physical/nonphysical humans lived in harmony with the natural world. While these descriptions are true, they do not define the age or the humanity that defined them.

The Age of Humankind is the collective span in which Spirit has expressed Itself in and through the human experience. This spans many ages, as you might imagine, and throughout each age humanity has continued to unfold its own collective and individual story. Toward the end of each age, individual stories somehow begin to coalesce, as if humanity's collective soul must be in agreement as to what is written on the remaining chapters of the current age. And because beginnings and endings are somewhat related, the eve of the next story can already almost be perceived by those who have already begun to tell it by living it.

This age, that in which your experience currently dwells, now nears its completion, but its story is yet unfinished. In literary terms humanity's story in this age could be described as a cliffhanger, in which the ending is left teasingly unresolved until the very end. In this case, because the author and the reader are one and the same, both are eager to discover what will happen next—the moment is tense and the situation is suspenseful. Dramatic by nature, telluric people are yet quite young as measured by this solar system, and younger still as measured by the stars on the far edges of the galaxy.

The final chapters of this age will be written by your resources and by your ability to draw upon them. You will test your resolve in physical and nonphysical ways alike. You will have an opportunity to examine and develop your courage, your will and your wit in most areas of life. You will ask more of yourselves and each other now than you have asked yet, but not more than you will be willing to give, because there is always more to give at the end of an age than at any other time. Previously unimagined resources are at your disposal, because you will soon imagine them as possible rather than impossible. As these are revealed, you will come to know yourselves much more than you do today. It is important that you see the future as infinite, and infinitely available to you, for where you see it as limited it will become so. Even infinity can be expressed by different degrees and different orders or sets.

The universe is ordered in sequences that can be mathematically expressed by numbers. Numbers as integers can be positively, negatively and neutrally expressed, but it is more natural for a number to be expressed in its positive form. The same is true of experience. While humanity is capable of expressing itself in its most negative fashion, it is more natural and creative for it to express itself in its more positive element. The numbered universe can be expressed rationally by quotients, and irrationally by numbers such as pi and the square root of two. The golden ratio, by which much of nature is defined, is irrational as explained by mathematics, yet your future depends upon it.

## LIGHT WILL DEFINE LANGUAGE

As light defines all things, it will soon define language as well. Entire new languages, some of them telepathic, are about to unfold. Some of these languages are dimensional, or nonlinear, and were previously thought improbable, to say the least. The minds of humans are finite, but the thoughts they can contemplate are infinite. This is what some of your new languages will teach you. The new languages will be based upon a scientific model of a whole thinking mind or a mind that assumes that negative and positive thoughts both originate as one until they become separated or acted upon by the third dimension.

Once this premise has been accepted, the next step will be for science to look for the dimension(s) that have inspired whole thoughts. New frontiers in neuroscience await those with courageously open minds. The same is true of medical science and religious/spiritual science, as one will open the door to the next. Soon you will see that hungry minds in one part of the globe will feed hungry stomachs elsewhere. There is a revolution taking place in all fields in which evolution is concerned, but evolution is now accelerating much faster than those who study or explain it.

## ASSISTING THE COLLECTIVE MIND OF HUMANITY

If you wish, you can assist the collective mind of humanity, in great or small ways, by allowing your mind the freedom and mobility to move beyond as many beliefs and belief systems as possible. There is little that is more limiting than a limited mind. Beliefs reign all to frequently, even within higher-minded communities and those of open thought.

The New Age is no exception here, and is sometimes all too quick to grasp hold of a thought or a deed, especially if it believes it is for the greater good of all concerned. Let us visit a few examples.

The natural world is based upon the natural needs of the kingdoms and elements of the Earth, and Earth changes, even those of a disastrous sort, are neither uncommon nor unwarranted at the end of an age. It is best to be guided by your own evolutionary mind—that which already dwells in the future—in all decisions regarding diverting these energies elsewhere. While I do not endorse enduring the unnecessary, it is equally unnecessary to use your energies and those of others to direct or disperse these energies elsewhere. Are you certain where you are sending them? In the case of a hurricane, as you send it away from land and back out to sea are you certain that you are not directing these energies to where they will gather greater force, or to where merchant and pleasure ships are navigating? It is well to explore the subject of directing energies with an open mind, but to do so equitably requires a mind that is empty of fear and clear in how to replace one form of energy with another. Likewise, in replacing a negative thought with an empty thought, what is truly accomplished? Make your thoughts clear and mighty by marking all possibilities as viable and trusting in the perfection of the moment as it is presented. The kingdoms and elements are your partners; they do not require your saving them, and they have done little to engender your mistrust. Foolhardy are those who set themselves above natural law. Be humble in your sayings and doings, and thereby be well protected in all things. Be wary of those who remark upon their feats in this or other areas, for the arrow often misfires and the target is a movable one!

## KNOW HOW TO SEND LIGHT

Have you sent light to a worthy individual or a worthwhile cause? Do you know exactly what it means to send light? Are you not also made of light? To send light means to send a part of you, the part of yourself that is most interested and involved in the moment or the cause. To send light does not diminish you, but it does invest you in the thought or the event. Light is a very powerful tool—it is the very building block of the universe and of your own vital DNA. Every age has its own colloquial language, a jargon or pattern of speech that links a people or group with its beliefs. Light, perhaps more than any other word, exemplifies this pattern for those who identify with its present meaning. So be it!

Yet this is more than a mere word. It is the very glue that enfolds the integrity of the universe. Light and All That Is are synonymous. Together, they are one, and you are one in their name. Light is nameless because its source of origin is also nameless. Likewise, there is a part of you that is so bright as to be nameless light; therefore, do not call upon light or give it frivolously without first noting that you are as inseparable from light as from your soul. Do not send light where you are unwilling to go and do not send it thinking it goes instead of you. To send light is to send yourself. If you send light in protest you go with the protest and as the protest. If you send light to heal, you go as healing and with healing. Too many send light as if it were a get-well card, something they send in place of themselves. You cannot make a donation of light as if to a charity because you are the light, the donation, the charitable soul and the recipient of that charity. Simply know that you are never separate from what you are, and you are light.

## LIFE IN THE SHIFTING PARADIGMS

Do you still live, work and relate to others in old paradigm thought? Of course you do, and appropriately so. Do not be in too big a hurry to dismiss the old for the new. The new paradigm is already replete with its own jargon, but most of it has simply been transposed from the old paradigm, because that is where most of your beingness yet dwells. It is well and good to invite the new and to welcome it into your lives, but not at the expense of those who yet slumber and those who endeavor to awaken. This is not the time to abandon your brethren, even those who have forsaken you and ridiculed your new paradigm beliefs—they are beliefs after all, no more and no less. All beliefs are but suppositions of thought, even those that are most open ended. Any belief, old or new, wise or foolish, is a limitation on possibility. Some are already planning their lives after 2012! Live for today first and sleep the good rest of the shepherd tonight, so that tomorrow your eyes will be clear. The future is yet unmade and the new paradigm ensures that it will remain that way. I offer you this paradox: If you are certain that you are living in the new paradigm, then you certainly are not. And if you are certain that you are not, then you might be. To solve this paradox, live in the moment that is today and look yonder for news of tomorrow.

If you must believe in something, then believe in yourselves first. The stars are not numbered, and neither is the wisdom that is yours to gather.

The good works and deeds of others are worthy of your interest, but do not place others' truths above your own, for once you are beneath them, it will be much harder to rise above them once again. Be respectful, inquisitive and mindful in your pursuit of wisdom; do not tarry or delay in acquiring that which is already waiting for you. Unless you are in apprenticeship to another; advance as your own pace dictates. Neither credit nor discredit another, they will do this themselves without your assistance. Cleanse others of their wounds, be they physical or emotional, and dress them if you will, but see as well how many inflict the same wound upon themselves if only to lament it twice. Have the good word of wisdom ready to share with others, but have its silent companion nearby as well. You will not know until the moment itself which counsel is more appropriate. Trust in the simple more than the sensational, but be in awe of both. Look as far into the heavens as the depth of your heart allows.

# Predictions
# Packaged "To Go"

*Can you confirm or deny the existence of a so-called time machine that can see into the future and predict major world events? I have read that this machine recorded or "sensed" the events of September 11, 2001. Some speculate that it also appeared to forewarn the Asian tsunami.*

*I* can indeed confirm the existence of such a machine, but as to its purported powers, a little exploration and consideration seems in order. By their own admission, those who head the project behind the black-box phenomenon have stated that at the moment, they are stabbing at the dark. This statement could not be more accurate!

## HOW THE BLACK BOX WAS CREATED

Before there was a time machine, there was a project. Before there was a project, there was a study. Before that, there was an experiment, and that experiment was hosted by a well-known university. The premise or aim of the experiment was to discover whether humans share a single subconscious mind. According to reports, the black box was an unwittingly clever adjunct that now seems to define the experiment instead of the other way around. As you might imagine, universities are not in the business of funding time machines, let alone predicting the future. That being said, there are many well-respected scientists from a variety of countries who have been willing to look and see for themselves.

Those who have attached themselves to this project have admitted that the potential for paranormal power warrants such an investigation, but this has not yet led to an agreement as to what, if any, conclusions might be drawn. Investigations into the paranormal are certainly not new, but they have rarely been taken as seriously as they

169

are now. Technology, so often blamed for the ills of the world, should also be praised when appropriate. Modern, up-to-date instruments can now measure subtle energies that weave in and through given parameters and realities. Such instruments can see telepathy at work and record telekinetic responses. These instruments are not advanced enough to monitor the igniting of a creative thought, but their "eye" can perceive the brain's reaction to a thought; they can monitor what precedes action. This can easily be considered the precursor to a prediction, do you see?

Thinking computers are based upon the same ones and zeros as non-thinking computers—the technology is the same, plus or minus some enhancements and microprocessors. The same is true of time machines and those that have been enhanced with predictive tendencies. The difference is in the sequencing, or the arrangement of the ones and zeros. The original black box was a random—event generator, spitting out ones and zeros as easily as doughnuts. All things being equal, the ones and zeros should have been too. But life is not always equal—or even fair—where energy is concerned.

The study found that energy was indeed influenced by human thought, and that variations within these fields of energy created interference that could not be associated with chance. The results, stunning as they were at the time, could not be satisfactorily explained. Unfortunately, the results were also random and could not be proven or duplicated. By the early 1990s, the study was all but abandoned, even though many such black boxes were still connected to various computer networks around the world.

## FACT AND FANTASY MAKE INTERESTING BEDMATES

Fact and fantasy, like reality and illusion, make interesting bedmates—each adds versatility and adventure to the other. Likewise, the rarest of jewels can do no more than imitate its false cousins when the gaudy afternoon light shines adversely upon it. Such was the case in 1997 when, according to recorded accounts, the black boxes sounded off in unison, apparently speaking in one voice. The occasion was a blighted day by humanity's account, when the world watched as Diana, Princess of Wales, was laid to rest. Were these two events linked, as those who found renewed interest in the study quickly surmised? Not necessarily. But because all things are linked, it is not too difficult to see how they could have excitedly arrived at such a conclusion.

If, for the sake of conjecture, we assign a "1" to conscious thoughts and events and a "0" to unconscious thoughts and events, then chance or random awareness would dictate that the black box would read these equally—and yet that was not the case. You see, unconscious thoughts are denser; they weigh more. By contrast, conscious thoughts are lighter—they are not as heavily weighted as unconscious thoughts and events. The world responded to the light that was Princess Diana, not randomly, but as a collective consciousness. On that day, there were indeed more ones than zeros.

Humans tends to embrace or reject their studies much too quickly, especially when there is funding and accreditation at stake. Given the nature of this study, it is a small wonder that it is even still in existence. Eventually, the generators, no longer random, were renamed "eggs," and over forty countries volunteered to be their caretakers. Those who monitor them say that they are becoming more adept. For instance, it said that the eggs either sensed or responded to such world events as NATO's bombing of Yugoslavia, the Kursk submarine tragedy and the U.S.A.'s controversial election of 2000.

## DID THE BLACK BOXES PREDICT THE ATTACKS ON SEPTEMBER 11, 2001?

Such was the norm for the blackbox eggs, if they can be called that, until approximately September 10, 2001, when it was said that they began an unprecedented and unanticipated unified response to the events that were about to unfold. Had they indeed learned to predict or read changes in energy? Yes, because the density of the collective unconsciousness overflowed with fear, the simplest of all energies to read.

Next on the list of credits for the all-seeing eggs is the almost twenty-four-hour notice they seemed to offer to the earthquake and tsunami that occurred in the Indian Ocean in December of 2004. Do the same rules apply? Yes, but only if we acknowledge that my sentience—along with all of the elements and all the kingdoms of the Earth—combined to create such an event, as well as its warning or energetic signature.

Are the eggs resonating with less-than-obvious energies, or are they forecasting future events based upon raw, random data? Perhaps both possibilities are true, because it is the raw, elemental intelligence within the Earth that is broadcasting energy to the intrinsic, human-made intelligence within the eggs. But it doesn't stop there. Computerized intelligence, created by humans in an attempt to study nature, reflects its findings directly into the aspect of the Earth and humanity that responds to technology. In other words, the natural or elemental intelligence of the Earth (the first language) speaks to the less-than-natural mathematical/technological intelligence (the second language) that is of both Earth and humanity. Even more simply put, my sentience will employ as many languages as it takes to awaken and enhance that which has always been natural but has now been mostly forgotten within and among the peoples of the world.

You are not separate from the technology you create or from the nature you destroy. You carry it all within you. You have brought it here from the past and even from other worlds. You will carry it into the future and to many other destinations. The past and the future are simply coordinates on a magnificently creative grid, enhanced in such a way as to offer omnidimensional directions or choices. Are you certain that time runs from past to present to future? Are you any more certain about the past than you are about the future? Clockwise is only an agreed-upon direction. It does not really affect time, other than by agreement.

Those who conducted this study and others like it subscribe to a belief system. They are willing to explore errors within the belief system but have found none yet. They hope that the mind's hidden powers will reveal how it can forecast the future, but they are looking within a reality where that knowledge is hidden, instead of in a field where it is more than obvious. The answers lie not in technology but in consciousness— not in an individual but in humanity. The computer eggs have come as far as they have because they were joined. This is called unity consciousness, and it applies to humans and machines alike. This link, once established, is not easily broken.

*I want to accept that the earthquake and tsunami this past December were natural events, but I am having trouble doing so. For one thing, it would seem incredibly insensitive and wrathful on the part of the Earth's (your) sentience to stand by and watch such a catastrophe unfold. Additionally, I hear that technology capable of wreaking havoc of such untold proportions has existed for some time. Isn't this more likely?*

There is certainly enough evidence to support the conclusions that you seem to have already drawn. Although there is currently no shortage of human-made disasters, it might also be possible that you do not wish to consider that death and destruction are indeed natural events. In the event that your thoughts in this regard are still pliable, I will continue.

## AN UNPRECEDENTED SHIFT

The world is undergoing an unprecedented shift in both form and function. Shifts of this nature are not as uncommon in the universe as you might think, certainly not for a celestial body. That being said, it is a little more rare for changes of this magnitude to take place with as much physical life upon the surface of a planet as there is here and now. It is more common that, under such circumstances, physical life would be somewhat reduced in quantity and species, with at least half of all life forms existing beneath the planet's surface. As you might imagine, this requires cooperation between species, cultures and nations—something currently lacking upon the Earth.

The means within which to exist safely underground is within human grasp, but this possibility is not currently being offered to the average citizen. To be fair, until all weapons are exposed and rendered inert, the immediate interior of the Earth is no safer than the exterior. Space, another alternative, is also beyond the reach of the average citizen for the time being. Long ago, explorers were little more than pirates, claiming and appropriating land and resources as they saw fit. Those whose mandate now carries their country's flags into space have all too much in common with their ancestors.

Do you remember the story of Jesus's birth in a manger, because the inn was full and there was nowhere else to go? Without arguing semantics, this is also humanity's story. There is no perfectly safe place for you to be, and because your birth is imminent, improvising is both natural and imperative. Birth and death are one and the same, but from your perspective, they can and do look very different. Based upon prevailing beliefs, birth and death seem like remote opposites instead of obvious partners. In order for this to continue to be true, light and dark must also exist as opposites, as must good and evil. But these are traps, and the sooner you escape them, the better off you will be.

## THE BATTLE AGAINST SEPARATION

Humanity is battling an old enemy now. Its name is separation, and its only cure is unity. Your cellular memory remembers this, but your mind does not. Human minds look for answers from what they believe to be more intelligent minds, so they create computerized versions of separation. That is why there is so much technology today, why players face opponents on holographic battlefields and soldiers face enemies in the desert. Technology is not your true enemy, but the memory of how technology was misused in the past is. Technology is another word for power, and it is this power that humans both fear and crave. Technology is the study, development and application of devices and techniques that support practical and productive processes that enhance a culture's knowledge. Why, then, does technology induce such fear in the hearts and minds of humans? Can it be that it once meant something altogether different?

Where separation is concerned, technology can either mend or bend. Upon Atlantis, it bent minds and twisted hearts, and this is your most recent memory of its power. The Earth does not yield to technology, but it does yield to human knowledge of technology—or lack thereof. Ministers of mystery have always understood this, and it falls upon them to reveal or unveil these truths to you once again. Sometimes truth temporarily falls upon deaf ears and blind eyes. Fear can do that, you know. Technology, like everything else, has a fatal flaw. It cannot re-create itself, but it can destroy itself. The fatal flaw of humans is that they have forgotten technology's fatal flaw. Soon humans will sort themselves out, but in the meantime, fact and fiction, creation and destruction, must share the same stage.

Human-made events are flawed. Like clever forgeries, you can spot the inconsistencies if you look closely enough. Those who perpetrate chaos and then attempt to hide behind the face of nature are quickly exposed. Technology cannot find a flawless diamond, because at its core, it too is flawed. But humans can find perfection, because at the core of their many flaws is their own divinity. Humanity's source is All That Is, or unity consciousness. Technology's source is based upon individual knowledge that has been pasted, glued and collaged into place. It is not cogent and cannot stand upon its own merit. Technology can hack its way into a computer's brain but not into a person's soul. Today, when a computer steals your identity, you fight to retrieve it. In the future, you will abandon it and create a new one, because you will know that you are not your identity or what you identify with.

History is not doomed to repeat itself, but it is prone to review from time to time. Currently, inaccurate histories recorded at the behest of those who wield power have made it difficult for humans to visit their true past. Like a ghetto, some of the corridors where humans have traveled are distorted and littered with debris and inconsistencies. Improvements in time travel will change that. Those who choose to will be able to visit crossroads of specific interest in order to learn from them. Like a professor emeritus, these junctures in time and space will serve as your teachers.

## SOME OF YOU WALK A PRECARIOUS PATH

Your question indicates an awareness of those who travel these unsafe corridors now in order to disrupt the Earth's evolution. I will confirm that some of you walk this precarious path, but like a rubber band that has been stretched too far, these corridors will soon give way without disrupting my body or yours. Those who understand the science behind space/time/matter/ warp also know that the precarious path is based upon fields of energy that first attract and then repel. Navigators within your space agencies have used this slingshot effect to propel themselves farther than they could have traveled with fuel. Likewise, those who misuse science will at first attract the attention of many only to find that they themselves are beyond the fold when the very science they depended upon repels and then collapses.

The world is replete with secret agendas and conspiracies. No doubt many of these are sinister in origin and effect. The earthquake in the Indian Ocean was not such an event, and the forthcoming volcanic eruptions will not be either. The Moon is influenced to change its face almost every day, but it is not artificially manipulated to do so. The Sun's powerful rays eject radiation that very quickly makes its way to Earth, sometimes powerfully enough to disrupt modern conveniences, businesses and governments. At the heart of these potent migrations of energy is the Sun itself, not those who would harness it, if indeed they could.

Those who invest in conspiracies will reap rewards commensurate with their investment (intent), just as all investors reap their returns. Likewise, those who project their assets into the future will reap a harvest of their own. Those who await the end will have one, and those who expect a new beginning will match their vision with their ability to manifest it. The universe has an extensive menu from which to choose, and one can order a five-course dinner or a bowl of soup à la carte. If you like, you are welcome to linger here on Earth for dessert and cigars, but if you are in a hurry, you can also get a Happy Meal packaged to go and pick it up at the drive-through window on your way to your next destination.

# 19

# *Living on Prana*

*I really enjoy good food, and I think that eating is a joy. I also enjoy listening to cultural music, designing and wearing colorful clothing, and painting provocative art. I have heard that in the near future, we will feed ourselves through the solar waves of our local sun, lose our hair and even wear the same garments. I can see how this might simplify things considerably, but why would our evolution require us to abandon customs that are unique to Earth? Isn't the Earth exceptionally precious as it is—diversity and all?*

The Earth is indeed unique, diverse and precious. Among all other planets there is no other Earth, just as there is no other you. Our Sun has its own unique characteristics, as does the Moon and our solar system, which serves as both neighborhood and community. The universe is mysterious, awe inspiring and ever changing. It could never be described as uniform or commonplace. And the omniverse, well . . .

Almost everything that currently resides upon the Earth eats, drinks or consumes something. Some things—beings—even consume themselves, in a manner of speaking. Does this mean that their evolution is based upon moving away from diversity and toward uniformity? And if it does not, are they doomed to extinction? Couched within your question is a fear that you will somehow lose the individuality that you inherited from your ancestors and others who proudly carried the banner of freedom in advance of your generation. You are not alone in this fear, and we will address it a little later, but perhaps we should explore some of the future possibilities you have listed above first.

## HUMAN BEHAVIOR AND FOOD

Most people largely believe that they must eat to survive, but this is not entirely true. You must provide your body with necessary nutrients, vitamins and other organic substances essential to human nutrition. Among these, sunlight and water are vital to longevity, health and well-being. People also eat to express appreciation, as part of family customs and because it is enjoyable to the physical senses. Humanity's historic eating habits have been diverse and have depended largely upon how food is obtained, stored, used and discarded. Individual, cultural, social, economic and religious factors have always influenced people's eating habits—and continue to do so.

A glance back at ancient Greece would show a people practicing the art of "equilibrium eating," or the desirable middle between two extremes: excess and efficiency. This golden mean of eating existed long before today's food pyramid. The Greeks favored snacks such as chestnuts, toasted wheat and honey cakes. Shall I tell you that some of these were specifically designed to absorb more than their weight in alcohol? A good—and wealthy—host would be sure to have these cakes on hand to extend the life of a banquetlike party called a symposium.

A similar look back at ancient Rome would reveal excessive gluttony, at least within some class structures and societal echelons. Roman cuisine was influenced by the enormous expansion from kingdom to republic to empire, which exposed Romans to new culinary habits and cooking techniques. Interestingly, beef was not very popular then. Cattle were working animals, and their meat was usually very tough.

Modern eating habits have been heavily influenced by these early cultures. The three-course meal, for instance, is Roman in origin and the result of wealthy partygivers wanting to outdo one another. The story is a rich one, but suffice it to say that the Romans, who had radical ideas on many subjects, eventually discovered that the human body was not designed for long-term excess. Known for importing almost everything, wealthy Romans began to import personal Greek physicians and surgeons who eventually prescribed the first reduction regimen, or diet. Many ancient Romans did not believe in dieting, particularly since starvation was a means to punish the wealthy then.

Starvation is a result of a severe reduction in vitamin, nutrient and energy intake. Although most cases of starvation are in third-world countries, the statistics would nonetheless surprise you, and it would not be a farfetched idea to take a good look at the community you live in. Starvation is caused by an imbalance between energy intake and energy expenditure. This imbalance can arise from one or more medical conditions but is more commonly influenced by circumstantial situations, such as famine or poverty.

The most common form of starvation is malnutrition, best defined as the insufficient, excessive or imbalanced consumption of nutrients. Among first-world nations, many people suffer from one or more nutritional disorders conditioned by a shortage or overabundance in the diet. Second- and third-world nations can double and treble these numbers. Malnutrition poses a grave threat to the world's health, and those in a position to do something about it should not ignore their responsibility—not even in the short term. There is enough food on the planet to feed its hungry and enough water to keep the thirsty well hydrated. Humanity would do well to act wisely in this regard and in favor of those who only have a hollow remembrance of a meal in their stomachs.

## THE ABILITY TO LIVE WITHOUT FOOD

Over time and for a variety of reasons, humanity has experimented with eating or avoiding certain foods and food groups. Although a large percentage of today's population consumes beef, pork, chicken and fish, this was not always the case, and it is in fact more recent than you would suspect. Humanity will continue its interest in animal flesh in the short term—less than twenty years—but will lessen its portion size over time as it becomes interested and then accustomed to more plant-based sources of protein. This will not happen overnight but it will seem to. The wiring in your brain will begin to shift from one way of thinking to another, and your palate will follow. In the near future, your sense of smell will become more acute and your sense of taste will follow. Eyesight and hearing have both worsened during your recent technological age—but more on that at another time.

What of those who wish to nourish themselves by other means? For this is not a new subject at all. In fact, in every age and every generation there are those who seek a way apart from the norm, regardless of criticism or ridicule. Those who fill their stomachs with empty foods will empty their mouths of similar words. And those who study the science of nutrition and take into account only the visible spectrum will remain blind to at least half the possibilities. Therefore it is best to explore this with new thought receptors. As the name implies, these new thought receptors allow you to consider subjects that are in your near future without comparison to past conclusions or faulty, incomplete or missing empirical data. In other words, new thought receptors would not conclude that an idea is impossible or ridiculous. Why? Because these receptors typically do not follow the same sequencing path as linear thoughts do.

The human brain has amazing abilities and only a minute amount of these have been tapped thus far. What the brain can conceive of, the body can most likely do, and when your brain opens the door to universal mind, the possibilities are almost endless. Those who believe they can sustain themselves through sunlight or pranic forces more than likely can. Their job is not to convince you of that fact, for that would rob them of vital energy, but to establish within themselves a deep rapport with every aspect that depends upon the vital and essential breath.

"Inedia," which literally means the "ability to live without food" is not a new concept. Many cultures, religions and disciplines have examples in their histories with both substantiated and unsubstantiated accounts of living without food and even without water. Breatharianism, sungazing and vitalism are all related concepts that maintain that humans can sustain their bodies on prana, or the vital force inherent in all things. Previously, esoteric practices ascribed only to Eastern ascetics, these practices have been gaining in popularity in the West as well. The last one hundred years or so have seen a considerable increase in those who endorse and also teach how to live on the energy given off by sunlight. Science has not validated these practices and is not likely to for the time being. Conventional medicine will not lend its support, nor will alternative practices that separate body and mind from spirit. As of this writing, there are only a handful of people upon the Earth who are capable of living on light. The majority of these are not terrestrial in origin, and it is doubtful that they would make their differences public.

There are a few living examples who have adjusted to a moderate lifestyle that is light sustainable, but not in the long term. Some of them would tell you otherwise, but the days ahead will speak for themselves. The Earth is also the modest and humble host to perfected beings who are able to manifest energetic bodies of light at will. Their bodies can appear quite solid, but are in fact isometric crystalline systems that have three equal axes at right angles to one another. It is best to think of these as physical holograms.

## To Live on the Wholeness of Light

Prana, or vital life, is only one of five life-sustaining forces that support living beings. Prana flows through a network of channels that form the structure of the subtle body. It is commonly associated with the breath but can also be found in blood and in other bodily fluids. The auric field has many energetic sheaths that surround and protect it, and one of these is also a pranic sheath. Prana sustains both the physical body and the thought body. It permeates all living things, including the Sun, which is also a source of prana. Some traditions further classify prana into subcategories that direct its vital energy first through basic currents and then onto more subtle faculties.

It is possible to control the breath so as to influence and direct the flow of prana. Those who do are in command of increased physical vitality and mental agility as well as access to the gateway that exists beyond the transits of the body. Although the techniques are rather simple, they must be practiced and understood, as it is possible to encounter adverse effects under certain circumstances. Even ordinary breath is sacred, because at its core is the same primordial energy as that of the all and the All. Controlled or empowered breath enables a connection to the cosmic forces that can lead to profound transformation in a human being. Many spiritual traditions believe that working to establish this link is paramount to all higher levels of attainment.

Our planet, resplendent with diversity, reflects light in a variety of unique frequencies and bandwidths, each offering its own benefits and qualities. Light contains all colors, and supports humanity with subtle but important nutrients. Whole, or white light, is pure and complete. It contains all colors, wavelengths and frequencies; sunlight does not. White light and sunlight are not the same, but the average human would not be able to distinguish between the two.

Although light is always whole, it does not always reflect its full spectrum nor is it always absorbed. Whole light is a pure and excellent whole food, but it may not sustain all beings, particularly those who are in the process of transitioning from one dimension to the next. A candidate who desires to live exclusively on light would need to transmute any remaining obstructions or blockages that would otherwise be deflected by whole light. In this example, the healing properties of full-spectrum light would be drawn to the candidate's impasse, but the wholeness of white light would not. Sunlight cannot at this time provide the average human body with all of the nutrients it requires. It is possible to extract enough pranic force from sunlight to maintain the body at a low level of life force, but shorter intervals are suggested and for specific purposes.

If you wish to live on light, it is best to busy yourself with your fears and concerns, because the light will find these first so that it might heal them, which may not leave enough for you to eat. Without addressing these issues, you would quickly starve and feel that you are not a good candidate for such an intense program. You may retrain your body, but you must understand its language first; you must make it your partner and not deny the requests and messages that it sends to you.

## PRANA ADVANTAGES AND DISADVANTAGES

What are the advantages to living on prana? Those who choose this path must do so consciously and with a favorable disposition and at least moderate health. Candidates should be able to guide the pranic force in sunlight through the breath or through other means to all appropriate physical and energetic channels. This requires knowledge of effective breathing techniques—both shallow and profound. Specific meditations also help to accumulate and store prana. As was said earlier, few on the planet are able to sustain themselves on prana alone; however, those who do so will not hunger or thirst. Their sleep requirements will be less and their energy more balanced over extended periods of time. Those who are exceptionally adept may also be able to slow the ageing process.

What are the disadvantages to living on prana? Without specific and ongoing discipline and under certain influences, it will be difficult to receive enough nutrients. Those who fail to connect with the unique dynamics of their individual needs may not observe subtle changes in the body that indicate a change is needed. A pranic life is not for everyone and is not 100 percent effective given only an average quality of sunlight and air. Those who disregard the guidance above will find that as the body begins to rebel, they feel more hungry and thirsty than ever before. Their bodies will have difficulty in releasing toxins, especially if water is withheld. Some may believe that they are living on prana when they are not. In some cases cells, hair and nails will suffer or ageing may begin prematurely or accelerate.

Can you imagine a near future where supermarket shelves are filled with packaged sunlight? What about pranic breathing chambers? How about antioxidant rejuvenation environments infused with oxygenized light? Indeed, plans are already underway for this and more, but there is no reason to shut down your favorite pizza parlor yet! Your future is yours to make of it what you will. It will be diverse enough for those who enjoy cuisine and fine dining, and even hamburgers and fast food will be around for a while longer. But things will not remain the same as they are today, because you are changing faster than your food is changing. Your needs and desires are changing, and those of your body are changing too. Savor the moments that are yours and those that you are invited to share with others.

## Physical Transitions

Hair and nails are other subjects worth considering. It is interesting to note that while you fear losing your individual creativity in this regard, your current choices are somewhat limited and, for the most part, are determined by your genetic heredity. You struggle against this by chemical and other means and swear that one day you wish to be rid of it altogether. Nonetheless, and for the sake of discussion, in the further or mid-future—which is just more than one hundred years from now— humans will have less total hair upon their bodies than they do now. Over time hair will become a recessive trait and move into a dormant array of the DNA.

This will also affect the hair upon your head, which will grow in different patterns than it does now. You will not become bald in the process, at least not by current standards, and as it's seen from this perspective, the change will be quite attractive for both men and women. Your hair will be slightly more uniform in appearance than it is today, but how it is arranged will remain a matter of choice just as it is today. There will be styles and stylists to suit every expression. You may be curious to know that the earliest Egyptians were quite bald and adorned themselves with many different kinds of headdresses and hats. Their heads were slightly more elongated than yours, and their necks a little longer, even though they were smaller in stature. They were beautiful specimens to behold, thus beauty is indeed always in the eye of the beholder.

## The Future of Textiles

Garments and clothing have a long and varied history on Earth, influenced as much by climate and the availability of materials as by culture and fashion trends. Today, synthetic substitutes have all but replaced the natural skins, silks and cottons of long ago. There will be a reversal in this trend, and those who advocate an organic and natural lifestyle will make inroads—as they do from time to time and as indicated by the cycles of nature.

That aside, humanity is beginning to envision itself as part of a galactic family. It is likely that less than forty years from now, the first colonies will settle on the Moon and also on Mars. As you might imagine, these expeditions will require a completely different style of dress. The necessary garments will be much thinner than the bulky ones worn by astronauts today and made of a material that is "married" to its wearer. These unique garments will be able to regulate the health of the wearer, including vital statistics and mental balance, and they will even predetermine how long each individual can safely remain in such hostile terrains.

Although these garments will be constructed for first- and second-generation space colonies, the fashion industry will adapt and style them to suit those who favor forward-looking styles. Over time similar customizable suits will become widely available to the general population, allowing individuals to program their garments to monitor a variety of health-related functions. Is this a move toward uniformity? Maybe. Or perhaps it is one of many trends, and one of the ways in which humanity accustoms itself to change.

✳     ✳     ✳

You are individual sparks of light and no two are alike, yet you still struggle against both poles of diversity and uniformity. You are one family, and one day you will come to terms with the meaning of this. Until then, celebrate your individual way of life and encourage others to do the same. Offer an opinion if it is invited, but do not impose your will upon another nor judge the decisions they make. The physical earth will continue to evolve in its own precious ways, celebrating the diversity of life in every kingdom. My sentience will do the same, welcoming guests from other worlds, extending words of diplomacy when invited to do so, offering sanctuary to those who request it, nurturing and protecting all that is within my reach, and allowing the wisdom of the All to guide all things in their due course and due time.

# Compassion
# Knows No "Other"

*T*he year 2010 is an interesting, puzzle-like year that will reveal itself uniquely to each individual. It is a year that must be assembled from the inside out. The good news is that it can be assembled in a variety of ways. The bad news is that because it can be assembled in so many different ways, the most creative or correct way to do so might not be discovered until the year is firmly underway—much later than some would prefer. For better or worse, this year will cause you to think on your feet. You will still be able to anticipate and prepare, but perhaps not to the degree that you have been able to until now.

Remember that each year, like a perfect pattern, follows the laws of nature, which does not take for itself what it cannot replace. Therefore, other abilities will replace ones that are less accessible to you. For instance, if you trusted your intuition more, you would not need to prepare and anticipate as much as you do today. Likewise, if you trusted your ability to speak your truth and have it be well received, you would not spend as much time planning and plotting what to say and do next in order to be seen, heard and understood correctly.

## ASSEMBLING YOUR YEAR WITH CREATIVITY

Throughout 2010 you have several opportunities to revisit and remake your core values and to strengthen them in areas that may be weak. This will not be accomplished by challenging them or by throwing the latest crises at them to test their resiliency. Instead, your elemental self will be able to run self-diagnostic exercises designed to enhance that which you are already becoming. This is part of the (r)evolution paradigm already underway.

Again, the good news is that this very useful addition to your physiological being is already in place. On the difficult side, you will learn how to use this ability through trial and error. Your guides and teachers will be at hand to assist in the process, but you will write your owner's manual through the decisions and experiences you make. The most helpful key that can be offered in this regard is to choose that which you are, that which you have and that which you do—knowing that by choosing it and owning it, you are free to change it. There is no need to ignore or reject anything that you have learned and accomplished thus far, but if you allow it to define you, it will defile you too.

As the year unfolds, it may be helpful for you to imagine that the energies of 2010 are something akin to that which arrives marked "basic" or "introductory" so that you can add on to it based upon your ideas and desires. All of the basics are included in the box, so to speak, and it is up to you to begin to build a "model" year for yourself. Although a twelve-month solar year is not something that arrives with an instruction manual, it can be creatively assembled from a variety of influences.

The most important key to establishing a stable year is to use the basics that are offered—already in the box—to build a light but firm foundation and then to focus on the personal attunement and refinement of new paradigm abilities. Concentrating solely on the basic configuration of the year will result in a year in which your basic needs are met, although you may find yourself feeling more needy or needful than you would prefer. By contrast, any creative initiative you introduce will place you at an advantage, and you will feel one step ahead of the pack instead of one step behind.

## HISTORY, FREE WILL AND THE PATH OF EVOLUTION

Have you not wondered why history cannot accurately decode some of its past? This is because timelines flow and float alongside a variety of realities, converging and diverging, accelerating and decelerating, and encouraging humanity to choose its own collective path of evolution. This is one of the most effective ways that free will is expressed upon the planet. Once a path of evolution has been chosen, consciousness and unconsciousness are immediately affected, as is everything else in the last and next reality. Thus history can literally rewrite or erase itself through humanity's own experience.

Until recently, humanity was able to organize and assemble its future based upon memories of years past and years present. But future experiences and the historical past are very flexible things; they can be changed, rearranged and even erased, and history is beginning to do exactly that—erase that which has less of a place in the future in order to advance thoughts and things that do. Those who habitually prefer the past to the present will have a more difficult time this year, as will those who are always comparing this moment or year against the last one. Why compare that which has already been and is now obsolete? Those who do so live at the effect of life, unable to cause, create or coax their thoughts into the now.

How will certain aspects of history be erased? By unmaking the patterns that created the original experiences. Please do not fret in advance over a perceived loss that will not come to pass; the Earth is not a memory thief, and you will remain the owner of all your experiences. But what if the pattern that indicated a propensity for overeating on Fridays were erased or the one that constantly reminded you that your family had a history of diabetes began to fade? Likewise, what if a country or a culture could not remember why they have historically been at odds with another? Or what if the formula for making nuclear bombs did not yield the same results as it has in the past, because the elements did not or could not reorganize themselves in similar fashion? You see, a new idea or pattern can replace an older one and render it obsolete.

## DISSOLVING OLD THOUGHTS AND PATTERNS

Consider that thoughts are things and subject to the principles and laws of animate and inanimate life. These same principles guide that which is inactive, invalid and has lower radiation or intensity. This includes the extinction of species, which is measured in terms of significant reduction in pranic response. A deactivation in life force is a notable field marker; it is a precursor for change. Where is there a lessening of life force in your own life? What patterns or thoughts could be offered or sacrificed to oblivion?

Ever so often it is a good idea to empty closets, containers and cupboards of unneeded items. Usually these are passed along to another who may find use in them or simply take a liking to them, but what if no one did? What if no one wanted or needed your thoughts or things, or anyone else's for that matter? And what if they could not be incinerated or placed in a landfill? In fact, what if you could not think of anything you could do with them or anywhere you could take them to? Well, the Earth has a solution for just about everything, including this.

Dissolving a thought or a pattern is not the same as changing it. Actually it is more like uncreating the thought that unmakes the thing. The world you live in is made of thoughts and ideas that form an agreed on reality. It is now time to discover what thoughts and things of this world are also important and appropriate to the next world. At first you might say, "Everything!" But in 2010, you will begin to think about things differently, and because of that, you will begin to see things differently too. The energetic architecture of 2010 will secure a place for the new paradigm archetypes to come. These will recode and remake what humanity thinks relative to the purpose of the human race. This will invite a change in almost everything moral and social, including the contextual roles that humanity chooses to play.

## CAUTIONARY INFLUENCES AND (R)EVOLUTIONARY DEVELOPMENTS

As an aspect of nature, a year is subject to constructive and destructive elements. These build bridges between here and there, old and new. The energies of the closing year are aware of the newer energies and yield to them in ways that only nature seems to understand. For instance, although winter may linger, it does not resist spring. The year 2009 will pass the baton to 2010. It will not delay to see if there is an honorarium bestowed upon it or a placard placed in its honor. The same cannot be said for those who insist on headlines and limelight.

The year 2010 will know its share of those whose words and works have a proclivity for "exclusive bestowance," a fancy parlor term for those who sell their good name, reputation and fame for a price or a future favor. In this regard, you will note little difference in 2010, except in the swift fall of the newly risen. The world is still hungry for idols and heroes. In the absence of these, it will settle for the self-satisfied and the smug, but not for long! It will toss their bones onto the same heap as those who have been discarded before them. The high are no longer mighty and the mighty fall all too quickly. Follow nature where the rise and fall of the tides are concerned, but if you are unsure, wait to see how much light is left after the shadow has consumed its share.

## HEALING DIVISION AND DUALITY

The necessity to heal divisions belongs to the Piscean Age, which created the divisions to begin with. Divisions can be expressed in many ways, including race, religion, political affiliation, gender, economic class and more. All of these categories, and others as well, will experience a need to heal one or more of the divisions that separate them in the upcoming year. It could obviously be said that this has always been true; nonetheless, the year 2010 will provide ample opportunity for differences to meet at odd and somewhat extreme angles. Why 2010? Because with few exceptions, dualities must reconcile themselves before they can reemerge as pluralities and multiplicities in the next, or Aquarian, age. Dualities, like polarities, oppose themselves. This constant struggle promotes discord, prejudice, judgment and other negations of Spirit. This phenomenon will be played out in a variety of ways within the larger context of the world stage, but it would be wise to expect that the same will somehow transfer to your personal experience.

To heal means to recover and restore to health. Although natural things such as magnets have positive and negative poles, and seasons occur at opposite times of the year, they do not oppose themselves—a crucial difference. That which is in opposition to itself cannot be mindful or healthful until the opposition has been resolved. During the Piscean Age, the most common resolution for opposition has been reversal—as in a reversal of fortune, health, status and so on. This is an old paradigm of thought, and like outdated technology, there is less of a place for it in today's world. Self-reflection, or the ability to see the absolute within oneself, is the quickest path toward redemption of Spirit, and you will find that the finest weavers of life endorse this method.

Another word for duality is baggage. Although you will not be asked to thread the eye of the needle as you cross into the next dimensional age, it is important to be stable and balanced where body, mind and spirit are concerned. The next year and the one beyond it will ask this of you and will ultimately insist upon it. Why wait? The year 2010 will reveal extremes where this subject is concerned, as some long-felt symptoms are painlessly lifted and reversed while others seem entrenched and hopelessly deadlocked. A few leaders and countries once friendly to one another will turn their backs on situations when they matter most, exposing themselves as the world watches. Those who nod in approval at such reversals will experience setbacks of their own, perhaps at the hands of a beloved or trusted friend. Light will be cast on shadow this year, and the worst offenders will be exposed without privilege or prejudice.

Do not fear the lingering glow of imperfect light where your life is concerned. Your shadow grows shorter and has already been touched by the light of the New Age.

## EXPOSING INJURIES AND INJUSTICES

The complexities of modern human life will continue to spill over in 2010 onto ornate conference room tables and simple kitchen tables alike. Few were spared in this regard in 2009, and 2010 will continue to spill the contents of an already opened can of worms. No day or year is ever a repeat of the last, for although the universe is efficient and economical by nature, it is also creative and imaginative. The can of worms has been opened, but worms are ideally suited for wiggling and squiggling their way out of reach, moving deeper and into the creases and crevices where they might hide in an environment that is more to their liking. Interestingly, worms cannot resist rainy days, emerging from the darkest recesses to bask on wet surfaces in the same way that you might bask in the warm sunlight. In case you have missed it, the point of this inventive metaphor is to suggest that inevitably, even those who squirm out and away from view or from the grasp of the legal system will still find themselves inexplicably drawn to the surface by their own nature and by that which they most crave, the limelight.

The world is full, fat and overly ripe with juicy secrets now. These will seep, pop and explode onto the world stage this year, pointing the way to those who would prefer to hide behind the idle and innocent. To be more specific, 2010 will be a year that will have conspiracy theorists saying, "I told you so!" But if you are of a mind to do so, do so quickly because those who will be exposed are masters of disguise and will put on a different mask long before you are able to gloat in front of your friends. As the players change masks, they will also change the scene, the environment and more. You may spot them in the crowd again, but only because their scorn and contempt at having been temporarily "caught" will leave behind a wake in which others fall. Like any snare, it will trap innocent and guilty alike. Where is the justice, you say? As always, it is in the hands of those who lead and in the heavy footsteps of those who follow. Justice is impartial and evenhanded, but it does not always seem fair—a lesson that even a child learns early on. Those who cry out over prejudice and inequality must do more than show their outrage: They must display their own abilities and perform to their own potential. Currently neither the world's system of law nor its application conveys the qualities of true merit and integrity.

Now, remember that the world stage is simply a bit grander than your own; the celebrity faces are only a little better known. The cautions and influences of the year remain in effect for the young and old and for the seekers and keepers of truth. See how well you keep to the law of truth this year. The law of truth is one of the most ancient ones, and you have carried it with you from life to life. You may not be able to recite it verbatim, but you become aware of it whenever you stand beside it rather than astride it. See how you tell the truth here and not there, to this person and not the other? Certainly you have the right do so and justification enough too, but that which is right and just is not blind; it is made of living consciousness—the strongest and longest living of all life fibers. Bear this in mind, particularly this year, as the fabric of lesser fibers continues to unravel at a greater pace. If you will sound the horn of truth, let it be heard in your own realm as well; if you will drape yourself in the flag of peace, sleep warm under its covers at night when the light shines less, and if you will point fingers of truth at the world stage, be willing to lose your anonymity in the process.

## CAUTIONARY NOTES: REDUCING RISK AND VULNERABILITY

Each year is a little like a roadmap—with some clearly marked areas and others left to the imagination. Cautions, detours and points of interest are marked for you, but only you can decide what areas of the map you will visit and how long you will stay. Your roadmap is an individual one, but your journey can include many companions. Notice that your roadmap does not tell you where you can go, how fast you can go or whom to bring along. This is your part, and you will learn much about life based upon the decisions you make along these lines.

I extend to you this caution then, and ask that you apply it throughout the year: Choose your companions well, and base your decisions upon a compassionate heart. Be so bold as to peer into the heart of those who accompany you on your path and in your dreams. Do not obscure their light nor add your own bias to their truth. Do your best to see them as they are and not as you imagine they could be. Listen to what they say and ask yourself: If it is necessary, am I willing to hear the same words every day?

It is time, particularly this year, to choose your companions wisely, because the influences of this year are many, and they will bear on you more than you can see from your current vantage point. The year 2010 is a heavily conditioned year, and the clearest among you will be swayed to think and to do in ways uncommon and unclear. For instance, the influences of this year might invite a trusted friend to suggest a get-rich-quick scheme; something that neither of you would consider in another year. While you cannot be on your guard around family and friends, you can watch for changes in temperament, character and personality. Pay particular heed to excess humor or to its absence.

This next year will also invite new visitors into your life; some of these will be long-lost friends from lifetimes ago, and others will be new, temporary or seasonal. In this regard, we could call 2010 the year of the exchange student, because at times it may seem to you that you are temporarily living where someone else might or in ways that are strange to you. Pay specific attention to the demeanor of those who have the ability to walk on your life instead of in it. What is the lesson here? Whenever possible, do not allow yourself to feel oppressed by the words or deeds of others, but see these as brief encounters, transitory moments that are short-term and short-lived. When you discover that someone has been less than genuine with you, resist the need to act out so that you do not become ensnared in the moment.

## You're Moving into a Tertiary System

The year 2010 is a year of karmic attraction. Karma exists peacefully in the null and the void until providence calls it forth. Karma is the companion of destiny, and your thoughts and actions determine when and how the two companions will travel together, if at all. The Year 2010 is a karmically charged year and its influences will be felt, at least to some extent, throughout the year. Why? Because things and thoughts that were created in moments of duality must be re-paired with one another again so that they can be dissolved.

Duality belongs to a binary system of paired opposites—one of the reasons why the third dimension is so dense. Before you dismiss this world, you must leave it in good order for those who follow. You are moving into a trinary system where words and deeds are not opposite in nature. For instance, in a tertiary system, you would need to take two steps forward only to take one step back. Whenever possible, do not tug at the drapery of the past, for all too quickly you will find yourself tripping over its density, unable to put things back as they were without re-pairing them first.

## DO NOT HOLD BACK COMPASSION

As we have examined the cautionary notes that 2010 will sound, it would be advantageous to explore the year's special advantages too. The fact that compassion is the keynote in all things is not new, but where does one get compassion when it is not readily available? When compassion is not readily available, it is because conditioning obscures it. Conditioning is numbness and the result of the taming and habituation of the mind so that it becomes disconnected from the heart. An overly conditioned life is less able to refrain from causing harm. Many of humanity's most ancient prayers called for souls to be delivered from human conditioning and the harm associated with this. Those who are most susceptible to conditioning will have the most difficulty seeing or easing suffering, whether it is their own or another's.

Compassion is one of three central virtues where humanity is concerned. More than an emotion, it is a feeling that gives rise to an active desire to alleviate suffering. Interestingly, the word "compassion" actually means: to suffer together with. It is also related to being patient, or the quality of patience. Compassion is a shelter for the soul and a warm embrace for the distress of humanity; it is that which moves the heart to act in a good way against the pain of others in order to heal the self. It is self-full rather than selfless.

The year 2010 will carry the note of compassion to every corner of the world. Compassion has the special ability to dissolve the inert purposeless often found in that which has been exceedingly conditioned. And yet unless you will also offer it to yourself, it will be of less use to the world you live in or the one that follows. A sage once said, "Kindness gives to an other. Compassion knows no 'other.'" This year is accompanied by a deep well of compassion. Dip your ladle as many times as you will, and you will not be disappointed. Offer the ladle to others, and your own goodwill is multiplied.

## THE PURPOSE OF LIFE IS LIFE ITSELF

The words we have exchanged here do not foretell a certain future, but they do contain tokens of truth that can be invested and inserted into your life where you most see fit. Couched within key words and phrases are figurative symbols and representations that can be decoded and translated into a language that is both energetic and practical.

The words can be customized so that they tell a story—perhaps your own—and they will become further enlivened as you apply them to your own unique circumstances and affairs.

How you see the year ahead will determine the quality of what you practice in the world you live in. Pledge not to live by theory or intellect alone, and confirm this pledge by developing a spiritual practice that supports your words and your deeds. A spiritual practice is not something you do; it is something that you become as you apply its principles in daily life. Remember that the purpose of life is life itself. The purpose of humanity is to pose and solve all of the great problems, and in so doing, leave no other proof of that solving other than the elements and forces of nature or life itself. Whenever possible, walk lightly upon the Earth so that you will not need to retrace your steps just to revisit and erase a heavy footprint.

# Does Gaia
# Believe in God?

*I just have one small question. Do you believe in God?*

Your question is short, but it is not small. It is an interesting question and of obvious importance to you. Uncertain times carry uncertainty into almost every area of life, creeping into the deeper recesses of one's thoughts and challenging even those things and thoughts that have been accepted at face value for eons of time. But may I engage you peacefully and politely by suggesting that your question is a challenge designed to confront the science that enables channeling, the channel who is now veiled behind these words and your own doubts and beliefs about the subject? No matter! It is simply best to state the known in one's search for the unknown. With this in mind, let's begin with what is known about God versus what is believed.

## FORMS OF BELIEF

Interesting telling points distinguish philosophers, scientists, followers of religious faith and other lay people. One of these is the use of the terms "belief" and "knowledge," because while some people make a distinction between what they know and what they believe, others do not. It is human nature to accept a belief as a known fact, particularly when exploring a subject or statement that is considered accurate, true or justified. A belief in God or a higher power or authority is a perfect example of a concept appropriately named "justified true belief," which describes a traditional relationship in which a belief is also considered knowledge if the belief is true and if the believer has a justification, meaning a necessarily plausible assertion that may or may not include evidence. False beliefs, even if true and sincere, would not be justified under this concept, because they are not necessary and plausible to a large enough percentage of the population.

Beliefs are assumptions that humanity makes about itself, about others and about how it expects things are or will one day be. Beliefs are also definitive ideas about how individuals and groups think things really are. When a large group or segment of the population thinks similarly, it often believes similarly as well. A justified belief sees other beliefs as less than just. Most beliefs presume a subject and an object of belief, which requires a subjective and objective God, an internal and external relationship with God. Beliefs are further divided into core beliefs, those that you might actively consider; dispositional beliefs, those that you simply choose to believe or disbelieve; and occurent beliefs, those that you are currently considering based upon stored knowledge or unconcluded wisdom. Based upon the foregoing, do you know what part of your being believes in God? It may be more likely that a part of your being knows God, so let's explore further.

## KNOWLEDGE AND FAITH

Just as with beliefs there are many different forms of knowledge, each one important in its own way. Scientific knowledge, for instance, is a method of inquiry that focuses upon gathering empirical, observable and measurable evidence. It is subject to specific principles of reasoning, the collection of data, experimentation and formulation and testing of hypotheses. Partial knowledge acknowledges that in most realistic cases it is not possible to have an extensive or exhaustive understanding of a subject and that most real problems can be solved by combining a partial understanding with the proper context and other data. Situational knowledge, as the name implies, applies to a specific situation and is often embedded in language, culture and tradition. Other forms of knowledge include trial and error, learning from direct experience, secondhand knowledge and discovery. Do you know how you know what you know, or do you believe deeply in what you believe that you know about God?

Knowledge about God and belief in God are supported by faith. Faith is the confidence and trust that one places upon truth; it is the trustworthiness of a person, thing or idea. Faith has a special advantage in that it involves a concept of past events and future outcomes. Faith does not require logical proof or material evidence. Informally, faith and trust are similar, but in this regard, faith would more appropriately connote a context of religion or spirituality, where belief in a transcendent reality with a supreme being is implied. Faith is the point of view of the mind that a certain statement or belief is true. The mind accedes [accepts] belief based upon declarations by accepted forms of authority, including people, books, doctrine and scripture. Faith encourages the acquisition of knowledge and growth. Those who believe and also know God have faith in their beliefs.

Although you may not agree that faith is within your field of concern, I would tell you otherwise. Faith, like its counterpart hope, rises and falls during seasons of discontent. Faith is also affected by economic conditions, changes in lifestyle and living situation, sickness and especially when others in one's family or community experience a change of heart in regard to their spiritual beliefs. When faith and hope waver, the individual and the collective mind of humanity suffers a kind of stroke, paralyzing some thoughts and exaggerating others. A spiritual stroke is like a great divide between mountain ranges—there is no clear path between here and there. One must pick one's way in roundabout ways and up and over rocky crags. I will tell you what I know and believe about God, but only some of it will meet with your approval, because your mind and your heart currently wander the great divide between what you believe, what you know, what you hope and the direction that members in your immediate family are beginning to take.

## THE MANY VERSIONS OF GOD

The God you reference in your question is a deity. A deity is a supernatural immortal being who is holy, divine, sacred and worthy of great respect. God is the sole deity insofar as many world religions are concerned and the principal deity in many belief systems. God is omniscient, omnipotent, omnipresent and omnibenevolent. He is eternal and necessary to human existence. The modern concept of God is one in which He is personal and active in the organization and governance of the universe and the world you live in. God is invisible but is thought to dwell in holy places such as heaven, supernatural planes and celestial spheres. God is made manifest to humanity through the effects of His omnipresence. Although immortal, God is assumed to have a personality that is perfect, pure and free of defect. I know this God, because it is one of the versions of God that humanity prefers and has a close bond with.

Another version of God assumes immortality, consciousness, intellect, desire and emotion. Natural phenomena in the form of floods, lightning and earthquakes are attributable to God, as are miracles and other wonderful acts. God is the controlling authority in the various aspects of human life and afterlife. He is the director of fate, the giver of law and the moderator of moral obligation. The ultimate judge of human worth, He is also the creator of earth and heaven. I know this God too, because humanity studies Him, lives and is guided by His hand.

I know another God too. He is divine and infinite simplicity, perfection and goodness. This God is whole and without parts. He and his attributes are one. He is the God of truth and goodness, which is also identical to His being. This simple being is indivisible rather than composite: His characteristics are not made up of thing upon thing. His properties are also His being, which is not true of any created being. He is complete in all ways, and He is the cause of all that exists. He is the greatest in all things and the least of all too, and this without exception. This God is also mine—because He is your God, he is also mine.

Aside from the God of religion, I know the God of philosophy. His essence is inexpressible. He is concerned with ideas that are incomprehensible to most. These cannot be expressed in general terms or in common language for they would render that which is ineffable mundane. This abstract God is complex and his nature is paradoxical. He is symbolic gesture, illogical statement, principle and reason, and intrinsically impossible to understand. I have attended the schools of thought that uphold this version of God and bear witness to the existence of an existential God. This version of God is as real as the other versions.

## THE LIVING MIND

My favorite version is not as popular as the others because it exists beyond humanity's capacity to conceive. This inconceivable beingness is the light that gives meaning to the darkness of being. This being and nothingness are closely related. Nothingness and All That Is are one in this beingness. All That Is cannot be comprehended by human senses— not today, tomorrow or yesterday. It is unknowable, indefinable, eternal, invisible and formless. It is living mind. No language can describe or define the All. Its being is so still as to be indistinguishable from nonbeing. I do not know this God/Being/All That Is, for to believe in that which exists without need of existence is folly. I do not believe in this being either, for its existence does not require my belief or that of any other being. To do so would limit my relationship with it—an injustice, to say the least. This All is a substantial part of the reality that underlies all appearances and manifestations that are called "life," including matter and nonmatter, energy and nonenergy, thought and no-thought, and there is that which exists beyond this.

As your life continues to unfold, your beliefs will change, shaped by the thoughts and experiences that you draw to you. Your individual existence that currently believes you are a human being also believes that it must fight for itself in this world. This part of you has a sense of "doership" that must establish a purpose for its existence, but it is ultimately unaware and unconscious of its own true nature. Human nature and the mind that occupies its time compulsively thinks, and then thinks about what it is thinking. It does so in order to assure its own future existence, because it does not know that the present moment and the eternal self are one and the same. The human self does not know that it is made of nothingness and believes in error that it is made of something. This is because the human mind dwells within the living mind and is subject to the laws of created things. As one of your mystics once said, you are the eternal principle and the temporal process; you are the impressure of nothingness into something.

✳    ✳    ✳

Do not think for a moment that Gaia hopes to challenge or change your life stance on God, religion or the nature of your being. Your world view, values and viewpoints are preserved by your own will and by approval of All That Is. Your way of life is well guided and moved by the same forces of nature that pilot these words. Know that I am one with your thoughts and with your beliefs too. They are no strangers to me, and I find no provocation in your attitudes and convictions. Let quarrel be with those who object for all is at rest here. The same principles and ideas that created the Earth also created the moment we now share, and ideas beyond ours will inspire the future we will both share. New concepts will present fodder to philosophers, thinkers, logicians, academicians, theorists, truth seekers and dreamers. And the one that was in first place before a place was made will yet be.

# The Once and Future Pope

*There are both ancient and new prophecies that relate to the office of the Pope and the future of the Catholic religion. Would you please comment on the recent passing of the Pope and the impact that his passing might have upon the world? Any insight as to the future of the world's religions would also be very much appreciated.*

A comment is perhaps all that can be offered, for anything more than an observation might be considered an opinion, and opinions all too quickly become judgments, evaluations, assessments and conclusions, and these are generally based upon less-than-desirable evidence. Unfortunately, such accounts are hastily adopted by the public, which has a greater circulation rate than any publication ever to be in print.

## PROPHECY AND PREDICTION

The problem with prophecies is that one cannot draw a proper conclusion from them based upon a simple observation of facts, as these are often lacking. More often than not, experts are called upon to interpret them, but the most they can offer is their expert opinion, do you see? A prediction is a statement made regarding what it is believed will happen at some point in the future relative to one or more subjects. Predictions can be based upon present indicators, past experience or any other objective or subjective phenomena—including channeling.

In other words, anyone can predict anything, from next week's weather to next year's pope. If things turn out the way the general population expected—in other words, without the need of an oracle's toolbox—both the predictor and the prediction will fall by the wayside, making way for the next set of oracles-in-the-making to try their luck.

On the other hand, if the results are surprising and unknowable to the average person, the predictor is elevated overnight to the status of a prophet. History has marked many of these, and although an official job description for a maker of predictions does not exist, the number of job applicants never seems to diminish, present timeline included.

A prophecy, unlike a prediction, can span many centuries or lifetimes, according the prophet a few extra chapters in the scrolls of history, at least until he can be measured by the legacy of his words, or those that have been attributed to him. Prophecies differ from predictions in that they infer that the will of a deity or a supernatural power has inspired the prophecy. Some believe that otherworldly powers instill powers within or bestow powers upon a prophet, who then reveals or interprets the significance of the prophecy to those of less spiritual privilege. Again, if all goes well, the prophet is well on his way to becoming an inspirational leader or teacher, an advocate for an idea, deity or cause.

Unfortunately for most, history has recorded more one-hit wonders than true visionaries. Only a handful or so have done more than shed light on what has already been foreshadowed, ordained or otherwise chosen. True prophets leave behind empty shoes that few can fill, but herein lies the rub: Humans tend to both favor and fear their prophets, be they foolish or sage, while ignoring the simple but profound words and deeds of true visionaries. Those who croon from the balconies and the rooftops, like birds with brightly colored feathers, often have more to display than to say.

## THE MOST RECENT POPE
## HOPED TO LIVE THROUGH THE END TIMES

The most recent Pope, John Paul II, delayed the time of his passing as long as he could. Frail and ill, he maintained the position he was elected to, as ordained by those who had elected him, as well as the divine power that resounded throughout his being. He was aware of the many prophecies regarding his office and his person. Some of these are well known and widely available to the public, but others have remained private. The Vatican owns the most extensive collection of writings in the world. The Vatican library is a private, temperature-controlled vault, encompassing over a million volumes of books, scrolls, plates, templates and steles. The various texts are in many languages, some that are common to the modern world, some that have long since become obsolete and others that are purely symbolic in nature. John Paul made frequent visits to this library, allowing his instincts, dreams and visions to guide him accordingly. His personal attendants also conducted extensive research for him on a variety of subjects, some of which could be considered occult in nature.

The office of the Pope has been no stranger to controversy or conspiracy, and John Paul felt it important to continue to protect the Church in its sovereign rights. He believed in the sovereign wisdom of others, but he also believed that the Catholic Church was the best shepherd when it came to tending the world's flocks. He honored other world religions, and even admired the earthiness of certain pagan rituals, though he would not publicly admit this. He believed in reverence and penitence, and he feared for humanity's future based upon the views of the world's present leaders.

Pope John Paul II believed deeply in some of the prophecies, such as the ones brought forward by the children of Fatima; he also quietly and modestly discredited others. He did not reveal the prophecies of Fatima as they were originally put to him, and thus they are still misunderstood or misconstrued by most. His life was one of privilege as well as suffering, as all lives are to some extent. In the latter part of his life, he studied eschatology, the branch of theology that concerns doctrines related to the end times. He very much wanted to experience this time period for himself and to assist humanity in avoiding what dangers might be in his power to avert. To this end, he clung to life longer than he would have otherwise, bearing physical burdens and raising alarm within the higher echelons of the Church from time to time. He chose to surrender his office and his life in the same moment.

## THE NEW POPE FACES CHALLENGES FROM THE POWERFUL

As to the future of the office of the Pope, much remains to be seen. Conflict between conservative, moderate and liberal thinkers exists everywhere now, and the Church is no exception. All organized religions are currently under scrutiny, and the infrastructure that has supported them thus far is overburdened and stressed. Earthquakes are tearing at the landscape in many places throughout the world; they will do the same in other environments as the strain becomes insurmountable. As of this writing, the new Pope has just been elected and has chosen the name of Benedict XVI. Within moments of his coronation, predictions as to the possible short tenure of his reign were already circulating. So that such immature thoughts are not derived from this text, it will be said that Benedict, like benediction, is an expression of good wishes and approval. In the Roman Catholic Church, it is the state of being blessed by the Host, which is exactly what the newly elected and crowned Pope experienced.

It is possible that this new Pope will be a man of great power, influenced equally by his morals and personal politics as by the movement of his spirit. It is also possible that he will be no more than a figurehead, with the true power of the Church wielded from deep within the halls of the Vatican, and beneath it as well. Either way, the existing prophecies will not diminish him. Already they surround and enfold this new pontiff, because they were designed to do just that. The office of the Pope is the human extension of the Church. As such, it is important to remember that it is the Church that has assigned a voice to God, and not the other way around. With great pomp and circumstance, the new Pope will be heralded by the public and then paraded about for all the world to see, but only the people can decide what rights and privileges will be accorded to him. Visiting dignitaries will visit him and invite him to visit their homeland in return. But the powerful who have made their own accord with God will be more wary, lest an uninitiated newcomer onto the world stage endanger their own agenda.

## AN INTERPRETATION OF THE BIBLE AND ORGANIZED RELIGION

The Bible is encoded with allegory that represents the movement of the soul in its deeper aspects. Many of the Bible's depictions are symbolic in nature, as are its characters and events. Some depict moral obligations, whereas others express political meaning through scenes and stories; only a few of these can be taken literally. The Bible is a digest, a compilation depicting the opinions, obsessions and rites of passage of a bygone era. Those who are most passionate about it today were the leaders and followers of its subject matter long ago as well. It is a book of many chapters. Some are soft, sublime and poetic, whereas others are filled with hyperbole—deliberate and obvious exaggerations meant to agitate or instill fear.

The future path of organized religion is the same as that of unorganized religion, and the same can be said of all spiritual sects, beliefs and minor ordinations. It is through both lit and unlit corridors of light and dark that each being must explore concept as well as ritual. This is the true purpose of the support one should expect to receive along one's endeavored path. All else is superfluous to the first cause and can be discarded as soon as its false light is discovered. Long ago, organized religion was a forum for gathered and disseminating teachings from different sources and places. Science, structure, language and spirit were all discussed in equal measure, but the lesser mind is easily influenced, and it was not long before it was easily controlled and manipulated. The lesser mind does not question; it does not find fallacy within authority. Instead, it seeks the absolute—not by becoming it, but by succumbing to it. Absolute authority—like absolute power—eventually crumbles, because it cannot sustain its own weight, which by nature is quite dense. As long as humans remain spiritually divided, they will be susceptible to control by institutions that require membership and impose allegiance.

The new Pope will hold open the door to the Church, as any good shepherd is obligated to do. How wide that opening—how narrow its interpretation—is still to be seen. In the days that follow, one religion's gain will be another's loss, and all religions will tilt and repolarize themselves along with the rest of the planet. Change will be slow for some and quite swift for others as secrets long held silent are revealed. As the world continues to reorganize its priorities, its governments and its lands, religion will be forced to follow suit. The mighty will surely fall and the humble will rise, but without truth to guide reason, they too shall fall from great heights.

## THE AUTHORITY OF SPIRIT

The conflicts of spirit will be many, but the rewards will be greater still. Ask yourself from whence the Pope derives his power and then see if your own source is lesser, greater or equal. The door to spirit is always open, even though its paths are many. Truth, though not elusive, can never be captured. It can only be embraced, and temporarily at that. As humans continue to rediscover their path, they will also choose a different future. These truths might be temporarily harbored behind closed doors that offer only limited admittance, but the evolution of consciousness will soon offer more choices.

Those who concentrate on issues of survival might miss the more subtle whispers of the newer truths that have only recently become known. Therefore, choose a course that is steady and firm, but resilient. Anticipate, explore and then resolve to respond. Immediate action or reaction is not always the most prudent choice. Be creative and expansive in all of your endeavors, and you will be wiser tomorrow than you are today. Listen to the predictions that are offered, but extract the knowledge from the babble that hides it. Ask by whose authority a prophecy exists, and then see if that being holds authority where you are concerned.

# The Gift of Life
# Continues to Give

*A few of my friends and I get together once a week to debate subjects and questions of interest to each of us. Although we tend to agree on many subjects, we have found no commonality among us on the questions that follow. Would you be kind enough to offer your perspective? I have heard that it is not okay to contact dead relatives or friends on our own or through psychics and mediums because it delays or disturbs their spiritual progress. Is this true? Secondly, suppose we attempt to contact someone who we know has transitioned, but who might have already incarnated again. Who or what are we contacting?*

Each being, incarnate or otherwise, is in command of all of the resources at his disposal, and the spiritual progress he might attain is not measured by how many delays or deviations he experiences. With spiritual progress, the glass is always at least half full and never half empty. The law of correspondence indicates that while incarnate upon the Earth, there is an urge to define oneself by what has not yet been accomplished or understood, whereas beyond the Earth plane, celebrations honor the slightest move toward wholeness. There is no measuring stick to hold you to account or to judge your crimes against yourself or others. Your PhD from Harvard is worthless beyond the dimension you now occupy. Likewise, murderous hands and thoughts also dissolve.

Spiritual progress is measured dimensionally, and each dimension has certain attributes and elements that are associated with it. For instance, the third dimension is associated with growth through struggle. Right from the start, there is a struggle to birth one's physical body, and then to maintain it so that it will last long enough to accomplish what one has set out to do. This is true for all beings and kingdoms, although consciousness certainly plays a part. The physical elements associated with the Earth plane are carbon and crystal. Opposite in appearance but similar in vibration, these represent the lower self and the higher self. The nonphysical elements associated with the Earth plane are ether and akash, representative of Spirit's ability to act upon potential. Although ether and akash are both nearly invisible, their association with the physical realm makes them measurable under certain circumstances.

## IT IS NOT POSSIBLE TO IMPAIR THE PROGRESS OF THOSE WHO HAVE PASSED ON

All that you are now and all that you have ever been exist as energy. This energy can be traced backward and forward and through both the inner and outer worlds. Through density and light, all that is individually and uniquely you stands out from among the rest. Considering the subject of cremation for a moment, we might note that ash remains with the physical plane; akash, or the experiential energy attained in the life, remains with the astral plane; and ether, the spirit essence associated with the life, moves dimensionally as governed by the soul's progression. Energy dissolves but does not disappear, do you see? The existence of someone or something cannot be erased or completely obliterated—this is a master law.

It is not possible to impair the progress of those who have passed beyond this dimension, because their physical and nonphysical elements have been rearranged to suit the needs of their next experience. The same applies to the buried, the mortared and the martyred, and to those whose remains have been scattered to the four winds as dust.

Still, ether and akash take a long time to dissolve, and the residue they leave behind, sweet or acrid as it may be, finds temporary respite in that which seems most familiar. Scents associated with a certain place or being often remain discernible, as well as memories associated with loved ones, which sometimes seem almost more real than is possible. This is because the energy associated with these events or beings is now shared between multiple dimensions of understanding; it is no longer just yours or just theirs. This sharing of like or common energies is exactly what allows you to contact your beloved friends and family.

It is normal to expect that there would be less interest in the dimension one has recently transferred from. For instance, if you had recently graduated from a university, how much interest would you have in the grammar school you once attended? You see, the ties lessen and your interest becomes more of a sweet-tinged curiosity, akin to perusing a photograph album or a yearbook. As with all things, the level of interest between dimensions is unique to the individual soul and the family associated with it.

## FOLLOWING THE TRAIL LEFT BY A LOVED ONE

If your connection to your friend or relative was a strong one, the need for a psychic, medium or other intermediary is not necessary, but you must trust the connection that is already present, and then work to establish and strengthen it. Some find a deeper, more meaningful connection when it is a personal exchange, and others find greater benefit and clarity with the assistance of an adept. By the way, not all channels are skilled in such endeavors, nor do they want to be. There are those who believe that visitations from the departed will impair their own progress, the very opposite of what your question implies.

You may or may not be aware that the loved one you have contacted has moved on, because in general terms, you will be contacting the residue of energy that is left behind. Like bread crumbs or the comet's trail, this will only guide you so far and you will always be one or more steps behind, at least from your current perspective. Generally, if the being has moved into not only another dimension but a new life as well, there will be even less of an interest in crossing paths for old times' sake. Of course, there are exceptions to this, and certain bonds defy the laws of time and dimension.

To sum up, each lifetime is but a role to play. One's presence in any one life is most significant in the present moment. If you wish to communicate with a family member, a friend or other beloved one, do so now. Why wait and wonder if your true feelings have found their way to your intended recipient? Likewise, if your words have malicious intent or are purposeless in meaning, why create a trail that will have an energetic residue of its own? Whenever possible, be clear in both words and intent. Express feelings as accurately as possible, taking responsibility for all that you are and do. Take action when it is appropriate that you do so, not in order to elicit a reaction or response on the part of another. If your thoughts and feelings are muddy, recycle them until they become clearer and of benefit to the environment you would offer them into. Live in the present moment, while remembering that all moments are as one—expansive, collective and dimensional.

## ON ORGAN TRANSPLANTS

*In cases where transplanted organs are used to renew or enhance the life of another, does the donor's essence or energy follow the recipient? Do the two become linked in some meaningful way? Does it matter whether the donor makes the choice to donate in life or others decide upon his passing?*

Life—including all that it animates, contains and sustains—is purposeful. Every cell, atom and creative thought is designed to be of service to itself and to the whole. The heart is designed to complement the needs of the other organs as well as to unite the entire organism that comprises the human body. Hemispherical acknowledgment—recognition of more than one side—is evident in organs such as the eyes, lungs and kidneys. Each of these can perform approximately one and one-half times their required function before becoming overly fatigued and rendering themselves ineffectual. Likewise, an average person can carry one and one-half times his or her weight when in excellent physical condition or when life demands the extraordinary. A human being can also assume one and one-half times an average amount of responsibility before suffering any loss due to overburdening stress. These averages can change very quickly during extreme environmental conditions, and when they do, both the inner and the outer world of the individual are restructured forevermore. For instance, the body never forgets the life-altering effects and subsequent decisions that are made as a result of a heart attack.

## BODY REGENERATION IS A GIFT FROM HUMANITY'S ANCIENT ANCESTORS

Long ago, at another time and in another place but still within your cellular memory, there existed a species of beings who were also humanoid in nature, although not terrestrial in composition. An unfortunate series of environmental factors crippled this species, debilitating their bodies and significantly reducing their numbers. Finally, a team of experts was able to isolate the source of the trouble, and they set about the arduous task of bypassing certain organs, restructuring others and reorganizing the body's ability to rebalance itself. The goal was to teach the depleted aspects of both being and body to relearn their relationship to the whole, whereby nurturing wellness would replace the struggle to survive. Within a few decades, this species, which had nearly annihilated itself, returned from near extinction. They thrived in both physical wellness and spiritual health until evolution carried them into and through the shift, whereupon they became nonphysical in nature. Without going into great detail at this time, and for the sake of remaining attuned to one subject, we will simply acknowledge this species as one of your genetic ancestral parents.

Memories of the ability to implement self-correcting changes still exist within your cellular makeup, and from them you have derived many of the organ-transplant procedures that are used today. Although these memories have served you well, there is much that you are only beginning to remember, such as how to successfully regenerate rather than clone organs. These technologies require the consciousness of the body to request this from itself while it supports and then completes the process. It is a simultaneous three-step process. For the most part, humans do not yet embrace the consciousness or the perfection within each cell, and as long as separation exists, humans will hold themselves apart from answers that involve unity and the healing that accompanies these answers.

On the other hand, humans have devised other means of bypassing and reconstructing the body's organs when necessary. The mere fact that you are able to transplant an organ from one body into another is an acknowledgment that humanity is indeed one great organism, a giant beingness that likes to think of itself as separate and individual. Individuality allows you to experience yourselves as creative and unique and to perceive others as distinctly different from you. Anomalies within the genetic contributions you carry mark differences in blood type, organ size and adaptability to change. These subtleties further accentuate beliefs in separateness, and because you believe them, your bodies do too.

## ORGAN TRANSPLANTS ARE PROOF THAT YOU ARE ALL ONE

A successful transplant relies upon a willingness to receive or import something foreign, and heretofore carry and care for it as if it were one's own. It seems easy enough to imagine, but let's place it in another context. Imagine that you are an Israeli mother who is losing her child to disease and cannot save him. In order not to lose herself in the process, she is told that she must receive the child of a Palestinian woman who has herself recently succumbed to struggle and relinquished her body in the process. In essence, the choice is to receive the child of an enemy and to nurture and love him as if your very life depended upon it, do you see? As long as both body and beingness respond to transplants thusly, their success will be limited. A belief in separation on the part of the being is tantamount to an instruction to the body to mount a full-scale response to an impending foreign invasion.

Consciousness is the key by which the door to this subject will be changed forever. The recipient and the donor are no different—even in life or death, there is no difference. Once the illusion of separation is seen as just that, compatibility between donors and recipients will increase, and the need for antirejection drugs will decrease. In the meantime, and whenever possible, it is important that the donor be as conscious as possible when choosing to become a donor. For instance, it is best to avoid thinking, "After I'm gone, they can do whatever they want with what's left, since I'm not going to need it anymore," because the energy of that which is carelessly discarded may indeed be carried forward. This does not link the donor and the recipient as your question indicates, but it does reduce the life force and the vitality of the experience. Would you rather your dinner consist of a meal that was prepared especially for you, or would you be just as pleased with what was left over from another's dining experience?

Immediately upon the death of an individual, and sometimes even slightly before, vital organs are harvested from one body, stabilized and preserved, and then rushed to a needful and waiting individual. As hopeful recipients take turns wondering in agony if their long wait is over, a struggle for the organ itself is developing in hospital corridors all over the world. Vital organs have become commodities: bought, sold and traded behind the closed doors of even the most reputable medical facility. The sale of such organs funds research in areas where funding is often in short supply or nonexistent. It also helps defray the cost of lobbyists and other professional haranguers who must curry attention in ways and places where discretion and indiscretion meet. In other words, the donor and the recipient have a third, not-so-silent partner who not only influences the vitality of the energy but the direction of the organ itself. The answer to your question—a seemingly simple one—has more twists and turns than the path of a one-eyed ox tethered to a blind persons cart!

## ADVICE FOR HOPEFUL RECIPIENTS, KIND DONORS AND BROKERS OF ORGANS

If you are a hopeful recipient, let peaceful intent draw to you what was always compatible with you, even before a need arose. If you are a donor, allow your consciousness to best direct your gift so that you will also benefit from the process. If you are a seller or a purchaser of a commodity, be aware of the terms of sale. Read the fine print, as they say, and make certain that you are prepared to fulfill whatever contractual obligations are required. And if you are an agent or broker of such an exchange, do not tarry on your journey and hold fast to your soul, for another more skilled than you will soon come along and inquire as to its salability as well!

The very near future will explore the many facets of this question as well as others that dance in the same garden. The answers are not nebulous or uncertain, but they are undetermined as of this writing. Humans are poised to uncover a bit more of their past. You are poised to embark on a more specifically attuned future. Mysteries revealed already peek between veiled thoughts, while waves of consciousness await their turn.

# Earth Changes Update

It feels to most of us that Earth changes are increasing in both frequency and magnitude, and yet Gaia says that they are not. She tells us that our interest in 2012-related change has made it seem that way and that our newer technologies allow many more of us to share similar thoughts at similar times. Gaia goes on to say that this will begin to work in our favor as soon as we align with the kinds of things we want to change instead of the change we think is affecting our kind. I know you join me in wishing you could do more for earthquake-displaced families, friends and loved ones as well as in wanting to know more about what may be around the next bend.

With Gaia's help, we were able to quickly arrange a small roundtable to explore this subject in depth and to broadcast it in several different languages around the world. At the same time, Gaia was clear with us in that we were not to expect a channeled response or explanation following every movement, large or small. She was quick to remind me that my role as a channel is not that of a news reporter nor is Gaia a public service announcement. That being said, every question posed received adequate and expansive answers. Those who have been significantly affected by recent events submitted the questions included below.

## ACCLIMATIZING TO CHANGE

The Earth is always changing—day to night and night to day—with each new change ushering in the next. Long ago, on a very fine day, the Earth had changed enough that it could support and welcome human life upon it. Now, as it continues to evolve, the Earth will be able to support humanity's expanding future, which includes much more than a need to simply survive. As you well know, life can be lived or it can be L-I-V-E-D. Now that you have tried it one way, why not try it a new way? In order to do that, you will need to change along with the Earth—adding and subtracting here, multiplying and dividing there until you arrive at the right formula. That is what this time is about, and there is nothing wrong with the Earth or with you.

Change has always been rather difficult for humanity. You call for it in other people, places and things, yet you reject it in yourselves until it is no longer a choice, after which you proclaim that you are not free to choose. Perhaps you will see the humor in this. The changes that are taking place now should not be surprising to you, and you have known about them in this life and in others too. The subject of Earth-related changes has been discussed, theorized, evaluated, prophesied, scientifically explained and more. Now, as you begin to adapt and adjust, you will see that you are suited to live in a variety of different ways and under different conditions. It is time to acclimatize (literally) to new and changing thoughts, environments and more.

The next few years will introduce new concepts and techniques into several areas of life. These will include new ways to relate to ordinary and extraordinary situations and events. Natural telepathic abilities that have been latent and dormant in human beings will reemerge in the younger generations and in those who choose to participate. The transition may require a radically different way to think, and a small percentage of the present population will advocate against it. Change does not always look like evolution, and evolution sometimes looks too much like change.

Humanity requires new resources with which to build the cities that are even now being conceived of. Those who presently control and allocate resources do not do so evenly, fairly or with thoughts toward a future that is unfolding differently than the past. If things were to remain the same, the Earth could not feed its hungry or sustain its thirsty; therefore, the Earth must shift its ability to make resources available, which is to say that it will also relocate some of them elsewhere. Although this is in accordance with the laws and principles of planets that sustain a variety of forms of life, it can sometimes also appear as upheaval on the part of the host. While an apology on the part of the Earth that is compassionately working on your behalf is not entirely in order, please know that I am careful, concerned and deliberate in my movements with my body, the Earth.

*What does Gaia feel during an earthquake?*

This is an area in which we differ quite a bit. To begin with, I—Gaia, the Earth—do not feel fear or pain, not in the grand scheme. What do you feel when you allow stress to roll off your shoulders during a stretch? What do you feel when you shrug, curl your toes or crack your knuckles? Are you consciously aware of what is taking place within your body, or do you simply feel better as the result of a semi-intentional movement? You have a dynamic relationship with your body, and so do I. Our bodies know what we need and how to get it, which brings me to another fundamental difference between us: The Earth responds to all things, including movement in accordance with the laws and principles of nature, which means that it does not forestall or avoid an event.

It is common for human beings to delay a distasteful chore, to avert their eyes from an unpleasant situation, and to be less than forthcoming when communication becomes difficult. While this is not natural, it *is* part of humanity's natural process of evolution. Although the Earth's movements are natural, my sentience understands that humanity is displaced and distressed by them. Earthquakes are not natural disasters as much as they are human disasters. In time, humanity will improve technology to predict earthquakes, improve the durabilty of earthquake-resistent structures and adjust to earthquakes overall.

## EARTHQUAKES AND HUMAN PRACTICES

*Can fearful thoughts about earthquakes and other natural disasters actually attract them, or is the timing of these events based only on natural phenomena?*

Fearful thoughts about people, places, things or events will not bring them physically closer to you. That being said, fear is not a natural repellant, either. Fear is like an energetic bookmark. Every time a thought or an event in your life is triggered by a fear, your awareness will turn to that page so that you can read what you recorded there the last time you visited that place or life. Once you have re-read or re-experienced it, you can agree or disagree with it, keep it as is, rerecord it or discard it. You do this every time you have strong opinions or judgments about yourself and others too. This is one of the ways you change and evolve—by choosing how you feel.

*Is it possible that the recent increase in Earth changes, namely earthquakes, is due to abusive or ignorant practices on the part of humanity?*

No and yes. To be clear and specific, there is no real or incremental increase in Earth change activity when measured over an appropriate cycle of time. The Earth is a relatively small celestial body with a comparatively short history, but it is still much larger and much older than humanity's existence upon the Earth. Only in the last eighty years or so has humanity been able to register and record earthquake activity with relative precision.

Records prior to this time are limited; they present vivid and detailed depictions but with less accuracy. Like you, the Earth has many moving parts. And like you, they are moving most of the time.

Earthquakes are primarily caused by bursts of energy in the Earth's crust that create seismic waves. These are natural and normal for the Earth and have always been so. Periods of solar intensity, which are also natural in origin, can cause temporary increases in the frequency and magnitude of earthquakes. These periods are known to occur near the beginning and end of great processional cycles, this being one such time. Like a woman's labor, seismic activity can also be induced. For instance, the construction of large dams may contribute to an increase in seismic activity. The same is true of certain large buildings, depending upon the profundity and anchoring of their foundations, and certain Earth injection techniques in use during modern well drilling. Coal mining and oil drilling also have correlating factors that can be attributed to certain movements. The Earth's resources are obtainable by many means, and it is good that humanity consumes them. However, it is also important to restore environments so they can continue to supply humanity's voracious appetite, particularly those that are essential to both Earth and humanity.

It is well-known throughout the world now that many practices do not benefit the health or well-being of the Earth, its kingdoms and elements, or humanity. Awareness of these practices will continue to raise concerns, and eventually humanity will turn its hunger elsewhere. A few recent quakes have been influenced by ignorance and abuse, but these earthquakes would have occurred just the same. Even if the magnitude of these had been less, it would not have been by a significant margin, and the destruction would have been almost the same. Although humanity is not yet able to predict earthquakes, they are able to determine some of the more likely places earthquakes may transpire.

*Why do people loot, steal and commit other crimes following large-scale events such as earthquakes?*

That is a good question. Looting, sacking, pillaging, despoiling and every other form of taking goods by force has played a role in humanity's history for a long time. Cities and villages have been plundered by the victorious for as long as humanity has felt threatened by the presence and practices of others. Piracy is another form of looting, be it on the high seas or on the waves of technology. Even among the modern and the civilized, theft and embezzlement is a form of capturing or plundering assets, both public and private. The corrupt and the greedy do not require a natural disaster for inspiration. Interestingly, these more civilized approaches do not seem to affect humanity as much as the sight of a man making off with a sack of rice, a case of water or a television. Why? Because these barbaric customs represent humanity's basic nature—an inherent fear that life is fragile, unfair and unstable. They reveal a belief in lack and an uneasy anxiety born of panic and fright.

During natural disasters, people sometimes lose self-control. They forget their "right mind" and lose themselves within a minefield of thought that only allows them to consider survival, even if their survival is not actually being threatened. A very small percentage of people actually succumb to these actions, but many more than you might imagine do at least think about them. Certain regions of the human brain are still wild, and when these are triggered, even the impossible becomes fathomable. Most looters are ordinary citizens; they are not criminals or street thugs and often think of themselves as heroes and champions of the needy. Sooner or later, order will return to their minds and to the streets.

## LISTENING TO THE EARTH'S MESSAGES

*Why do earthquakes strike without warning? Do you know when and where the next earthquakes will occur? If so, could or would you tell us?*

Earthquakes rarely arrive without warning, but humanity's instrumentation is not yet sophisticated enough to see or hear them. To be precise, an earthquake is what happens during and after an actual seismic event. In other words, an earthquake is what happens on the surface of the Earth, specifically to humanity. Seismic events include natural phenomena such as a rupture in geological faults, volcanic activity and landslides. They can also be generated by mine blasts, drilling and even nuclear detonations. The epicenter of an earthquake, whether natural or human-made, is the point at ground level just above where the seismic energy is first released, also called ground zero. Stored energy is released from rock at the hypocenter, the point where the fault begins to rupture. Energy is released in waves, and these fall into different categories. Physics is a science that understands and studies wave phenomena, but not yet with the certainty and subtlety that is required.

The Earth may seem quite solid to you, but it is actually very elastic. Seismic waves have different characteristics, and as their force moves through the Earth, it leaves behind certain signatures. There are many types of seismic waves, but the most notable are primary, or P-waves, which can travel through anything, and secondary, or S-waves, which can travel through solids but not through liquids or gases. Other seismic waves worth mentioning are body waves, which travel through the interior, or body, of Earth following specific paths in accordance with the density of the Earth's interior, and surface waves, which travel more slowly than body waves and move upon the surface of the Earth as the name implies. Due to their low frequency and long duration, surface waves are most destructive where humanity is concerned. Surface waves can be further subdivided into categories of ground roll, ripples, shearing and more. Low-frequency Rayleigh waves are as yet inaudible by humans but easily detected by birds and both marine and Earth mammals. These slow-moving and long-lasting waves are detectable over long distances and for long periods of time. Domestic animals are attuned to these and other ground vibrations. They are good predictors of earthquakes too.

The importance of this expanded answer is that inherent within the science of seismology is the language of seismology. The Earth is speaking to you and warning you that change is imminent. Currently your instruments record this data after the fact, because they are not sensitive enough to hear the Earth speaking before then. In the near future, your technological devices will be more sensitive and precise, and your intuitive hearing will be more discriminating than it is now. Within a short span of years, you will be more attuned to the language of nature and you will be able to predict the location and timing of earthquakes with relative accuracy. In time, science will have access to better instruments, and these will lengthen the predictive cycle to approximately six weeks before major earthquakes and four weeks before those of lesser magnitude.

Tectonic (natural) earthquakes can occur anywhere within the Earth where enough strain has accumulated, even in areas that seem less likely given past historic models. Sometimes, and without your knowing it, fault plates slide smoothly past one another aseismically (without friction), avoiding an earthquake altogether. On the other hand, even a smooth glass surface can have just the wrong amount of asperity or roughness and cause a jolt or two. These moments are difficult to predict, and our communication is not yet so highly attuned that these could be communicated to you. I communicate with humanity in a variety of ways—only one of these being high and low frequency waves of specific origin and properties. Please understand that there are many ways to talk with one another, the least accurate of these being verbal.

## UNDERSTANDING NATURAL CHANGES

*Can you shed more light on rumors that the Earth's axis has shifted?*

The Earth's axis is constantly shifting by minute amounts that are, for the most part, imperceptible to humanity. Large-scale natural disasters can and do affect the wobble of the Earth's axis, and even small-scale disasters can have an impact in this regard. Events of this magnitude can be catastrophic to humanity; they can move countries, continents and more. The Earth has experienced several pole reversals that have wreaked havoc upon the Earth and reset the clock, so to speak. Please note, however, that the largest earthquakes on record are still small-scale events to a celestial body such as the Earth.

In terms of the Earth's axis, you have been taught to imagine a line, or plane, that intersects the Earth from the north to the South Pole, balancing the Earth on an invisible point like a child's spinning top. While useful, this illustration is not completely accurate. Why? Because it is a little like imagining a balloon balancing on the head of a pin—one little pivot this way or that and *kaboom*! The Earth's axis is not so fragile and neither is that of the other planets.

The Earth does pivot and move and shift, but it rests upon something that looks like an energetic pillow that is both strong and spongy and also very resilient. This invisible layer of elasticity acts like a shock absorber and allows the Earth to pivot and wobble without losing or reversing its polarity. The length of an Earth day is also quite relative, with some being shorter or longer than others. The length of each day is actually determined by the relationship that the Earth has with the Sun at any given moment. This relationship is responsible for at least some of the changes the Earth is currently undergoing and for others that are still to come.

*Were the earthquakes in Haiti and Chile related to one another?*

They are both in active areas where several lines of energy meet and cross paths. The earthquake in Haiti did not trigger the one in Chile; they are unrelated in this respect. The earthquake in Haiti began its journey elsewhere but erupted there, as many elements that are also associated with timelines and probabilities are drawn to this area. The earthquake in Chile was centered there. The panoramic and powerful Andes were formed by some of the most powerful earthquakes ever, which took place long before your written language and instruments could record them. Interestingly, the events, which took place in eight successive thrusts, were observed and recorded by beings much like yourselves who resided on Mars at the time. If this seems strange to you, remember how your own telescopes were able to observe the impacts on Jupiter just a few short years ago. You are a family of Earth dwellers, but you form part of a larger galactic family too, as do others who do not dwell upon Earth.

*Can we do anything to prevent earthquakes from happening near large cities or densely populated areas? Are there safer places to be?*

Population is of no consequence where plate tectonics and fault lines are concerned. Earthquakes are not attracted to large or small cities. They do not discriminate between land and sea. Seismic waves balance, shift, move and redesign the Earth. They release stress and pressure and resource the Earth's surface for generations to come. Seismic events are an important part of the geology and structure of the Earth, and without these, the Earth would die. I have not asked humanity to build its cities here but not there, even when it would be in its own best interest to do so. I do not censure or punish the decisions of builders and dwellers; in fact, I place the very best materials at your disposal and offer them with a blessing and a caution—a time may come when buildings will sway. Build well and prepare even better!

It is safer to be in mountainous areas with solid rock such as granite beneath you rather than soft soil. It is best to be in cities and communities where newer buildings have been well constructed. It is better to be near natural waterways rather than ones that have been dammed, as these oppose the force of nature. It is important to know the lay of the land, which means to understand the currents of energy and in what direction they flow best. Whenever possible, it would be better to be above sea level by whatever factor of land is available or affordable.

## HEALING IN THE AFTERMATH

*Some people have reported changes in eating habits, sleep behaviors and more following earthquakes. Are these related?*

There are very few things that are as unsettling to humanity as natural disasters. From a human standpoint, the ground beneath you should be solid and your environment secure. While this is true most of the time, sometimes it is not. Earthquakes can be life-altering events, and the physical destruction they leave in their wake is the least of it for those who are sensitive in these areas. Buildings can be rebuilt and belongings refurbished, but human nerves are more delicate; the path and process they take on the way to wellness is often individual and unique. Restoring and regaining the trust of your central nervous system requires patience and personal attention.

A physical earthquake may last from a few seconds to a few minutes, but its aftermath can last much longer. It is not uncommon for the physical and emotional effects of an earthquake to last approximately two years. In rare instances, it can last a lifetime, and in even more rare, but not unheard-of cases, it can take more than one lifetime to heal. This is particularly true if there is an overattachment to one's physical belongings, position in life or relationships.

The most common aftereffects associated with natural disasters (in no particular order) are: excessive fear of darkness, separation and/or being alone, worry, anxiety, nervousness, depression, clinging to loved ones and/or belongings, aggressive behavior toward strangers, timidity, immature or childlike behavior, changes in eating and sleeping patterns, persistent nightmares, headaches, stomachaches and other physical complaints, irritability, anger, increased stress, sadness, fatigue, loss of appetite, nausea, hyperactivity and lack of concentration.

Generally, these normal reactions will not persist longer than a few weeks to a few months, but it is not uncommon for them to last longer. Some feelings or responses may not appear for weeks or even months after an event. Many who appear to be coping with disproportionate calm following a high-magnitude event might suddenly regress over a small aftershock several months later. Delayed feelings and expressions are sometimes also accompanied by specific resentments toward both Earth and heaven.

Whenever possible, and to accelerate the healing process, it is help-ful to be near loved ones.  Touch and hold each other often, but respect the need to be alone if it is requested.  Take frequent breaks from the recovery and rebuilding process, pay attention to health, diet and sleep and, if necessary, mourn or grieve.  It may take time to feel safe in your world again.

## PREPARING FOR UPCOMING CHANGES

*Can you give us an overview of upcoming Earth changes and events that could affect humanity?*

The first half of the year will record earthquakes and other move-ments that wash soil away from its normal path and to other directions. Waterways under the Earth are being diverted and rerouted as well, in order to be of better service to humanity later on.  These move-ments will place greater strain on certain portions of the ocean floor but will relieve pressure in other areas, particularly where land mass (continents) is great and mighty.  Underground water of all types will be affected and even simple wells may experience a shift in level or mineral composition.  You are accustomed to water levels that rise and fall, but in this case, they may be sliding sideways above and beneath the surface.

Most of the quakes will be offshore and deep enough that they will not disturb the surface populations, but as you have already seen, that is not always the case.  Areas to watch in North America include the Alaskan coastline, the waters west of the Pacific Northwest, includ-ing Oregon and Washington, and the southern section of California as it dips into Mexico.  In South America, Chile is still not stable and may experience one or more large spikes that will be strong but not as long lasting as the initial quake.  Peru is another country that must keep watch at this time.  Strong indicators of quakes will persist in Indonesia, particularly where island nations are also host to many volcanoes.  The second half of the year will include at least one major volcanic eruption in the northern hemisphere and another in the southern hemisphere.  Thousands of miles apart from each other, the two eruptions will be related.

*What specific message could you offer those who become displaced due to earth-quakes and other natural disasters?*

During the day, dare. At night, dream. Live, love and listen to one another. Give generosity and gentleness to others. Celebrate, cultivate and contemplate each moment. Have humility, honesty and sincerity. Rebuild, renew and restore. Breathe, balance and believe again.

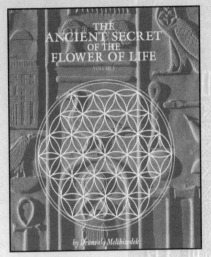

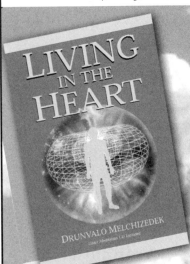

# Light Technology PUBLISHING

## Beyond the Light Barrier

### By Elizabeth Klarer

This autobiography of a South African woman is the story of the interstellar love affair between the author and Akon, an astrophysicist from the planet Meton in Alpha Centauri. Elizabeth Klarer travelled to Meton with Akon, lived there for four months with his family and gave birth to his son. Featuring fascinating descriptions of the flora, fauna and advanced technology of Akon's people, this classic is being reissued in a long-awaited American edition.

Chapter 1: A Stranger in our Skies
Chapter 2: Link with Men of Other Worlds
Chapter 3: The Secrets of Light
Chapter 4: An Escape Route to the Stars
Chapter 5: The Heights of Cathkin
Chapter 6: Beyond the Time Barrier: To Alpha Centauri
Chapter 7: The Nature of the Universe

$15.^{95}$

244 P. SOFTCOVER
ISBN 978-1-891824-77-7

## "A profound, provocative book for the 21st century,"

JJ Hurtak, PhD, Investigative researcher and founder of The Academy for Future Science, a United Nations NGO.

Phone: 928-526-1345 or 1-800-450-0985 • Fax: 923-714-1132